PENGUIN BOOKS

GERALD
A PORTRAIT

Daphne du Maurier is the second daughter of the famous
actor and theatre manager-producer, the late Sir Gerald
du Maurier, and grand-daughter of George du Maurier,
the much-loved *Punch* artist and author of *Trilby* and
Peter Ibbetson. After being educated at home with her
sisters and then in Paris, she began writing short stories
and articles in 1928, and in 1931 her first novel, *The Loving
Spirit*, was published. Two others followed. Her reputation
was established with her frank biography of her father,
Gerald: A Portrait, and her Cornish novel, *Jamaica Inn*.
When *Rebecca* came out in 1938 she suddenly found herself, to her great surprise, one of the most popular authors
of the day. The book went into thirty-nine English impressions in the next twenty years and has been translated into
more than twenty languages. Sir Laurence Olivier starred
in the film under Hitchcock's direction.

Since then, besides several best-selling novels, she has
written plays, short stories, and a biography of Branwell
Brontë. Her latest publications are *Not After Midnight*
(1971), *Rule Britannia* (1972), *Golden Lads: A Study of
Anthony Bacon, Francis and their friends* (1975) and *The
Winding Stair* (1976).

Her three most popular novels were all inspired by her
Cornish home, Menabilly, where she and her family lived
for over twenty years. Daphne du Maurier was married to
the late Lieut-General Sir Frederick Browning, war-time
commander of Airborne Forces. Their three children, two
daughters and a son, are all married.

D0608727

DAPHNE DU MAURIER

GERALD

A Portrait

PENGUIN BOOKS

Penguin Books Ltd, Harmondsworth, Middlesex, England
Penguin Books, 625 Madison Avenue, New York, New York 10022, U.S.A.
Penguin Books Australia Ltd, Ringwood, Victoria, Australia
Penguin Books Canada Ltd, 41 Steelcase Road West, Markham, Ontario, Canada
Penguin Books (N.Z.) Ltd, 182–190 Wairau Road, Auckland 10, New Zealand

—

First published by Victor Gollancz 1934
Published in Penguin Books 1970
Reprinted 1977

—

Copyright © Daphne du Maurier, 1934

—

Made and printed in Great Britain
by Hazell Watson & Viney Ltd
Aylesbury, Bucks
Set in Linotype Baskerville

CHAPTER ONE

WHEN the du Mauriers were first married, they lived in rooms in Great Russell Street, Bloomsbury. The house was new, and rather damp, and not very comfortable, but these things did not worry them because they were young and happy. Surroundings did not matter very much to Kicky then. He had never known luxury, and did not expect it. The studio he had shared with Whistler was scarcely furnished at all, and had a rope slung across it, hung with a piece of brocade, to shut off the corner used as a bedroom. There had been little furniture in Antwerp either, or in the old Quartier Latin studio, but so long as there was room for an easel, and perhaps a chair to sit on, one did not demand anything else. The du Mauriers lived carefully in Great Russell Street, for Kicky was never a spender, and he reminded Pem that, although he was contributing regularly now to *Once a Week* and occasionally to *Punch*, and was to illustrate *Sylvia's Lovers* for Mrs Gaskell, the future could never be an absolute certainty because of his eyes.

He was only twenty-nine, but his left eye was lost for ever and there was always the dread that the sight of the right eye might go too.

There was, though, no immediate worry, and in the meantime life was a pleasant enough thing, what with work, and one's friends, and dear Pem proving herself a wife in a thousand.

Friends were necessary to Kicky's existence. He needed the warmth of their voices, the quick laughter. He did not mind how many of them crowded into the small studio, chaffing him, arguing, criticizing.

There were so many things to discuss and to question, so many riddles that would never be solved. And it was fun working like this, with a friend at his elbow and two more on the floor; and he would smoke innumerable cigarettes while the light slowly faded, and Pem would scold him for using his eyes so late, and remind him that supper was getting cold and would be spoilt.

Then two of them – Tom Armstrong, perhaps, and Lamont – would stay, and there would be more talking; of books, of pictures, of old days in Paris, of music; and one of them would say, 'Sing to us, Kicky. Sing "Noel". Sing "Vin à quatre sous".' And he would sing to them in the sweet tenor voice that had been his father's before him, while Pem would bend over her needlework and murmur the words silently with her lips, looking up now and again and catching his eye, smiling, and very happy. 'I think I should make a better actor than I do an artist,' Kicky would say later when the others had gone. 'I've often fancied myself on the stage'; and he would strut up and down like a young cock, very pleased with himself, full of talk and in excellent spirits, and Pem would agree tactfully that he would have made a splendid actor, thankful in her heart that he was no such thing.

It had been a jolly day, he would say; full, with no empty moments; and tomorrow would be the same. There would be work in the morning, and lunch with *maman belle-mère*. Then more work, with Tom or one of the others dropping in perhaps, and dinner with Millais and his wife. He had had no eye worry then, thank goodness; the ghost lurked in the shadows and had not shown its face. And he could lean out of the window and wink at a star, singing softly, '*Je n'ai jamais autant aimé la vie*,' and kiss Pem on both eyes and whisper '*Bon soir*.'

For all the doubts and fears that arose in him at times,

8

his sight remained good. It was not long before he was sending weekly drawings to *Punch*, and, on Leech's death, he succeeded him at the *Punch* table, a great honour and tribute to his workmanship. From that moment success was his.

This was in '65, and, with better prospects and a growing family, life progressed calmly, with no financial worries. The children were a great delight to him, appearing regularly every year like the lambs and the first snowdrops. First Trixie, then Guy, then Sylvia; crawling on the floor, knocking against his easel, breaking his spectacles, they never worried him, and he liked to have them near. Of course, they were an anxiety at times. There was the time when Guy was sick all night and when Sylvia broke out in a rash; and they were for ever catching colds and giving Kicky and Pem a fright that it would turn to bronchitis. Pem was like a hen clucking after her chicks, wrapping them up for fear of draughts and dosing everyone within sight, including Kicky, with cod-liver oil; scolding the irrepressible Trixie when she made too much noise, quelling Guy's occasional outbursts of temper. Then, when they were safely tucked up in bed for the night and work was over for the day, she used to come and sit beside Kicky in the studio and read aloud to him. They dined out a good deal and made more friends every year; there was Leighton, and Millais, and Val Prinsep; Jimmy Whistler, of course, and Swinburne; William Morris, Burne-Jones, and Arthur Sullivan. There were musical evenings at Arthur Lewis's where Kicky sang Gounod and was much applauded, and, fanned with success, borrowed somebody's hat and sang comic French songs in a high falsetto and was not funny at all. There were evenings at the theatre to see John Hare or Charles Matthews, and once a week the *Punch* dinner, where discussions were lively, the gaiety sometimes uproarious, and Kicky, with his friends, would drive back very late in a cab,

9

rather tight after two glasses of burgundy. 'Who would be *père de famille*?' he used to sigh, as Trixie, excited as usual and refusing to sleep, called to him from her room, 'Papa! Papa!' and in he used to go to kiss her good night while the dawn was already in the sky.

Next day he would be in bed until lunch, having caught a cold from the draughty cab, and Pem must wrap a stocking round his throat and give him gruel, and put his feet in hot water – all very depressing and lowering to the spirits. And, although he drew for *Punch* in the afternoon, he would feel dissatisfied with his work, declaring he was not improving, that he was paid too well for his *petits bons hommes et bonnes femmes*; that his eye was worrying him. *A quoi bon vivre? Ce n'est pas gai.*

His demon of depression was always ready to close in upon him and stifle him, shutting out the beauty and loveliness of life, reminding him that blindness would one day be his, turning his little world to darkness. He used to hold out his hand before his eye. 'Pem, it's not so clear as it was. I can't focus when I look this way. It's getting worse, I tell you.'

'Nonsense, love,' she would sooth him, 'it's your imagination. Neither can I see if I hold my hand that way.' And she would make a little play of showing him to prove him wrong.

'Are you sure?' he used to ask anxiously, like a child demanding comfort, 'Are you sure?'

Little by little she would calm him, chatting quietly, bringing his mind round to other things, questioning him on the *Punch* dinner, discussing the children – how forward Guy was for his age, how Trixie was growing – and gradually his nightmare would withdraw to the shadows, his cold would no longer be so heavy, and because it was a fine evening, they would venture for a stroll in Soho market, Kicky well wrapped up in a muffler. At dinner they would have a little celebration to themselves, tapping a bottle of Hock for the occasion and feeling very extravagant, and afterwards at home, perhaps, Pem would read aloud Froude's essay on the science of history. This would lead him to talk of the stars, of the universe, of the queer unsatisfied longings that one could not explain and did not understand (which, Pem would say, shaking her head, she did very well without; and, anyway, it was past bedtime). And she would go upstairs softly, so as not to awaken the children, while Kicky would follow slowly behind, at once elated and depressed, and yearning for the infinite.

Apart from eye trouble and occasional secret depressions that arose from the depths of an unknown inner self, his spirits were tremendous in those days. His enjoyment of life was spontaneous and his gaiety infectious. He had a bubbling sense of humour that saw something ridiculous in every sort of situation: the tedium of a musical party enlivened by the outbursts of an ignoramus; the snobbery of the *nouveaux riches* when giving their first 'At Home'; the passionate declarations of preciosity from the young aesthetes when contemplating their own works of art; the embarrassing naïveties of his own children before strangers; and the indiscretions of his friends. It was inevitable that he should use these personal impressions for his weekly page in *Punch*, and the world and posterity benefited accordingly. Du Maurier's drawings became the fashion, the latest thing, the usual light topic of conversation in society drawing-rooms. The very people who were ridiculed were amongst his most fervent admirers, and clamoured for his acquaintance.

It amused him to move amongst them, listening to their superficialities, remarking their insincerities, observing the beauty of the women and the self-satisfied pomposity of the men.

He watched them, a smile on his lips, his eyes twinkling behind his glasses. And then back to his own home and his studio, with veal cutlets and curried sole for supper, and a tremendous romp on the floor with Trixie, as usual on top of the world and growing like a *rose trémière*; and afterwards smoking innumerable cigarettes, which he made himself, and thinking of tomorrow's work at his easel, while Pem read aloud *The Scarlet Letter*. Every day brought scenes that appealed to his sense of humour and which sooner or later served for *Punch*.

There was the time when a Jewish friend of his was married, and he and Pem attended the wedding at the synagogue, Pem in a dress of her mother's, hideous but rich-looking and well suited to the occasion. The service was impressive, but he did not feel much moved, and keeping his hat on seemed very strange. There was music, and all the improper parts of the service were in Hebrew. Kicky felt *Baruch* was all very well, but *Shallaballah* was not a word to say before ladies.

They had hired a brougham for the occasion, and drove in the Park to show themselves, but unfortunately none of their friends were about, so they went on to the wedding breakfast, where they sat down sixty to table. 'Beastly wealth,' said Kicky at the *Punch* dinner that night, 'horrible colours, and, by gum! the curtains and carpets. I took a Miss Elias in to breakfast, and there was turtle soup and speeches. An old rabbi praised the well-stored minds of bride and bridegroom, and Oh Benjamin got up and bowed and raved for hours about friendship and pecuniary success. The young couple left in the middle, so I and some others joined them, and kissed the bride, and flung a shoe when her back was turned, and Pem whispered hopefully in my ear, "They may be happy yet."'

Then there was the memorable occasion when Kicky's acting ambitions were realized and he played in *Box and Cox* for charity at the Adelphi Theatre, with the permission of Arthur Sullivan. The performance was given entirely by amateurs (they did it later in the year again in Manchester), and Kicky played Box.

He used to rehearse his part every evening with Pem, who told him he was not natural enough, and forced his voice, and over-acted generally, and he said he found it far easier acting before a large number of strangers than in front of an audience of one, who was his wife at the same time. The whole company gave a dress rehearsal at Arthur Lewis's, Kicky very nervous and managing the singing successfully, but a hopeless bungler at the funny business – he was damped by one or two people being cold in their applause.

The night before the great performance he slept with a cold water compress round his throat and gargled with ginger essence. He was fidgety all the morning, and arrived at the theatre as early as half past twelve, taking a glass of stout to calm his nerves. The theatre filled in an incredibly short time, and before he knew it had happened he was alone on the stage and singing the 'Lullaby'. It was a terrible moment; the theatre all a mist because he was not wearing his glasses, and in one brief second he caught sight of Pem in a box. During the duet he recovered his self-possession, and the scene went off in grand style amidst loud applause, the serenade duet being encored. Kicky was delighted, though secretly relieved when his performance was over and he could change and go round to the front of the house and visit his friends in the stalls, all of whom were very civil and highly flattering, protesting he could not have played better had he been a professional. The Terrys were there, and Meggie Coyne, and John Hare; and Hare it was who suggested that when he did it again he should paint his nose red, which Kicky thought rather unkind.

The evening finished with more songs, Kicky changing again and appearing on the stage to sing 'Les Deux Aveugles'. While he waited in the wings for two of the company to finish a last duet he felt so elated that directly the curtain fell he tripped on to the empty stage and performed an extravagant *pas seul*, whereupon the stage manager amiably made a sign to the curtain lifter and up it went again, disclosing Kicky for all the world to see, clad in a flannel vest and a dirty pair of white ducks.

It was a tremendous success. After dining with a crowd of friends and discussing the performance from start to finish, he and Pem went home in a cab, dead beat, Kicky so overwrought and excited that he did not sleep at all.

Those were the days, said Kicky, irresponsible, lively, gay; days when to be a Bohemian meant that you were genuinely artistic and not a fourth-rate idler *sans* talent, when wit was spontaneous and not offensive, when manners were informal but never forgotten, when women were attractive without being vulgar, when laughter was effortless and boredom unknown.

Pleasures were simple then, and Kicky's world found happiness in little things. There were summer days when, treating himself to relaxation from his work, he and Pem and a party of friends took cabs to Waterloo and train thence to Richmond Bridge; and, there embarking in three boats, they rowed up to Teddington, the ladies seated gracefully in the stern and on the way back begging to take an oar and performing uncommonly well in spite of their frills and furbelows. And then to dinner at the Star and Garter, finishing the evening at a friend's chambers – potatoes and pie and music – and so home in another cab, Pem much disgusted because a young widow who was sharing it with them had the audacity to put her feet up on the opposite seat.

'But it was such a pretty foot,' pleaded Kicky. 'I don't care for forward women,' said Pem, shaking her head. 'I very much fear J— is sweet on her.'

It was quite true, Kicky admitted afterwards to Tom Armstrong, that the way one of their friends had licked his lips over the widow's beauty was in no sense fit for the drawing-room.

'It all depends how that sort of thing is done,' he argued; 'the way I lick my lips would not call a blush into the cheek of seventeen, and the way you lick yours, old fellow, would not desecrate a church!'

Kicky loved beauty. He clamoured for it in women and children, and even in men. People had to be tall; they had to be graceful; they had to have a certain charm and dignity about them, whether they were street urchins, duchesses, or cab-drivers.

'We called on the Fenns this afternoon,' he wrote in '67, 'and then drove in the Park to see the folk and to bow to our carriage acquaintances should any pass. Met Mrs F. and her sister-in-law. *Qu'elle est jolie, jolie, jolie! Mais pas mon genre.* Haw-haw and that sort of thing. Met her once before, years ago, and she has since been to Tasmania and got prettier. We chatted for a while, and then it came on to rain, and Pem got her feathers ruffled. Then in the evening to Mrs Graham, to meet the Duchesse d'Anmal by express invitation. The D-d'A didn't come after all thro' it being some Bourbon's death day, but ordinary English duchesses were plentiful enough, and a few countesses and that sort of thing – they were so common I lost all my native respect for them. Grisi sang very well, so did Mandin, I refused to sing after such swells, at which Pem was disappointed!

'We went on to the Haden's. Mrs H. played and Madame Lehman sang exquisitely.

'Then home in a cab with the Poynters, delighted with our evening and with everybody.'

For all his eye worry and consequent mental anxiety, there was a sense of tranquillity and peace possessed by Kicky that those who came after him would never know. He belonged to that age of sublime security when the present appeared enduring and the future held no fears.

Time was not an enemy then. It was a friend with whom he dallied; a friend who moved in step slowly, sedately, who saw to the furthering of his plans. Faith was not lost then, nor belief in mankind; friendship was lasting, and men and women trusted one another.

Prosperity could be counted upon then; there was a certainty that after the lean years came harvest, and it was with a complete trust in his own judgement that provision was made for the grandchildren, some of whom he would never see.

The countryside was not yet desecrated, nor had turmoil come to the streets of London. Walking was pleasant; there was a sort of sweetness in the air in summer; a scent of pink chestnut, and later lilac unharmed by dust or petrol fumes; the good honest smell of horses; and with this were curiously mingled the pleasing sounds of London, distinct from mere noise – the roll of carriage-wheels, the crunch of gravel drives, the light and easy patter of a hansom cab. Flower-boxes, gay with geraniums, caught the passing eye, and window-blinds at noon. Luncheon was leisurely and agreeable; conversation was intelligent; parlourmaids passed silently, wearing billowy aprons and large caps with flying streamers.

Gossip was amusing and occasionally malicious, but there was no breath of slander, no interminable plunging into the privacy of others. Voices were softer; the nasal twang and the high-pitched cackle were not yet born. Hustle was an unknown word; people thought more slowly, moved more slowly, lived more slowly. Women knew how to listen, how to be motionless; they had not yet learnt stridency nor restlessness; and their skins were clean. Nails were not dipped then in coloured varnish, nor dresses saturated with scent. Women took pains with their toilet. Their hair was brushed for twenty minutes at a time. Even the gowns they wore were not impersonal, but belonged in some unmistakable way to

16

the wearer, impregnated with her individuality, her body, bearing for ever the odour of unscented soap, rain-water, and sweet lavender.

The men of Kicky's day respected their women, courted them and won them. They lay side by side at night; they confessed their little hopes and fears and looked forward calmly to another day. Not for them the hunger before dawn, the doubting hours of midnight, the ever-present fear of the future and the shadow of insecurity; worries about money, worries about plans; the very uncertainty of life itself, born from the horrors of wars.

Kicky was blessed in his generation. He enjoyed great beauty, and was spared much pain. Patience was his, and dignity, and a quiet kindliness. They had strength, the men and women of his time, but their fortitude was un-tried and of another kind. The burdens that they carried were cast in a different mould. Their sorrows and their joys were personal, were familiar; the little occurrences of day to day. No universal hunger bore them down; they trod their prosperous paths with measured steps, untroubled and serene, trailing a bright, unfevered gaiety, smiling with God as their sons would never smile.

The du Mauriers decided that they were outgrowing the rooms in Great Russell Street, and moved to Earl's Ter-race, in Kensington, where they lived for four or five years.

The children, especially Trixie, were becoming obstre-perous, and needed more room, and in Earl's Terrace they could live on a slightly larger scale. Extra help would be needed, of course. Servants were inclined to be difficult. Martha objected to late dinners, and Jane was known to have gone out one evening without permission. It was all rather fussing. Kicky did not like to be too severe with them, because they sat to him willingly when he wanted

17

a model, and he could not complain that the cutlets were underdone if Martha had left her cooking to oblige. The children liked Kensington because it meant occasional journeys in the underground, and frequent visits to the gardens. Pem, too, was within easy calling distance of her mother.

Earl's Terrace was not ideal, however, and when the next baby came – another girl, May (christened Marie Louise) – both Pem and Kicky were conscious of hankerings towards the country: somewhere not too far, because their friends must visit them, and within easy reach of town and the *Punch* office. The children were looking pale, though; they needed fresh air and space. Kicky went once or twice to Hampstead, and fell in love with the old houses, the great expanse of heath, the bare unspoilt beauty of it. Somehow it reminded him of Passy and his boyhood; the ponds where the children sailed their little boats were like the small lakes in the Bois de Boulogne where he had played so often as a boy, and it came to him that he must live in Hampstead; that it was his place, his plot of earth, his home; that he would be happy there, he and Pem and the children; that somehow they would all belong there as once he had belonged to Passy.

He succeeded in letting the house in Earl's Terrace. It was not entirely a success, because the people who moved there had the audacity to hammer picture-nails into the precious Morris wallpaper, and 'Although we spoke them fair,' Kicky wrote to Tom Armstrong, 'and never made any remark about it, we are boiling over with indignation. To nail pictures on to the bard's paper without consulting us seems a great liberty. What do you think about it? We sent in to the landlady of this house to ask whether we could put a nail in the bare wall of the pantry, and were by no means sure of her answer. Well, here we are since Saturday, "than which", as they say, a lovelier situation, a more genial old house, and pleasanter state of things altogether, if it could only last, could not be found anywhere.

'There is a spare bedroom facing the west with the most beautiful view in Middlesex, so mind your eyes; you will want to live here altogether.'

This was Gangmoor House, standing on the very summit of Hampstead Hill, facing the White Stone Pond, with a clear, uninterrupted view towards every point of the compass, the peace and seclusion seeming wonderful to them after the bustle of Kensington. (Gangmoor stands today untenanted; even the walled garden is no proof against the constant stream of traffic towards the north, and on most days in summer the cars are parked in rows beside the pond where Guy and Trixie sailed their boats.)

It may be that Gangmoor was too exposed to the four winds and Pem feared bronchitis for the children, or perhaps the house did not altogether suit them, for they were living further down the hill in three years' time, at No. 27 Church Row, and they did not settle into their final home, New Grove House, where they lived for twenty-one years, until 1874.

Church Row is a short avenue with trees in the centre, leading out of Heath Street, and terminating in the parish church, and on either side there are still tall, sedate Queen Anne houses, that might have graced a novel by Jane Austen. No. 27 had a flight of steps leading to a green door, and the front windows looked out upon their placid neighbours, while to the left the squat spire of the old church gleamed between the leafy branches of the trees. There were several floors to the house. Leading up was a long flight of stairs, and from the top windows at the back you could catch a glimpse of London lying far below, long and straggling, like another world.

When Pem and Kicky had dined with friends or maybe visited a play and had come home late at night – and this not often, because the drive was a lonely, tedious one, not altogether safe after dark in that slow climb up the hill – they would peer from those top windows and endeavour to trace the way they had come, which seemed to them now, from their summit, a jumble of chimney-pots and little winking lights.

And Kicky said sometimes, with a sigh, that Hampstead was healthy but a little dull, and they were too far from their friends, and, sensed from above like this, there was a glamour about London that you lost when you were near; a glamour that was partly the lights of the theatres and the street lamps, and partly the bustle and chatter that you heard, music, and the laughter of your friends.

He wondered always if he were missing something that might be happening in London below. It lay so full of promise, like a jewel, and he feared they had lost the art of good living, of conviviality, of social understanding, through breathing the pure air of the four winds. Had they gained so very much in exchanging the lights of London for the stars? He was never quite certain, never quite reconciled. But Pem was very well pleased. Pem professed herself content. Already, in her big generous heart, she planned parties and gaieties for the children; she saw them grow steadily and happily to maturity, held in check by her wisdom, wrapped in her love and secure from all danger. And Kicky stood by the window, looking down upon London, the thought coming to him that next birthday he would enter his fortieth year, that he would be middle-aged, that in spite of his success as an artist he had not achieved all that his dreams had whispered.

There was so much that he would never do, so many worlds that he would never know. He thought of Paris with a ghost of a smile – the noise and clatter of the studio, all the old gay carelessness of youth that would never be his again. He was settled now, a man of means, anchored to his family and his profession, and he did not want to wander again. Fate had been good to him, giving him Pem and the children, and sparing him his eye. He had no grudge against mankind, and he was happy in his friends. Somewhere, though, he did not know why, for all his gaiety and contentment, there was a little seed of melancholy in him, fretful and unappeased.

The last of Kicky's children was born on the 26th of March, 1873. He was a boy, and they christened him Gerald Hubert Edward. For some reason Pem kept the wire that the *Punch* office sent to Kicky. It ran: 'Welcome big little stranger. Health just drunk with all the honours. Homage and congratulations to madame.'

CHAPTER TWO

AT first view there is nothing remarkable about New Grove House. It is of a certain age, and stands in a by-road, attached to another house older and more attractive than itself. The entrance is on the very road, and the house is not set back in any way.

You would call it tall and yet poky, large yet awkwardly planned. There was no bathroom, and when the du Mauriers lived there the back rooms looked out upon a little square of slum houses.

From the front they could see the high wall of Fenton House opposite, and to the right the road led to the summit of Hampstead Hill and they might catch a glimpse of the White Stone Pond.

The best room in the house was the studio, with its many windows, and directly below this was a tiny space of garden screened from the road by a high brick wall. The studio was used more or less as a living-room, because it was the largest in the house, and because Kicky did not mind five children tumbling over his feet as he worked.

'This is a regular house for children,' he told Tom Armstrong, 'a kindergarten for all ages.' And, with his usual exaggeration, he went on to say, 'I took about a dozen for a long walk across the Heath on Sunday, and found them more amusing than most grown-up people one meets.'

They were a riotous band at any time, with Trixie reaching double figures and Guy approaching school age, and Sylvia for the moment the ugly duckling, not quite certain of herself, and May the delicate one, thin and passionate and highly imaginative, ordering small Gerald to do what he was told. The youngest of a family is always rather a problem. He is not quite big enough to do the same as the others and yet he feels neglected if he is not allowed to join in their play.

It was this way with Gerald. He hated to think he was missing anything. In fact he objected strongly to being treated as a baby, and for the sake of peace they allowed him to enter their games. From the studio Kicky heard their clamour in the small garden below, Trixie ring-leader as usual. When Pem went down to see what they were about, she was informed by Trixie they were playing at railway trains. 'I'm the engine,' she explained, 'and Guy is a first-class carriage, and Sylvia's a second-class carriage, and May's a third-class carriage. And Gerald, he's a third-class carriage too — that is' — she lowered her voice — 'he's really only a truck, only you mustn't tell him so, as it would offend him.'

Gerald, from the end of the row, looked up sus-piciously. They were no doubt saying something about him. He was not as yet very steady on his legs, and he was obliged to hang on to May's pinafore to balance himself. If there was going to be any unpleasantness about this game, he knew who was going to get it in first. Carefully he watched his mother's eyes. You never knew. A tear at the right moment sometimes produced results of a con-soling nature. He wrinkled up his face ready to cry. Pem obeyed the signal and swooped upon him, bearing him off to the house with suggestions of finding kind Martha, who kept chocolate Suchard in her store-cupboard. The others shrugged their shoulders at one another.

'Mummie and her ewee lamb,' said Trixie, shaking her head. (The family pronounced it 'ewee' in the years to come.) Gerald watched them over his mother's shoulder as though butter would not melt in his mouth.

He was a plain little boy, with rather lank brown hair

and a long upper lip, and a pair of large, very innocent blue eyes. He looked so innocent and guileless that it was difficult to imagine him anything but very simple and very good.

Pem was deceived from the start. He was the baby; he could do no wrong. Besides, he looked rather fragile, as though he might easily catch bronchitis, and she would watch him anxiously for the first sign of a cough. He had only to sneeze and she would rush to the medicine-chest for camphorated oil. The du Mauriers were a terrible family for colds. If any one of them caught a cold in the head, the whole household behaved as though they had been visited with plague.

'I fear Gerald is starting a cold,' said Pem with wrinkled brow; and, 'Oh, dear! Oh! dear,' groaned Kicky, '*les enfants – toujours les enfants*. Now it will spread through the house.'

The children slept with stockings round their throats for fear of infection, and with cries of dismay they would learn the next morning at breakfast that May had felt a tickle in the throat.

This nervousness became general, and the fear of colds in the head was to stick to all of them throughout their lives, making them unnecessarily fussy over little ailments.

Gerald would be caught up in the general fever. This alarm over colds was instilled in him by his mother, and although by nature he was a careless, happy-go-lucky little boy, he was forced to take his health seriously like the others, being wary of east winds and chills on the liver, perhaps seeing in them a certain excuse for the attentions which he always enjoyed. Although Pem called him her ewee lamb, meek and mild, his brother and sisters were not deluded. His spirits were almost as high as Trixie's, and he was not easily suppressed. He was undoubtedly funny, but would take advantage of the slightest encouragement and proceed to show off shamelessly. He knew he could make them laugh if he chose, and he loved to be the centre of interest. He developed a naughty habit of mimicking people who came to the house, and, although he succeeded uncommonly well, the others felt it was not a trick to be encouraged.

'Don't look at Gerald; he's showing off,' whispered May, and they proceeded to turn away their heads while the small boy capered in front of them, very pleased with himself, and watching them out of the tail of his eye.

'It's no use,' sighed Sylvia. 'He knows it amuses Papa'; and Kicky, who had always rather fancied his own imitations, chuckled at this youngster who appeared in the studio dressed up as the gentleman who had lunched with them on Sunday, and, unnoticed by the model who was sitting for the weekly *Punch* drawing, pulled faces behind his back.

'Shut the door,' said Kicky, because the boy invariably and maddeningly left it open; and then Gerald came and stood behind him and watched the careful sketch come to maturity – a sight of which he never tired – to be asked in a few moments whether he would also sit, as there was to be a child in the drawing.

Gerald assented, at once demanding sixpence and ninepence if he sat for two different positions, which seemed to Kicky a fair bargain, and when he had finished he was very prompt in his payment.

The model received five shillings a morning, and lunch, which Gerald considered princely payment, completely thrown away, as the model's expression was totally unfitted for the seasick traveller he was supposed to represent, and which Gerald himself could have done much better.

He wandered to the chest of drawers in the corner of the room and pulled open the bottom drawer, turning over in his hands the three or four suits that were kept there as 'wardrobe' for the model. There was a suit of dress clothes, a knickerbocker suit, and one or two others. Kicky never kept more, and, though fashions might change, the 'wardrobe' remained the same. These suits were a source of fascination to Gerald and served for purposes of dressing up.

Then it would be time for lunch, the whole family assembling in the dining-room, Kicky reluctant to cease work and invariably late, so that Gerald, as youngest, was sent to summon him. 'Papa, Papa, Mummie says will you come; lunch is getting cold.' There was generally an uproar at the table, because all the du Mauriers were great talkers, even as children; they had a vocabulary of family expressions and family jokes, as usual quite unintelligible to outsiders, and they brought to the conversation also a smattering of badly assimilated French, fluent for five minutes and execrable for the next five, speaking a strange Anglicized version with perfect accents, much to Kicky's amusement.

In the afternoon there was a general exodus to the Heath, Kicky taking any of the children who cared to accompany him, escorted by his beloved Chang, the enormous St Bernard dog, and meeting on the way either of two greatest Hampstead friends, Canon Ainger or Basil Champneys.

Kicky had favourite walks, and little routines to be observed; he must descend from the top pond down hill, through the trees towards the Leg o' Mutton, then, branching right, strike up in the direction of the fir-trees above the Bull and Bush; or on wet days there was the brisk march along the Spaniards Road, tapping the first tree at the end with his stick, and so back again the way they had come.

It was on one of these walks that Kicky performed his famous rescue act for which afterwards he was unmercifully teased by his family. The whole crowd of them had been for the usual Sunday walk, Kicky, Pem, and the children, and were returning home by the White Stone Pond. It was winter, and the ice frozen upon it about an inch thick, and as they came to the pond they noticed a mob of people shouting and pointing to the centre, where a miserable dog was slowly drowning, the ice having given way beneath him. Nobody was making the slightest attempt to save the wretched animal. Kicky, short-sighted without his glasses, was only aware that a dog was in difficulties in the water – he could not even see the ice. Stripping himself dramatically of his coat, his eyes flashing, he ran a few paces back and then took an enormous header on to a thin layer of ice that barely covered two foot of water. It was a tremendous sight! Cheered and applauded by the crowd, he plunged to the centre of the pond (still only three foot deep) and rescued the yelping dog, which covered his face with licks of gratitude. Kicky, still without a word, brought the dog back to shore, gave him to his master, and proceeded to walk straight home, followed by his admiring but slightly embarrassed family.

He had scarcely gone a hundred yards before the owner of the dog caught him up, tapped him on the shoulder, and said, 'You're a brave fellow. Here's half a crown; go and get yourself something hot.' Kicky, very red in the face, thanked him politely, assured him that it had been a pleasure, and that he lived quite close. The man would take no refusal, protested that he would gladly make the sum five shillings, that he had never seen so brave a fellow, and insisted so much that Kicky suddenly lost his temper and exclaimed, 'Oh, go to hell, you damned fool!' The man immediately became very apologetic, very humble, and, taking off his hat, bowed low and said, 'I beg your pardon, sir, I didn't know you were a gentleman.'

27

The next morning Kicky received a letter which began, 'Little did I know who it was that saved my canine pet from a watery grave. ...' Poor Kicky, he never quite lived the episode down, and it was the doubt about his breeding that pleased his family most!

He was incredibly easy to deceive, as Gerald discovered later when he grew older, and more than once the boy dressed up and was shown into the studio as a stranger come to call, generally to borrow money, and Kicky, rather annoyed and ill at ease, was obliged to keep up some attempt at polite conversation, until Gerald, from very pity, had to acknowledge himself.

Those were the happy days, the careless days, when Gerald could dream and idle the whole time long, thinking of nothing in particular, leading the monotonous yet incredibly full life peculiar to all the small boys that have ever been – climbing trees on the Heath, sailing boats, squabbling with May over the choice of games, May determined and inclined to boss because of her few years' seniority; planning the delights of the now annual holiday at Whitby, an ever-increasing joy, when the days were never long enough; watching Papa draw, and skilfully inveigling from Mummie the promise of a new tennis racket; cheeking the girls and baiting them about their choice of friends; standing on one foot in an ecstasy of delight and embarrassment when Guy returned from Marlborough for the holidays, grown very handsome and tall, and with pleasant affability called Papa 'the gov-nor' and Gerald 'old fellow'.

Books were an excitement. There were *Treasure Island*, *The Three Musketeers*, *Robbery Under Arms*, and *The Wreck of the 'Grosvenor'*. They were so real that Gerald felt he was Hawkins or d'Artagnan, or Edward Royle saving Mary Robertson from the wreck, and sitting on a corner of Chang's sofa in the studio he remained gazing into vacancy, with his mouth hanging open, dreaming impossible adventures, dimly aware of Papa's laugh and his remark to Mummie, 'Look at Gerald, giving his brain a rest.'

Life was a genial, casual thing, where Gerald did more or less as he wanted, where it was easy to assume the quality of vagueness, thereby escaping all sorts of boring errands for grown-up people, and unconsciously thus earning for himself the title of 'vague' which would cling to him for ever until he became absent-minded through sheer force of habit. He discovered that it was one of the easiest things in the world to fool people, especially his own family, and that it only required a few minutes' concentration for him to have his own way over everything.

Mummie was easy game. He had only to sniff a little, and cough just the slightest, shiver a little and rub his hand across his nose, and at once she would be after him, questioning him, coaxing him, suggesting that he stayed indoors out of the cold wind and he should have what he liked best for dinner, and because he was not well he need not go out with the others or speak French to the governess, but might sit comfortably up in the studio with herself and Papa, and have his favourite books to read. Trixie might scoff, and Sylvia and May shrug their shoulders in disdain, but they would walk out primly along the Spaniards Road when he would be before the fire, flourishing an ostentatious handkerchief, and sucking a particularly pleasant brand of throat lozenge.

'Oh, Mamma, how you spoil Gerald!' exclaimed Trixie. 'You don't give way to the rest of us like that.'

'Nonsense,' Pem would answer – quite sharply, too, for her. 'Gerald is the youngest, and he has always had a delicate chest, and you are all of you far too inclined to tease him as it is'; and she sat beside him on the sofa, flushed and rather defiant, while the small boy in the sailor suit blew his nose for the twentieth time, and, peering up over his handkerchief, winked deliberately at his eldest sister.

Unwelcome invitations could generally be avoided with a 'I don't feel very well, Mummie; I think I won't go out to tea with Bertie and Cecil this afternoon'; or when the occasion pleased, and friends were in demand, 'Mummie, my headache seems to have gone, and I believe if I went up and played cricket with the Stedalls it would prevent it coming back again.' Of course, Mummie's fussiness could bring its annoyances as well. When he was thoroughly enjoying himself on the sands at Whitby she would make a dash at him with a wretched muffler, and wind it round his throat, or she would pursue him and May, as they went from the rooms in St Hilda's Terrace to the tennis courts, with jerseys and overcoats over her arm and strict injunction to leave off playing at the first speck of rain. What fun Whitby was, though! What an unending delight and discovery, with the big seas that broke over the end of the pier, and the slime and smell of herrings and cod in the fish market; and bathing, and cricket on the sands, tennis tournaments, picnics on the moors, with Mummie clinging to her hat and her skirt, and Trixie, too, while Papa smoked and sketched, and Guy read, and Gerald and Sylvia and May scampered about in the heather with Chang padding slowly at their heels.

Another year it would be Dieppe, which was almost as amusing but not quite, because the band of small friends would not be there and there was not quite so much to do. It was not very exciting pottering about the shops, even if the girls liked it, and sitting at a café was slow work when the last drop of grenadine had been sipped through its straw. But it was a great lark playing tennis and showing off before the French children, who gazed at him and May with open eyes of wonder as they played pat-ball to each other across the strip of net, and cried,

'*O, là-là, quelle merveille!*' when he succeeded in returning a volley.

'I say, May, I'm glad we're only half French,' shouted Gerald in disgust. 'These people can never have seen a racket before in their lives'; and, with all the arrogance of the young Briton abroad, he swaggered and capered about the court, throwing the ball much too high in the air and bringing his racket down with a crash on top of it, watching his little audience out of the tail of his eye, while May called to him impatiently to get on with the game. It was fun for the children, with their own perfect accents and proficient, though not entirely fluent, command of the language, to watch the other English tourists struggling with their vowels, and the children began a game amongst themselves of speaking '*à l'Anglais*', like the people in the hotel, much to Papa's amusement, who foresaw possibilities for *Punch*.

Oh, but living was pleasant, and living was fun, and back at Hampstead it was equally full and triumphant. Cricket matches with the Stedall boys, skating in winter on the private pond in Spencer Wells's garden, trying to cut figures on the ice in front of a girls' school who passed in crocodile, and crashing on his head as they turned to look at him. There was much laughter always, much good-humoured ragging and chaff, and only occasionally did less pleasing things happen, such as eating too much plum pudding at Christmas and being sick all the following day, and Mummie fussing with castor oil, and Guy looking scornful and cold as though he despised him.

Soon, only too soon, the necessity of school loomed on the horizon. Heath Mount, a boys' preparatory, was only two doors away up the road, within shouting distance of New Grove House. What could please Pem better than that her baby, her ewee lamb, should become a pupil at this school, so conveniently, so thankfully, close? Why, she could peer through the railings into the playground when she went for her morning walk, and call to him to be careful if he became overheated. Pem was delighted with Heath Mount. So Gerald was sent to school, and went his own way, as most small boys do, and was bad at geography and worse at mathematics, and none of his family was much the wiser or took particular interest in his life as a scholar; and why should they, when other more exciting things were happening, such as Trixie coming out and Guy talking of leaving Marlborough and trying for Sandhurst and the Army?

We have been more than usually dissipated, [wrote Kicky in '81] thro' Trixie coming out. Last night we took her to a large ball at the most noble Marquess of Salisbury's, and the night before to the most delightful music at Tadema's, Henschel, Rubenstein, etc. The night before that to another dance, a most gorgeous affair, and she may be said to have definitely come out for good. *Le rôle du père ne manque pas d'agréments – mais le lendemain – les lendemains! Aie aie! et ainsi de suite jusqu'à nouvel ordre!* The gay *monde* seems as yet to exert little fascination over Trixie, however, who thinks nothing so festive as a small dance in bourgeois respectable Hampstead, where she calls her partners by their Christian names, or even worse.

Gay, obstreperous, irresistible Trixie, with her eager curiosity about life, about people, her huge sense of fun, her bubbling voice, her quick laughter – Kicky was terribly proud of her. He did not keep her long, though; she danced her way through her little world of girls and boys and discovered herself engaged at the age of nineteen. Nineteen and twenty-three – they were very young. Of course, a Victorian parent must be pleased when his daughter decided to marry; the younger the better, no doubt, and a score had been made against other disappointed parents whose daughters were still hanging on their hands; and yet ... 'Trixie has made up her little mind,' said Kicky, 'and has engaged herself to one Charlie

Millar, a very nice boy who has been fond of her for some time.

'He is six feet high, *et gentil comme un chérubin*. Three years ago he meant to go into the Army, but the thought of Trixie prevented him, and he has become a merchant in the city. They seem very jolly and happy, and if they only get on together as well when they grow up they will do very well. I think Trixie a most fortunate girl and he is such a dear boy. *Pourvu que ça dure . . .*'

He so loved this daughter of his, he so longed for her to be happy in her life as he and Pem had been; but, however open and familiar he was with his daughter, how was it possible to tell her about marriage, about men, about the little irritating happenings of daily life that sometimes meant so little, that sometimes meant so much? They were young, these two; they had never suffered; they did not understand. Poor Kicky, when his firstborn was married, twenty years of age, and walked the aisle of St George's, Hanover Square, with a smile on her face to welcome the future, he stood watching her in a sort of dream. And then, as she went away from him, he shed tears like any other Frenchman.

The rest of the family departed in high spirits to play lawn tennis, while Kicky and Pem packed up the wedding presents to be sent to the new little house in Harewood Square, and, as Pem talked fondly of Trixie's happiness and contentment, Kicky kept thinking of his daughter's face when she had turned to him in the carriage on the way to the church, and taking his arm, had said to him with a puzzled frown, 'Papa, dearest Papa, if one marries a good-looking man, does it necessarily mean one will have good-looking children?'

With Trixie married, and Guy away at Sandhurst, and Gerald at school all day, New Grove House seemed very empty and forlorn, and during the next few years Kicky and Pem decided to let their home for the summer months and take a smaller furnished house in Bayswater. They were nearer to Trixie and their friends, Sylvia would meet more young people, and May would be closer to her singing lessons. So Gerald became a weekly boarder at Heath Mount, not without several injunctions from his mother about changing his undervests and bewaring of colds. He must also write to her twice a week. The life, of course, was the same as at any other preparatory school of that time, and Gerald was perfectly content, but he had the family trait of exaggerating little discomforts and pretending himself ill used.

'It's not much of a life,' he said, watching his mother's eyes; 'up at quarter past seven, and then prayers, and then breakfast, which is nothing but weak coffee and bread and scrape, and then putting on our boots, and then morning school, and then football.'

But Pem must know if he was substantially fed midday, and he was obliged to admit that dinner was 'first class, and tea was very fair.'

'But the Head, Mr Walker, takes us in school,' he grumbled, 'and I have to slave like a nigger. There's prayers, too, in the evening, an' we all have to line up and say good night to him before going to bed. Going to bed takes a quarter of an hour, and, although they come up to put out the gas, Nicoll and I [Nicoll was the crony of the moment] keep up a lively conversation afterwards. Then Mrs Walker comes and tucks us up and gives us a kiss, which keeps everybody awake all night. Prison life, I call it.'

Of course, he had caught the inevitable cold. 'Well, anyway, Mrs Walker rubbed my chest so hard it made me think of you, and I had to have my breakfast in bed, and was given Eno's Fruit Salts. Ugh! But in the evening it was even worse, 'cos I had some gruel which was full of lumps.

34

'No, it's quite gone now, thank you, and please I want you to go to Whiteley's and get me a swagger pair of reins; me and the other chaps have got a new game of driving each other. No, it's all right, I won't keep my coat on and get overheated.'

School apparently did not have the sobering effect upon Gerald that his parents had intended; if anything he became more cheeky and pleased with himself, ready to show off at the slightest sign of appreciation, and he wrote facetious little letters to Pem and the girls, fully aware that they could not help but laugh at him.

We went to a lecture on Monday evening, [he wrote] and the money was given to the Sailors' Daughters' Home girls. The girls sang at the beginning, I think they must have done it to get rid of some of the people, if so, it was a jolly good dodge. Anyway, I've made up a new song which begins 'He polished his gums with oat-meal cake' and it's got twenty verses. You sing it to the tune of 'Just before the battle mother'.

We had such a fearful pudding today that I hid it with my spoon, it was made of blamanche and plums, bad clotted cream and small black beetles. Tell Sylvia and May I hope they are behaving well, and are neat and modest withal. Matnong Adu, as the Englishman said when he went to Paris, j'ai tant bezwang de tes leves.   Your loving son,

                                    GERALD DU MAURIER
P.S. Don't forget apple pudding on Saturday night or you will ru the day.

Perhaps Guy was not often enough at home to squash this irrepressible young brother. Guy, who had just passed out of Sandhurst and was about to become a subaltern in the Royal Fusiliers, had presumably other matters in hand, and Trixie, who generally spoke her mind, had become the mother of her firstborn, Geoffrey, fulfilling in every way her anxious expectations, for he was one of the loveliest babies imaginable.

Of course, it was up to Kicky to administer parental

correction when necessary, but this was one of the things Kicky had always shirked. He was, and would be to the end of his days, lenient with children. So long as they were happy, so long as they looked attractive and amused him, he could not be hard with them; they would get knocks enough when they had to face the world. So when Gerald was too full of himself, bubbling over with health and high spirits, Kicky would look at him and shake his head, and then go back again to his easel, drawing away all the time, with his one blind eye and the sight of the other going, and say, 'Wait till you come to forty year, and see how you like it.' With a temperament like Gerald's, he thought, growing old wasn't going to be much fun. He would expect too much out of life, and would never understand why he did not find it.

But, anyhow, Gerald as yet was only a half-fledged youngster, like all small boys though slightly more original; and Kicky at fifty-three found the elder ones of his brood rather more companionable.

Trixie was adorable, though a wife and mother, and Guy was doing so well and making him feel very proud; and Sylvia was growing lovely with a rare, indescribable charm, gentle, wistful, touching; and May with her quick brain, her understanding, her French sense of perception, and her flaming devotion to him, was becoming the true daughter of his dreams.

It was Pem who must devote herself to the baby and see to Gerald's education, and it was Pem who wrote to Bowen, house-master at the Grove, to find out when there should be a vacancy for Gerald at Harrow.

It is to be assumed that Pem preferred Harrow to Marlborough, where Guy had been, because of its nearness to Hampstead!

So in the April of '87, Gerald, aged fourteen, was sent to Harrow, where he stayed until he was seventeen, spending three very happy years.

I've passed into the Lower Shell, [he wrote to his mother when he arrived] which is three above the bottom form, so it's not too bad, darling, is it? Please come and see me soon. As soon as some of the fellows knew my name was du Maurier they said, 'Oh, are you any relation to the *Punch* chap,' and the master made me sit down and be looked at for having so great a father. I am very happy here, though some of the things are very hard to understand.

Poor Gerald! Life at a public school was going to be rather different from easy-going Heath Mount and the freedom of New Grove House; and it looked as though his introduction as du Maurier's son, which he naïvely recorded with pride, was in reality in the nature of a rag.

He soon found his level, however. He made a number of friends, ragged and was ragged, did as little work as possible, took to football and swimming, consumed an incredible quantity of jam, sardines, and pies, sent regularly by the faithful Mummie; and if he learnt a lot he had never learnt before, and still less suspected, she was none the wiser, and he none the worse. It cannot be said that Gerald distinguished himself at Harrow in any particular way, in class or on the field, and he felt it was not likely that his name would go down to posterity as one of the great Harrovians. Nevertheless, he managed to squeeze the maximum of enjoyment out of his three years, and he saw to it that he made his friends laugh in the same way as he did his family – by imitating those whose peculiarities of speech or form lent themselves to mimicry, from his house-master down to the youngest fag.

He received several scoldings from Pem through spending his pocket-money on 'grub' or whatever took his fancy – he never at any time had the slightest idea of how to save money – and in his very first term he was supplying every boy in his pew at chapel with pennies, because it was hospital Sunday, and all the small fry but himself had come ill prepared.

From the start his letters to his mother began with an apology for the low place he had taken that week in school, continuing with a fervid promise 'to do better next time', and quickly going on to something else – something amusing if possible – so that she might forget.

Bowen [his house-master] has just gone out of the room, [he wrote, after admitting he had taken tenth place] and asked me who I was writing to, so I said 'to my mother' and looked up to Heaven dutifully. Then the head of the house came in and asked if I was a treble, to which I replied 'sometimes'. He then asked me what I sang generally, to which I replied 'middling'. He then laughed and said I was cracked. I have seen the plays rehearsed in 'Speecher', and they are rather good. They have got a Greek play, a German play, and a French one. I think the German is done the best because the chaps have such splendid accents, but the French accent! ! Ugh! Oh lor! An old professor came down this afternoon and jawed about cricket, that Temptation was the bowler, and Honour, Purity and Truth the three wickets, and I was so flabbergasted at his hockbottleness that I was nearly ill. ... Look here, I'm awfully sorry about tenth place but I really will do better, and in the meantime will you be a darling and send down at once a large square tin of milk biscuits, a cake from Buszard's, some Cadbury's chocolate, a Roll tongue, chicken and ham sausages, two tins of sardines, some more jam and honey, and anything else you like. And while you're about it, what about a little – oh, well, never mind! I'm longing to see you on Saturday, come early, and we will lunch at the King's Head, which is very much à la mode.

From his confident tone it did not look as though he expected Mummie to be very angry! Pem took her duties as mother seriously, though, and at the end of his first term was writing to his house-master to enquire how her boy had done; and Bowen replied with caution that he had had 'a satisfactory first term' and was 'likely to do well', though it was 'too soon to form proper judgment upon him'. He continued by saying that 'he seems to possess more than average ability, though not in the first rank, and it is a pity he seems so weak in mathematics. However, the boy appears to get on well socially, and is good tempered and modest.'

None of this was of much interest to Gerald himself, who could think of nothing but the holidays and his adored Whitby, where they were going as usual. The announcement that Guy was coming to spend a fortnight's leave with them filled his cup of happiness to the brim.

Gerald was beginning to realize that Guy was a very valuable possession. The girls were dears, of course, and May had been a great companion up to school days. But after all, he thought to himself, he wasn't a kid any longer, and sisters couldn't understand or appreciate half the things that happened at Harrow, which, of course, Guy did, and he was most terribly decent in telling one what one could do and what one couldn't, and when one behaved like a fool on certain occasions; and he was never beastly superior or put on side or anything like that, but talked to one in a very kind, gentle Guy-ish sort of way, as Papa might have done but never did; and though one never said anything about it one simply adored Guy. He was such a hell of a fellow, though he could be jolly frightening when he was angry.

Of course, Guy was frightfully good-looking, whereas some other people would never be anything but hopeless. He said one ought to take a pride in one's appearance, and brush one's hair and clean one's ears – after all, Harrow was a pretty important school. So the next term Gerald was writing to his mother for 'a thick waistcoat like the other chaps'.

Now just because I say that don't go sending every undervest I've got, [he said, knowing her] it's not because of the cold I want it, but because everyone has one. So couldn't you send a piece of paper saying 'my son can have an order for a thick waistcoat' because he won't give me an order for one until I have a letter from home. And darling, I left my rug behind on purpose, it was much too big for the train, and chaps hate a squash, that's why I didn't bring it.

Ask Guy to come down on Saturday, there's heaps I want to tell him.

It was obvious that Gerald, like any other school-boy, hated to be the slightest bit different from the others, and Guy was not likely to encourage individuality in a brother of fifteen.

Harrow was not, alas, ceaselessly amusing; this business of being low in form was a constant strain, because Mummie got so fussed and kept asking for the reason, repeating that he had not been sent to school only to enjoy himself, and what he did with his time she did not know, for he certainly did not spend it in writing to her.

I wish you wouldn't write letters that are nothing but one long curse, [he replied, thoroughly fed up] especially when it isn't my fault.

I was low this week and shall probably be low next week, but honestly I mean to do better in the future. I haven't been feeling too well anyway, I was ragging the other evening (there wasn't any work that night, so there!) and I got a very bad headache, about the worst I ever had, and when I got up it was no better. Going out made me feel worse, and I kept feeling sicker and sicker and finally I was sick, which made me better.

But it's a lesson to me not to forget my menthol another time. I've also had a stinking cold, and felt awful, and that's what really accounts for me being nineteenth this week.

So please write me another letter, and don't write it as though you had been to church on Ash Wednesday.

Whatever were Pem's private feelings, this epistle from the ewee lamb had the effect the sender intended, as a hamper containing roast duck, two roll tongues, and several pots of greengage and apricot jam arrived exactly

40

two days later. It was acknowledged with shouts of delight and an immediate effort to be amusing with pen and paper.

Thanks terribly for the hamper, darling, and do try and come down next Saturday, I'm longing to see my 'iky Mamma'! I will swat like a 5th rangler at trials and get up at four every day. I went to tea with Miss B. as you asked me, and liked it very much, but she's got such ghastly brothers, sort of leery brutes, don't cher know! Mrs B. is rather one of those 'do you think she is a lady?' sort of persons, and there was another old soul there, fat and rather jolly. The actress, Mary Anderson, came to chapel on Sunday, she evidently knows Weldon [the headmaster].
By gum! she is pretty! I looked at her while that moaning old goat Cannon M. preached to us. It's ghastly weather, raining like a sewer, but my cold is better, and I'm longing for the holidays, the first night of which I mean to celebrate by getting tight.

It is hardly to be wondered at that Bowen, his housemaster, was writing to Pem during the holidays:

I venture to send you a note about your boy, as I have been rather anxious about him during part of last term. I was not satisfied with him, as it appeared that frivolity was too much in the ascendant with him and conscience falling out of sight. I hope that this will pass away. He has again come out much lower than I should wish. But towards the latter part of the term I noticed an improvement in his behaviour, as though his face was set in the right direction, and I trust that he will yet grow to set a good example to the house.

Poor Pem, this baby of hers was more anxiety than the other four had been, put together. If only he would sometimes take things seriously! He appeared to do well at games, winning the house football prize for boys under fifteen during his first year, and later the house football prize for boys under seventeen, but really that was not going to be enough to equip him in life. It was a great source of worry to know what they were going to do with him when he left. As Kicky said, Gerald did not seem to show any aptitude for anything, unless it was play-acting, and of course that was out of the question; it was tactless of Kicky to laugh at him and encourage him with his foolery. This talent for mimicry had been allowed to go far enough; Gerald was continually boasting how he made the boys in his house laugh by imitating Irving up and down the passages, and alas this was where Guy was no help to her, because he himself was very keen on amateur theatricals and was always ready to take part in some such performance if there were any likelihood of one taking place. People were always only too ready to get up a show for charity at Whitby, and, although it was nice to hear May sing, it was another matter when Gerald blacked his face and capered about the stage as the whistling coon. Poor Pem was nonplussed. Gerald did seem to enjoy it so, bless him. It was gratifying to hear the applause, but oh! dear!

Pem was beginning to think she preferred going to Dieppe for the holidays instead of the usual inevitable Whitby. It was a nice change, and anyway Gerald was too young to be allowed in the gambling-rooms at the casino. However, the problem of what to do with Gerald when he left Harrow was still unsolved. At seventeen he was clamouring to leave; all his friends were going, and he kept saying how pointless it was to stay on, but did not seem to like the idea of going into the City, which was what she and Kicky intended. Not, as Kicky observed, that he was likely to do well there, but as far as he could see he was not likely to do well anywhere! Kicky was finding life very full just now; he had not the time to bother himself very much about his youngest son.

Gerald could leave school and enjoy himself staying with friends for a while, playing about at amateur theatricals, before earning his living in some capacity;

but Kicky had started lecturing over England, and was finding it rather a strain. It helped him financially, however, as his eye was a constant worry these days and interfered with his drawing. He had family troubles too; his only sister was in poor health after an operation, and his only brother, who had been in the French army and had never succeeded very much at anything, was constantly and wretchedly ill, and scarcely likely ever to recover. Sylvia, the gentle, had become engaged to one Arthur Llewellyn Davies, the son of a well-known clergyman, and was making plans to be married and leave home. *'Il est joli garçon comme l'autre,'* said Kicky to his friends; *'j'ai toujours l'œil sur ma postérité!* In fact, he is all that the most difficult-to-please parents could wish for a much-beloved daughter. *Il n'a que vingt-sept ans,* and has his own way to make entirely – as a barrister. Sylvia is very happy, but we shall miss her most dreadfully.'

But there was one other thing in Kicky's life at the moment which was occupying his mind to the exclusion of anything else. At fifty-six he was writing his first novel, and finding it a very absorbing experience. Ideas for stories had constantly passed through his mind, but he had never until now put them on paper. And now that he had started he found it simple, almost too easy; he wrote, in fact, with dangerous facility, as somebody once put it. The words poured from his pen. He looked back into his childhood; he shut his eyes and smelt the old scents of Paris, remembered the sounds, the spent voices, the dead faces. He conjured up once more the old ideals, the laughter, and the tears. He remembered the pageantry of his past, threaded with stray thoughts and long-forgotten dreams, and so *Peter Ibbetson* was born.

Kicky had much pleasure in its begetting. It served, he said himself, as a much-needed and powerful distraction through all the anxiety and trouble of poor brother

Gygy's illness, and his sister's too. And when it was finished, and had found a publisher in England and in America, it proved a very satisfactory way of making money.

'I'm glad you approve of my literary style,' he told Tom Armstrong. 'I took pains, of course – most delightful pains – and now see that I should have taken more. It all came too easily, and I found it far more difficult to illustrate than to write! Whether it will go down with the British public is another matter. I count a great deal on people's curiosity to see how a poor devil of a *Punch* draughtsman will acquit himself in a new line.' The British and American public apparently approved, and showed themselves willing for more, because a few months later Kicky was hard at work on his second novel, *Trilby*. Sometimes he thought it good, sometimes he thought it bad, but it never at any time came straight from his heart, as Peter had done, and he was conscious now of trying to write, instead of simply remembering. When it was published in the autumn of '92, and it received an ovation that had hitherto been unknown for a novel – it was the first of the modern 'best-sellers' – nobody was more surprised than Kicky himself. He had long been a celebrity, but now he was famous, and had made his fortune as well. The *Trilby* 'boom' was one of the most sensational literary events that ever happened; people went mad about the book in England and America. Its popularity was enormous, and Kicky became quite apologetic. He felt it was all rather vulgar, and he knew in his heart of hearts that *Peter Ibbetson*, written with the spirit and not with an eye to the public taste, was by far the better book.

The family, of course, became very excited; they none of them – with the possible exception of May, who was more intimate with him than the rest – had taken Papa's novel-writing *au sérieux*. At any rate, everybody was

44

delighted and exceedingly proud. Dear, funny, lovable Papa had become a household word. Gerald, who was secretly very impressed and proud of his father, pretended to take the matter light-heartedly, and asked his mother cheekily whether the governor would now consider putting electric light in the lumber-room, or if his French caution still held the upper hand!

Gerald, during all this time, had been doing pretty much as he wanted. He had a short and highly unsatisfactory period in a shipping office endeavouring to learn the business and making extremely heavy weather of it. Matters, in his opinion, came to a head when he was asked by the head clerk to remove a greasy dinner chop, upon which he immediately complained to the senior partner and received abject apologies. Finally, he announced his intention of leaving the City for good, as Papa and Mummie must surely realize it was in no way the sort of life for which he was suited.

He did not see that there was any desperate hurry about earning his living, for that matter. There was always plenty to do in London and elsewhere; friends to visit, week-ends at country houses, dances during the season; and, more fun than anything, amateur theatricals at Whitby and other places. Guy would back him up in these engagements, too.

By now Gerald was making quite a name for himself as an amateur actor, to Papa's amusement and to Mummie's distress, and in every respect the ewee lamb was finding life highly amusing. He saw himself at twenty as a young man-about-town, rather dressy and amusing, don't-you-know, strolling down Bond Street with silk hat tilted ever so slightly, cane in hand, and an eye to every pretty girl that passed.

'How are all my girls?' wrote the *blasé* youngster to May, who was up at Whitby whilst he was holidaying elsewhere with a friend. 'Have you noticed if they are looking sad, or at least anxious? I'm glad Margery is unchanged and still affectionate. The complexions here are marvellous, and tonight we are going to a dance where there will be two or three nice girls. I daresay you will see me at Whitby soon. Ta-Ta.'

He joined the family a few weeks later, looking rather tired and pale, and with the inevitable cold, to be nursed at once by Pem, very much concerned for her darling's health. His indisposition was trifling, however, as Kicky remarked drily, and occasioned by a rather too festive week at Canterbury with the 'Old Stagers'. Gerald was full of amateur engagements, as usual.

All the du Mauriers were up at Whitby; Trixie with her family of three boys, herself in tremendous spirits as usual and quite unperturbed by the fact that she had nearly died of typhoid earlier in the year. She was reconciled to her youngest's being another boy when she had longed for a girl, for he was so touchingly beautiful that his sex did not matter; Sylvia, with her first baby, George, and the devoted Arthur; Guy on leave from Woolwich, a Captain now, aged twenty-eight, very smart and good-looking, always writing plays for himself and Gerald, for they were inseparable; May clinging to Papa as usual, witty, talkative, with a better brain than any of them; and, last but not least, the generous, large-hearted, over-anxious Mummie, hovering with extra woollies and cod-liver oil, already warning Trixie not to let young Geoffrey and young Guy venture too near the railings for fear they should spike their noses.

In the autumn Gerald won laurels for his performance as William III in *Lady Clancarty* at a charity function, the local newspapers giving him high praise, and even his mother had to admit that he seemed better fitted for the stage than anything else. Perhaps if they let him do it for a little while no very great harm could come from it. Perhaps if he could be with some nice manager – a gentleman, of course – it might after all be quite a good idea. So Kicky, who had been reconciled to this all along, asked his friend Johnny Hare whether he could do anything for Gerald; the boy had been acting with amateurs all over the place, and seemed disposed to turn professional, and Kicky and Pem would be very grateful if he would give Gerald some little part in one of his plays.

Hare, a great friend of many years' standing, professed himself delighted, and on the 6th of January 1894 the ewee lamb appeared for the first time on the stage of the Garrick Theatre in *An Old Jew*, a comedy by Sydney Grundy. Gerald played Fritz, a waiter, the smallest part out of a cast of sixteen, and, though he had little to do and still less to say, he did both to the best of his ability, obtaining a certain amount of publicity because he was his father's son, and receiving a note of recognition from one critic, who observed that 'Mr du Maurier in a very few words showed that he had probably found his vocation, and that this was only the earnest of better things to come.'

So Gerald was launched on the professional stage; light-hearted, happy-go-lucky, and twenty-one. There had been nothing difficult about it; if anything, it had all been too easy. Mummie, the disapproving one, had proved herself amenable, and Papa and the rest of the family seemed highly amused.

Acting professionally was not perhaps as wildly exciting as he had imagined; it was, in fact, after the opening night, even a little tedious; he was not aware of any emotional ambition to sway the world as Hamlet or Lear and had no deep desires to change the face of living drama.

But the whole life happened to be rather amusing, rather fun; it was, to a gay, happy-go-lucky boy, a heaven-sent opportunity to indulge in an orgy of showing off. Beyond the gaiety, the gossip, the light and frothy tittle-tattle of back stage, there were so many new friends to laugh with him and at him, and oh, gosh! it was such fun to be liked. ...

For the next six months or so Gerald continued to play small parts at the Garrick Theatre under the management of John Hare. He never had very much to do, but managed in some way – achieving a momentary characterization by a little trick of make-up – to catch the wandering eye of a critic. He did it light-heartedly, to amuse himself and his friends, and never for a moment took himself seriously, but it pleased him all the same when somebody said, 'Mr du Maurier has done exceedingly good work at the Garrick, and, although he has not yet played any big part, he will be fully equipped with experience when the crucial moment in his career arrives.'

'It's all too easy,' Gerald thought. 'If putting on a beard and wearing a wig and speaking in a husky voice makes one a genius, I can't see there is anything to it'; and it came to him how easily critics and the public were fooled by a ginger wig and a tremor in the voice, and how little they understood that it was the simplest thing in the world to do. But ask a fellow to stroll on looking like himself, and without putting his hands in his pockets – that was asking something. John Hare, however, did not seem to require that of one, which was just as well, and there was the amusement, instead, of making up like a Cruickshank drawing for the small part of a shoemaker, or strolling about with bowed shoulders and a cough as an old club member; and it was all very much like what had always been since the days when he had given imitations of Irving in the corridors at Harrow, or, even earlier, when he had staggered around the studio in borrowed clothes to make Papa laugh.

He had to cut Whitby or Dieppe or whichever it was that year, and go off on tour with Forbes-Robertson in *The Profligate* and *Diplomacy*. It meant dirty lodgings and probably fleas in one's bed, and the inevitable bacon and eggs for supper, but a lot of fun on the whole, even if it was the custom to grouse about discomfort.

It was a novelty playing in the provinces; the people were so enthusiastic, and one became quite hysterical when they shouted out warnings from the pit, yelling, 'Don't take it!' to Forbes-Robertson as he lifted the poison to his lips in the last act. Gerald found his part rather tricky, as he had to serve through a whole dinner in the first act, take way the plates, and put on clean ones, and brush the cloth; it was by no means easy, but he managed to get through without a hitch. He was certain very few people could have done it with so few rehearsals and not smashed anything.

Algy, in *Diplomacy*, required different treatment; it was his first attempt at a 'straight' part, and, according to the local Press, he was found to be exceedingly fresh and entertaining, as well as 'every inch a gentleman' – to his intense amusement. He played Algy for the first time at Derby, and was in a great funk that he might make a hash of the part, but everyone appeared to like him and he was much congratulated by the company. After all, it was not very frightening playing to a provincial audience, and once his little role was over for the evening there was ham and eggs in his rooms with the rest of the smaller fry, and songs at the piano, and heated discussions, a lot of smoking, and a great deal of card-playing, and, to wind up the evening, Gerald giving imitations of every member of the cast in his and her respective parts.

There was a tremendous amount of ragging and chaffing, Gerald usually the leading spirit. He fitted very well into this pleasant, haphazard life, where he could do just exactly as he pleased without being made to feel uncomfortable by a reproving glance from Mummie. 'Tell Papa I am NOT drinking too much,' he wrote very indignantly after a warning letter from home. 'I'm enjoying it all very much, apart from the fleas and the bad eggs, but nevertheless I long for the bosom of my family. I'm returning to the Garrick for the season at Three pounds a week. That's all right, isn't it?' His mother folded the letter and put it carefully away with the Press cuttings which informed her that her son showed promise and had pleased the Edinburgh audiences; and she sighed and shook her head and hoped that the sheets in those horrid lodgings were properly aired, otherwise he would go catching one of his colds, with, of course, nobody there to look after him. She did not see any of the women in the company rubbing his chest with camphorated oil.

'Has the mummer distinguished himself again?' asked Kicky. 'Or is it another sick·headache?' And when Pem reproved him for being heartless, he sighed, and took off his glasses, and said that success was all very well, but being sixty was another matter. *Trilby* was at the height of its fame, was to be dramatized next year by Paul Potter and win fresh laurels; but he, Kicky du Maurier, was tired and depressed, and his eye hurt him, and he had been happier far when he was a little draughtsman in the early days of *Punch*, and the children were young, and poor darling Trixie had not lost her baby from meningitis and broken her heart at the same time.

Life was not all play-acting and singing songs at the piano and having little mild flirtations, as Gerald would discover, he said; and then he looked out of the studio window and up at the passing clouds, and reproached himself for being hard on his youngest, to whose mind and body he had given so much of himself when he begat him; and he prayed to whatever gods might be that Gerald would not know the little solitary demon that dwelt in his soul sometimes, who cried, and yearned, and knew no comfort.

Trilby was produced for the first time in Manchester, in the September of '95, by Beerbohm Tree, and Gerald was one of the company, playing the small part of Dodor, the French dragoon, a character founded on his poor Uncle Gygy, who had died a few years before.

There is no doubt that *Trilby* is an enormous success [he wrote to his mother after the opening night] some people think the greatest Tree has ever had. The applause was tremendous. He of course made the biggest hit of the evening, but Taffy and the Laird were very much liked, and Miss Baird is simply charming – her likeness to Trilby in her first dress is quite astounding. You will be glad to hear that Tree is very pleased with my Dodor; he says I am the life and soul of the *cancan* scene, and has put me right down in the front, and I have got the best girl to dance with too.

The make-ups are all amazingly good, Tree and Taffy especially being right out of the book. Tree has got the whole thing on the brain and can talk of nothing else. We were all delighted to get Papa's telegram, and Tree made a speech before the curtain, and the governor's name was loudly cheered when he mentioned it. I think perhaps Papa ought to ask Tree to thank the company from him, don't you? Potter spoke very nicely to everyone, and I must say he has been devilish clever over the adaptation, but he is nothing like as great a man as the governor. Lots of things are going to be altered now that the first night is over. I'm suggesting heaps myself and they are all going to be done. That's what comes of being the author's son! In fact when people want things altered they come to me and say, 'I wish you'd ask Tree,' etc., etc., and so I go up and say, 'Mr Tree, it would be much better for *you* if So-and-so did such-and-such a thing,' and he says, 'We'll see,' and a few minutes later he says in a loud voice, 'An idea has just occurred to me,' and does what I've told him. In fact the whole thing is such a success that we shall play little else but *Trilby* now on this tour, and we shall probably bring it to the Haymarket next month.

I had a most fearful cold after the first night, but I spent a morning at a Turkish bath and am all right now. I hope you've not been bad with your cold. You tell me to take care of myself, why don't you take care of yourself? Be well, darling, by the time this reaches you. I've written to dear Trix to congratulate her on the new arrival, though I should have preferred a niece. Let's hope he will make up to her for the loss of poor Leslie. Love to May and Papa, and tell him he has the chance of making a lot more money.

After riotous preliminary weeks in the provinces, Tree brought *Trilby* to London and produced it at the Haymarket on the 30th of October. It ran for two hundred and sixty performances and was an enormous success. Gerald, who had definitely left Hare and was under contract now to Tree, continued to play Dodor.

So Kicky, at sixty-one, had the experience of seeing his own creation – adapted, it is true, but nevertheless his own immortal Trilby in flesh and blood – take London by the proverbial storm. He sat in a box and through a mist saw the excited faces smile up at him, and heard their applause; was aware of the hundred voices murmuring congratulations and the eager, outstretched hands; watched Gerald dance wildly about the stage looking exactly like poor dead Gygy forty years ago, and he thought: 'How very elated and above myself I should have been if this had happened then, or even later in '67, the time we played *Box and Cox* for charity; and now – I don't know; perhaps it's something to do with being sixty-one, and nearly blind, and not having been well for the last few months, but I don't feel nearly as gratified as I ought to; it's all rather fussing and slightly embarrassing and I want to go home.'

He felt he did not deserve all this adulation, and he was convinced that the success of both *Peter Ibbetson* and *Trilby* was nothing but a fluke. Nobody would understand his next novel; they wouldn't like it anyway; there was too much of the melancholy demon in it, the lonely self, blindness and spiritual longings all mixed up inexplicably with his deep attachment to May; a difficult, personal book. . . . He blinked nervously behind his glasses, and then took them off and polished them, and said, 'Oh! dear,' when Pem nudged his arm and whispered that he had smiled at somebody else in mistake for Mrs Tree. *'On devient vieux,'* he thought; *'on a trop fumé de cigarettes, et trop bu de petit bleu – et voilà . . .'*

Gerald, very flushed and excited with the family success, wondered what the governor thought of it all. 'Papa's getting more short-sighted every day,' he considered, 'and Mummie clucks round him like an old hen. What dear, funny old cups of tea they are, and how awful it must be to be old.' And he rushed off to change from Dodor back to his natural self again, so that he should not miss a moment of the champagne supper.

Whilst his father at sixty-one was wondering *à quoi bon?* about life, Gerald at twenty-two found it tremendous.

He had achieved no brilliant success in himself, but the very fact of being young and alive had gone to his head. He enjoyed every moment of his day – and night too, for that matter. There was always so much to do and to see. Besides the theatre there was golf when there wasn't a matinée, and cards and gossip at the Green Room until all hours. How peacefully Mummie slept, thinking her ewee lamb was safely in his bed when he was nothing of the sort.

Already he was boasting to Guy, home on leave, that he was far more of a man-of-the-world than he was with soldiering, and the older brother smiled and agreed, and let him have his head. He managed to squeeze the utmost out of everything; there was so much fun to be had, and even a crazy, uncomfortable bicycle tour, during the run of *Trilby*, with Harry Esmond and Charles Hallard appeared to him to be the height of amusement.

Thanks terribly for the ten pounds, darling, [he wrote to his mother] when I come back I shall give several little supper-parties to the – well, perhaps you had better not know! I have had a simply glorious week, and never enjoyed myself so much in my life. We bicycled all day, and ate and drank of the best, and all feel like new men. I did everything; paid the bills and got up at eight-thirty every morning, and went off to the station with our things to *expédier les bagages*. We all got on beautifully, and never a moment's unpleasantness from start to finish. We had punctures which we mended on the road-side, and which the whole village came out to watch, and there were no three more popular men in France than the genius, the gentleman, and the young Greek god. Of course you guess which I am; I invented the title and starred myself. Esmond is writing a story round it for private circulation only. Oh! it's been a glorious week, and we've done nothing but laugh and drivel the whole time, and there's nothing jollier than that when the weather's fine. Dodor once more tomorrow, and then *Henry IV* rehearsals. I'm sorry it's cold at Folkestone, but the change will do you a lot of good, and pick you both up for the London season, which I suppose Papa is looking forward to. Give him my love, and take care of yourself, darling.

The long run of *Trilby* finished in the summer. Alternating with it were matinées of *Henry IV*, in which Gerald played Gadshill, and then came a holiday in Scotland and the beloved Whitby, followed by a second tour with Tree in the provinces prior to taking *Trilby* to America.

Gerald wrote home in the usual high spirits, undamped by the discomfort of theatrical lodgings, and made occasional appearances to cheer up Papa, who had been off colour ever since he had returned from Whitby.

Kicky had been troubled by giddiness for some time. He supposed it was walking too much in hilly country, and his doctor ordered him complete rest in bed for three weeks. He hated this, but, as the only alternative appeared to be a business of carrying him from his room should he wish to go downstairs, he preferred to stop in bed.

He took a dislike to all food. As his gums were swollen

from a bad tooth and his mouth was very sore, he could only be induced to take slops. He had only been in bed a few days when there came a fresh spot in his remaining eye which caused him very great worry and distress. At the same time he developed a type of asthma, the cough tearing at him and exhausting him, so that he found it difficult to breathe.

Nevertheless he was talkative, and appeared to have no great pain, and the family hoped that with rest and care he would soon be himself again. Even the doctors did not realize that there was an accumulation of matter in his heart and that nothing could save him.

Gerald came and sat on his bed, and told him the latest gossip, and what Tree had said to somebody the night before. He reminded him of how he had saved the dog in the White Stone Pond, and of the time when they were travelling to Dieppe with trunks, suitcases, and hold-alls, and somebody's parrot bit him in the finger, and Papa rushed up to Mummie in a passion, as though it were her fault, and said, 'Don't you realize that if I had been a pianist this would have ruined my career, and you and the children would starve?' He spoke of the time when Kicky was drawing a masher-about-town, and asked Gerald to sit for him; Gerald put on the most extraordinary mixture of clothes imaginable – a frock coat, an evening waistcoat, white flannel trousers, an impossible tie and a straw hat – and walked into the studio without a smile; and, on Papa asking why he was dressed up like that, he replied that this was the latest fashion. He had asked for a well-dressed man, and this was what everyone was wearing in the Park. Papa answered, 'Do they? I call it very ugly,' and began drawing him at once, blinking away behind his glasses ...

'You ought to be a proud man, you know, Papa,' said Gerald, flicking ash off the bed and watching the governor's eyes; 'the whole of London has gone mad over

Trilby, and here they are in the provinces just lapping it up. You should hear them cheer and nearly lift the roof off after every performance. Tree says he has never known anything like it'; and he began to give an imitation of Tree as Svengali, rolling his eyes and stretching out his fingers in strange sinister gestures – grossly exaggerated, of course, but he had to do something to chase away that tired and weary look in the governor's eyes that he did not remember ever seeing before.

It came to him for the first time that perhaps Papa was going to die. The idea frightened him, and he began to talk faster and joke more wildly in a last and desperate attempt to keep the idea hidden. It could not be – not dear, darling Papa, with his funny old-fashioned ways, his set routine, his songs, his laughter, his odd words of wisdom. Other people died, perhaps, but not one's father, not the person one remembered before anyone else in the world, before Mummie even, standing in the studio at New Grove House with his back to the windows and the light upon his easel, smoking his innumerable cigarettes and humming *'Plaisir d'amour'* under his breath; Papa who used to give a whistle to Chang snoring upon the sofa, and then turning with a laugh to the small pale-faced boy who stood in the doorway, would say, 'Ah, Gerald, my Gerald, wait till you come to forty year. Come and sit to me for *Punch,* old fellow; *tu as l'air d'un tout petit microbe sans tête – je te comprends plus que tu n'y pense.'*

How little he knew of Papa – of his secret thoughts, of his dreams, of all the little happenings that had gone to make up his daily life. Why had he not taken more trouble, sat with him more often, asked for his advice? One was so infernally selfish. One never stopped to think. One took everything for granted: holidays at Whitby, walks on the Heath, lunch on Sundays, evenings in the studio; one hadn't tried to know this man who had written books at sixty from the dreams he remembered.

So Gerald fooled and acted, for the first time in his life aware of pain, his heart wrung at the sight of Papa in bed, small, incapable, and strangely pathetic; Papa, who, exhausted with coughing, put up his hand and shook his head, saying, 'No, no, stop; you make me laugh too much'; Papa, who, when Gerald stood at the door and said good-bye before catching his train back to the provinces, looked up at him for the last time with his poor blind eye and smiled, and held out his hand and whispered, '*Si c'est la mort, ce n'est pas gai.*'

Kicky died on the 8th of October, 1896, between two and three in the morning. He was quite unconscious and without pain. He was buried in Hampstead churchyard, ten minutes from New Grove House, and within a stone's throw of that first Hampstead home where Gerald had been born.

On his grave were written the last lines of *Trilby*:

> A little trust that when we die
> We reap our sowing! And so – good-bye.

CHAPTER THREE

KICKY'S death meant a great upheaval in the happy, peaceful home, and the family knew that life for them would never be quite the same again.

Trixie and Sylvia had their boys to console them, and the little daily round of their own lives, but, even so, the gap could never be filled. May was heartbroken, her world fallen about her, and it was her mother who found courage first and fought against the misery that overwhelmed her, with this breaking up of thirty-three years of peace and content. Guy was a tower of strength, gentle, comforting, and firm, shouldering his responsibilities as head of the family, and with the help of Charlie Millar, Trixie's husband, saw to the wretched necessities and all the pitiful aftermath of death.

Gerald, on tour with Tree and preparing to sail for America, could only write boyish words of comfort which he knew to be inadequate and hopeless.

You mustn't get too depressed about my going away, [he said] remember it's only for a short time and I will write very often.

Of course, darling, you must miss Papa terribly; it's bad enough for all of *us*, but what it must be to you! We must all live together, I think, Millars, Davieses, and the rest. I wish to heaven I was at home with you as well as Guy. I'm getting morbid at the thought of this beastly tour.

Everyone is being very nice, of course, and their sympathy is genuine. We are playing *The Dancing Girl*, and Tree says I have made a hit, but what is that to me? It's pelting with rain and foully depressing and cold. I'm wearing all my combinations at once, you will be glad to hear.

I wish we were all on tour together, darling, though I can't for the life of me think of a part that would suit you. Tree seems to be in a very good temper, and dear Kate Rorke is as perfect as always. A very pretty French girl, Miss Sylva, is also in the cast.

It is difficult to be weighed down by sorrow all the time, when you are twenty-two.

Gerald sailed for America in the *St Louis* with the rest of the company in the middle of November. He felt very depressed when Guy disappeared over the horizon at Southampton, and the only sight that cheered him was the vision of Mrs Tree and young Viola weeping on the pier head and throwing bunches of violets after the departing Herbert, who, striking an attitude in the bows of the vessel, cried, 'Adieu, England'.

Certain members of the company began to be sick as soon as the ship was clear of the Solent, but Gerald, recovering rapidly from his depression, was at the top of his form throughout the whole of the very boisterous passage. He played cards and deck quoits and shovelboard; to amuse Tree, he started a scurrilous magazine full of scandal about everyone on board, and got up a concert with some of the others and sang his famous song, 'Frosty Weather', aided by the friendly and decidedly ravishing Miss Sylva. The tour started off in Washington, and went on to New York and Baltimore. Gerald made something of a hit on his own account, but was noticed in the main because he was du Maurier's son and was entertained everywhere for that reason. It was the first time he wholly realized what a great man Kicky had been, and how colossal was his popularity in America.

The responsibility of his position rather weighed him down. He began to feel homesick and miserable, and, in a wild attempt to keep up his spirits, he started a heavy flirtation with Marguerite Sylva. Before he knew how it had happened he had asked her to marry him, and imagined himself to be desperately in love. As ill luck would have it, some newspaper got hold of the story before Gerald had time to write home, and he did not know that the family was aware of the news until he received a stern telegram from Guy saying, 'May I contradict report of your engagement?' followed by a stream of hectic reproaches from Mummie.

Gerald was terribly upset, and their very antagonism made him cling more fiercely to his Maggie. Mummie and Guy were unfair, were unkind; they made no attempt to see life from his point of view. They might at least give him a chance to explain.

You know, Mummie darling, I put you before everyone and always shall, [he wrote at fever heat] and if you could only speak to her for five minutes all your unhappiness would vanish. The only fault you can possibly find is that she is French in appearance, in voice, in everything. Why in Heaven's name she has fallen in love with me, nobody knows. She wears her hair parted in the middle, and it wants a bit of beating, I tell you, but I won't send her photograph as it makes her look forty, and bold at that.

Anyway, it's no use talking any more about it. I love her and you must too. I'm sure May will like her. Please don't write as though I was a son who had gone hopelessly to the bad.

Poor Gerald, raging and tearing over his first love-affair, swearing a little too loudly that Maggie was the only woman in the world, and wondering in his heart whether they were both making fools of themselves!

People think I am very lucky [he insisted in his next letter]. New York is full of it. She *is* younger than I am, though you say she doesn't look it, and what's more she has a beautiful voice and speaks three languages and is devoted to me. I suppose the girls think I'm hockbottle and have no sense of humour; well, I just don't care. They are beasts not to write. For God's sake tell me I am not making you unhappy, Mummie darling, because it isn't fair, and if you knew how miserable I felt when I got Guy's last cable you would be sorry for me.

He simply could not understand why, when he had been given in to over everything so far, his family should put up resistance the first time he showed signs of being serious.

Meanwhile the tour was proving a dismal failure; nobody, not even Tree, had received good notices, and the only play that went at all well was *The Dancing Girl*. Gerald found New York extremely expensive. He did not care about the people, and Maggie kept threatening to get another contract and to stop out there for good.

Neither of them gave way an inch to the other, and there were fierce arguments between them from morning till night, which did not speak very well for the future. The next thing was that Maggie received a furious letter from her mother telling her that if she married young du Maurier, who was nothing but a penniless young actor and a waster, she would disown her and have nothing more to do with her. For a while this fanned the flame. The pair of them swore vows of eternal love, and Gerald wrote to Mummie trembling with indignation, saying that he was going to stop out in America with Maggie, and she must come out with May and be with them, and they would make a lot of money – he was always being offered parts with good salaries, especially since they had played *Trilby*, which proved to be the biggest success of the hitherto unfortunate tour – and then they would all go back to England. He loathed the idea of remaining in America; he was desperately homesick and longing for his family; but he could not leave poor Maggie out there all alone. Surely Mummie saw that his plan was the only possible one? Why must she and May be so difficult?

His head was nearly splitting with his efforts to think of a way out for all of them. But Mummie remained firm. Nothing would induce her to leave England, and the suggestion that Gerald should stop out there, marry this Marguerite Sylva, and both of them go in for musical comedy – which was the latest idea – filled her with horror. She spent a miserable Christmas, the first lonely bitter Christmas since Kicky had died, and Gerald spent an equally unhappy one on the other side of the Atlantic. Of course, the inevitable happened. It was only to be expected.

DARLING MUMMIE, – I suppose you got my telegram saying that the engagement was broken off? Please don't tell anybody, for the sake of peace and quiet. The fact is this. We are absolutely devoted to one another, but as a married couple, as far as I can see, we should be impossible. I do not understand her and she certainly does not understand me. We are as opposite in character as the two poles, so what's the use of being engaged? If in the dim future we find we cannot do without each other, well and good. It's been the most awful week to go through I've ever had, and Maggie has behaved in a perfectly splendid way. I asked her to break it off. All I ask you is to say nothing about it, let it die of itself. She is going to stop out here, which will be pretty awful for her alone, and the rest of us come back about February the 3rd. I will cling to my family henceforth and for ever, the ewee lamb is no good away from the fold.

This is the first real trouble I've caused you, darling, and you mustn't be too hard on me. I think once will be enough for me in that line of business, so try and forget all I've done to make you unhappy. Never finish your letters in that way again, like last time; you know you wouldn't dare say that to any of the others. I shall never again travel without the family photographs, you've no idea how dreadful it is not to see anything even like you. And when you sent me that one of Sylvia and the kids the other day I nearly cried. Don't meet me at the station. I want to burst into the dining-room and find you all there at lunch or something. Oh Lord! what an eternity it

seems since I've seen you all, and I thought of making it
longer. ... Good-bye, darling,

Your loving son,
GERALD

So that was that, the whole episode, rather hasty and
unnecessary and foolish, leaving Gerald with the uncomfortable feeling that he had not behaved too well and was
something of a shirker, but too damned relieved that it
was over, and therefore no more rows and worry, to care
really very much.

Poor Maggie, he would miss her terribly, of course,
and she had been a darling; but being engaged was too
much of a strain to be pleasant, and it was a good feeling
to be free again. Before opening at the new Her Majesty's
Theatre in April with *The Seats of the Mighty*, Tree
took his company on tour for a short while; and, now
the excitement of America and his engagement had died
down, Gerald felt rather flat. The provincial towns
seemed dull, and he could not get any golf. Altogether
he suffered badly from reaction. Guy was away, and
would not be getting any leave until the summer. And
then May suddenly went and astonished them all by
getting herself engaged – May, who had been so broken
when Papa died that no one thought she would ever be
the same again; and here she was apparently devoted to
this new acquisition, a charming fellow, Edward Coles,
whom everyone took to on sight, quiet, dependable,
clever, and with a capital sense of humour; just the man
for nervy, highly strung May.

Still, it was just the slightest bit galling to see how
pleased and delighted the family were that May had
found her happiness, and to remember the fuss and com-
motion there had been about himself and Maggie. He
couldn't help feeling just a little bitter.

'I'm glad May is attached to Coley, or whatever you
call him,' he wrote. 'I suppose she knows what she's about.

I hope we will all get on with him. Can she look into his eyes and say "My king" without feeling a fool? Oh, well, God bless the loving couple. I'm sorry his income doesn't run into four figures.'

He felt superior, and rather old and *blasé*; after all, he had been through a much more hectic time than May would ever experience with this chap she was going to marry.

The family were a little tactless in their enthusiasm. 'Poor old cup of tea,' he said to Mummie, 'all your children seem to want the plain gold ring. The male portion of your brood play the game quite differently. You needn't be afraid of my young fancies turning to thoughts of love for some time, believe me.' It is so easy to speak when there is no one attractive in sight, and life for the moment is centred on the opening of Her Majesty's Theatre and the run of plays for the London season: *A Man's Shadow*, *The Silver Key*, *Seats of the Mighty*; and then the inevitable autumn tour, with its usual round of comfortless lodgings, golf and cards between performances, gossip, grousing, and back-chat. But when the months slip by and somebody turns up in England with fair hair and a tip-tilted nose, very spoilt and independent, aged nineteen, called Ethel Daphne Barrymore — well, it's a different matter altogether.

The worst of a man's being susceptible is that, each time, he thinks she is going to be the one and only woman and he swears eternal fidelity, and tears himself to pieces, and most of the time he draws largely on the imagination, striking dramatic postures and fancying every sort of tragic passion.

Perhaps with Gerald it was a question of not having enough to do, and feeling himself wasted playing small character parts at the Haymarket and on tour. At any rate, poor Maggie Sylva was barely forgotten before the ewee lamb was head over heels in love with this newcomer, and plunging himself and his family into the turmoil of another engagement.

Mummie, who had settled into a flat in Portman Mansions and was prepared to make it a happy home for her youngest, where he would be carefully nurtured under her tender eye, had the worry of seeing her darling fall once more from her careful clutches. Oh, dear, oh, dear, why must Gerald behave so stupidly? None of the others had given her this trouble. Look at dear Guy – a model son, writing to her nearly every day of his life from wherever he was stationed – and here was this boy taking up with another actress and talking wildly of an immediate marriage.

True, things might have been worse. Daphne was very young and pretty, and undeniably charming, and of course one knew who were her people, and she seemed very talented and all that; but really these things did not mean that she would make Gerald happy, and how could she possibly know her own mind at nineteen? She was very self-willed.

What did Guy think? Well, Guy thought it all over very carefully and produced many arguments against a hasty and improvident marriage, which he said would convince anyone who was not seriously in love, but the question was whether Gerald was seriously affected or not? Time would show; it was no use nagging him; that was just the way to send him off the deep end. So Gerald and Daphne and Harry Esmond and Charles Hallard all went off to fish in Ireland, a strange, unconventional thing to do, which Mummie was not at all sure she approved of. But presumably the children would discover whether they were really fond of one another or not.

Daphne wrote little letters to her future mother-in-law and wondered whether she was saying the right thing, and, because she was only nineteen, she was a great favourite with everyone in the Bay View Hotel, Waterville, besides Gerald. She played the piano, and was temperamental, and wore her hair in a pigtail with a crimson tam-o-shanter, and looked elfin, and adorable, and never more than fourteen.

Gerald fished with Harry, and bathed with Charles, and begged Daphne to marry him as soon as possible; but she was very wilful, and would not make up her mind, and asked if they couldn't be like brother and sister, and said that after all she thought she wanted to go back to America.

Whereupon Gerald, dramatizing the situation at once, threatened suicide, and, rushing down the Kerry beach, waded in water up to his neck, fully aware that Daphne was sobbing wildly, 'Gerald, Gerald, come back!' White and stern, he stood with folded arms, waiting for the tide to lift him from his feet. 'Now perhaps she'll believe I'm serious,' he said. It was a situation after his own heart.

But perhaps the tide did not come in quick enough, and he grew tired of waiting; perhaps Harry the dreamer, who was fond of them both, suggested that they were making fools of themselves; perhaps Daphne did really want to go back to America. The result was a letter to Mummie saying that they had decided against getting married, at any rate for the moment. Daphne could not make up her mind, even if he could, and he would come back to the flat and be her blue-eyed boy once more.

Mummie was furious; not with her darling, but with Daphne. She had just managed to accustom herself to the engagement, and believe that marriage would be the best thing for Gerald after all, and now the girl had the impudence to turn down the poor darling boy, perhaps breaking his heart, and talked calmly of going off to America and leaving him to get over it. 'You mustn't be hard on her, Mummie,' said Gerald when he returned; 'after all, she's very young and hasn't found her level yet. It won't do me any harm, perhaps a little good. I don't bear her any grudge, and you musn't say unkind things about her before me, because I won't allow it. You must not be intolerant, darling, and anyway, I haven't given up all thoughts of it yet, whatever she may say.'

But the wilful Daphne returned to America, and Gerald travelled north once more on another autumnal tour with Tree, not very much the worse for his second disheartening love-affair, though somewhat wounded and cynical nevertheless – a state of affairs which the chatty, sisterly letters from Daphne did little to cure. However, he plunged himself into the part of Aramis in *The Three Musketeers* and Casca in *Julius Caesar* and did his best to forget her, and wrote to Mummie about how he longed to be back in the flat with her alone again, to soap and water, and clean shirts, and the true ewee lamb existence. The following summer, when the London run of the *Musketeers* was over, Gerald left Tree and was at a loose end for a while. He played in a light comedy under Hawtrey in September, and was now getting nine pounds a week. In November he joined under the management of Mrs Patrick Campbell at the Royalty Theatre, and remained with her, both in London and on tour, for two years.

It was a period of transition, a time for growing up. During these two years he became a man instead of a boy, and if he hurt himself at times, and was angry, and passionate, and miserable, he came out of it stronger, with greater understanding, possessing a knowledge of human nature he had never known before, a comprehension of men and women and the realities of life that had hitherto not touched him, an added judgement, a certain philosophy, and more than a little wisdom.

He learnt during this time, as Kicky had foreseen he would, that life is not all play-acting, and fun, and doing as you please; that both mind and body must have discipline if they are to serve you well; that, as Papa once

said, 'It will take some little time and training before
you are fit to play well the trade you've chosen'; that
there is more happiness and satisfaction in working for
the sake of the play, the profession, and your immortal
soul, than there is in working for the glorification of
Gerald du Maurier. Even if he did nothing brilliant
during his time, nothing by which he could be long remembered, at least he put the best of himself into what
he did, and tried as he had never tried before.

It would always be something of a game to him, of
course; he was not then, and would never be, one of
your true actors. He lacked the intensity, the concentration, the necessary self-conceit and passionate eagerness
of those who talk about their Work and their Art; and
even then he was not known to say, 'Ah! what I would
give to play that part!'

It was possibly a strain of cynicism, inherited from
his forebears and undoubtedly French, that prevented
him from ever taking himself seriously. And his sense
of humour, Kicky's priceless gift, developed to an even
greater extent in Gerald, and at times, positively warped,
prevented that ecstatic and artistic abandon that is generally associated with the actor.

Had anyone asked him in '98 or any other time why
he went on the stage, he would have replied quite truth-
fully that it amused him, that he was too idle to work in
an office, and that he was quite unfitted for anything else.
And at that time he had certainly never heard the words
'self-expression' or 'ridding the system of inhibitions'. In
those days the actor's job was to provide entertainment
for people, not to work off surplus energy and private
complexes in public.

Gerald did well during those two years at the Royalty
and on tour, and gained very valuable experience. His
friendship with Mrs Campbell was the best thing that
could happen at this period of his life. She was eight

years older than he; very beautiful, very exacting, with a temperament like one of Racine's heroines, an angel one moment and a fury the next. Her personality was dominant, dwarfing those around her, and as a companion she was fascinating and exhausting.

There was no peace with her, no quiet moment; it was either heaven or hell, ecstasy or despair. When you were with her you wanted to be away, out of sight, alone; and when she was gone it was torture until you heard that voice again, rather full, rather sullen, the voice of Athalie or Phèdre. You adored her and hated her in turn. You sat at her feet and worshipped, or rushed from her presence slamming the door and calling damnation upon her name. She was disturbing and possessive and impossible, but it was better to be frowned upon by her than ignored.

It was worth while to endure the tempest for the knowledge she imparted. She was a mistress of stagecraft. She knew every trick of her trade, and her lessons were invaluable. She taught Gerald how to act and how to live, and he was eternally grateful. Under her tuition he became a man of certain depth, understanding, and subtlety, instead of a spoilt, irresponsible boy. He learnt how to talk, how to be silent, and how not to be consistently selfish. Much of his charm, his delicacy, his ease of manner and his assurance he owed to her. She worked tirelessly, taking infinite pains with him, and, being every inch of her an actress, she realized that this spoilt, restless young man might do almost anything if he chose to take a genuine interest in his trade and his own talent. There were scenes, of course, blistering rows and fierce reconciliations, days of sulky silences and days of riotous successes. And in this weird mixture of excitement, anger, and frequent disillusion Gerald developed his mind, his intuition, and his little grain of genius.

'I have taught a clown to play Pelleas,' said Stella in 1900, when they were touring in Dublin, and Gerald, in a fever of nerves, believed he had made the biggest success in his career in a part that was quite outside his line. But, although nobody was ever to remember this particular Pelleas, the work he put into it and the encouragement he received from the proud Stella were the real things that mattered.

In *Mr and Mrs Daventry*, *The Fantastics*, and *The Second Mrs Tanqueray*, which were three of the plays produced at the Royalty by Mrs Campbell, he did well but not brilliantly, bringing a certain freshness, a certain *flair*, personal and unique, to every new part he played, and, even when he did little, this little was noticed favourably by the critics.

Of *The Fantastics*, for instance, one said:

No one was light enough, quick enough, extravagant enough – with one exception, Mr Gerald du Maurier. He alone seemed to catch the spirit of the piece, and to understand what was wanted. He acted with infinite humour, dash, and grace. How much there is in heredity and parentage! Mr du Maurier is French in family, and had a delightful humorist as his father.

And in *Mariana Superba*, one of the finest things Mrs Campbell ever did, a minor part was, according to Clement Scott, played quite perfectly by Gerald.

He has inherited his father's great charm of manner, [he wrote] and certainly his gift for music. With a sweet voice he sang naturally and charmingly, to the manner born. This young actor promises to take a very high place on the stage, for he improves with each new part he undertakes.

By this time the family were well accustomed to Gerald's choice of a profession, and were taking a great interest in everything he did. Mummie cut out all his notices and pasted them carefully into a large red book, very indignant if he only had a word or two of praise. She listened with interest to his little scraps of gossip, smiled at his jokes, and frowned in sympathy at his complaints.

She approved of his friendship with Mrs Campbell,

hoping that it would prove a steadying influence. It was, after all, very flattering that so famous an actress should take an interest in her boy, and then Mrs Campbell had inquired after her so thoughtfully that time she had her accident, and was so very sympathetic and nice.

With Gerald, it was 'Mrs Campbell' at first for quite a while, and then it was 'Stella'. It was hard to say when the change took place, but then all stage friendships were like that, said Mummie comfortably.

She remembered it was only a little step from his first letter saying he had dined with Mrs Pat for the first time, and she was very much what he had expected, and spoke naturally and unaffectedly about everything, and was encouraging about his work. Then, after a few rehearsals (Mummie was away at the sea at the time) he wrote to say how he and Mrs Campbell had driven up to Hampstead in a victoria, and had strolled on the Heath, and he had shown her where they had lived all those years, and she was very jolly, and they had enjoyed themselves hugely. 'And I am being very good,' he added, 'not sitting up late or drinking too much, so don't alarm yourself.'

Then came the tour. Gerald wrote fairly frequently, because Mummie had had a carriage accident, and it was easy to trace the little thread of his friendship.

I have just been out shopping with Mrs Campbell [he wrote from Leeds]. I've never seen such a person for buying old furniture, and things. My knowledge is getting vast on such subjects as Dutch and French antiques. Afterwards I played golf, and she walked round and sat about, it did her tons of good, and she's never been so well. Her son Beo is with us too, and is a fine fellow. May would adore him; he is a midshipman, all muscle and a profile like Pharaoh, and captain of everything. There is to be a supper-party to the company this week, and Mrs Campbell says I am to do all my tricks!

This was followed by another letter, a little downcast, rather damped. Poor Gerald, had he been snubbed, one wonders?

This is an awful place, [he wrote] rain all the time, and dirty lodgings without baths, and stale grease paint on the pillows. Mrs Campbell isn't very fit, I don't think the air suits her, and she is all down and depressed. I am well, and oh, dear, I suppose I'm happy, as there is a lot of work and the parts are good, but I sometimes wonder if everything is worth while. Give my love to Sylvia and the boys, and tell 'em it's not worth growing up.

That he was beginning to concentrate on his job was apparent, however, for he wrote later:

My success as yet in the part is not pronounced, but I mean to do better in about a week. It's such awfully nervous work and so impossible a part to be natural in. I think acting is the most difficult and heart-breaking work, but splendid for the inside. I'm trying hard all the time, and Mrs Campbell is untiring with me.

And then, somehow or other – she could not remember when; perhaps after they returned to London – Mummie was aware of 'Christian names, and 'Stella and I are dining with the Trees tonight, darling'; or 'Stella isn't looking too well, spraining her ankle seems to have upset her'; or, 'Stella sent you her love, Mummie, and wants you to have tea with her.' And so it went on during the winter and spring and summer of 1901 and the second tour in the early autumn, but Mummie, who was very anxious and worried about Guy in South Africa, was inclined to read the long, daily letters from her eldest with greater care than the little weekly scraps from her youngest. Guy's safety and that of his regiment, his accounts of the war and his own experiences, were more important just now than the fact that Stella and Gerald had driven to Bath in a double horse shay, and she was looking marvellous, and the play was doing excellent business.

During the autumn she noticed that Gerald's letters

were not always happy. He was sometimes bitter and angry, and he wrote once saying that he longed to be home with her, and that this was a stinking tour in every respect and that he was vague about his plans for the future, and that everything was in the air. And then suddenly, in November, Stella went off to New York, and the company broke up, and Gerald came home to his mother, older and wiser than before.

I'm twenty-nine, [he wrote to Mummie four months later, on his birthday] and I look it too, and the wind is in the east, so I feel it also. I wish I were at Ramsgate with you, leading a peaceful existence with my old mother, who may be an old cup of tea but she does put up with a lot from her dissipated ruffian of a son. I'm afraid there's not much of the ewee lamb left in me now, darling, and my disposition is not the angelic one it might be, but I cling to you, so take care of yourself. Thank Sylvia for her dear words of wisdom, and tell the boys to stay young while they can.

This was rather a different Gerald from the one who had played light-heartedly on tour with Forbes-Robertson and Beerbohm Tree, who had bicycled twenty miles in an afternoon with Harry Esmond, and slept at the end of it like an exhausted puppy. Something of maturity had come to him now, and he realized that life was not always the desperately amusing thing he had believed it to be. One did not always get one's own way. Wanting a thing did not necessarily mean that one got it. He had at this time little streaks of bitterness in his make-up and definite moments of irritation.

He spent a great deal of time at the Green Room Club, playing cards, and being funny at other people's expense, and staying up to all hours, and drinking rather more than was good for him. He was acting in a success called *The Country Mouse* at the Prince of Wales's, and the part of the Hon. Archibald Vyse did not require more of him than ease and naturalness, which he had already to

perfection, so there was nothing in the way of hard work
to fill and occupy his restless mind. And, because he
lacked personal conceit and because he had that careless,
indolent side to his nature, he shrugged his shoulders and
made little effort about anything, finding this profession
of his too easy again, too simple. Stella was no longer
there to drive him, to mock him, to force him to work,
calling him 'Clown' and 'Mr Walk-About', goading him
to throw aside his indolence and show the world that he
could do more than stroll on to the stage with his hands
in his pockets, and light a cigarette, and make love
casually.

Besides, *à quoi bon*? – as Kicky used to say in his own
moments of depression. Why make any effort? To what
end was it all, when everything was said and done?
People were born, and they worked, and slept, and then
they died, and nobody cared or was much the wiser. Sometimes Gerald felt like chucking it all, leaving the stage,
going abroad.

There was no background to his life, no one to make
things worth while. There was Mummie, of course, and
darling Mummie could not always see things with his eyes.
She belonged to a different generation. She did not realize
that the order of things was changing with the new
century; the Victorian era had gone for ever, and it was
not only he, but everybody, who was altering, developing,
finding their feet in a changing world.

It was all very well for Trixie to rail at him, to call him
a waster, to say he had always been hopelessly spoilt, and
to blame Mummie and his upbringing. She did not
understand; no woman understood. Let her try being a
man and see what sort of a success she would make of it.
She accused him of making a fiasco of his life, just because
he was not settled and smug, he supposed. She dragged
Guy's name into it too; poor old Guy, because he had had
one or two little attachments that had come to nothing;

74

but he had fought for his country and had won the D.S.O. damn it all! But, then, Trixie was always a boss, a manager, from the earliest days when she had organized their games, and now she would order her brothers about, if she could, in the same way, seeing them much in the same light as her own boy Geoffrey, rising seventeen, and tied to her apron-strings as a matter of course.

So the summer wore away, and *The Country Mouse* came off, and Gerald fished and played golf, and spent a week with Sylvia, the gentle, who was always comforting and maternal, smiling adorably, with boys of all ages clambering over her. Here he recovered his spirits and seemed better in health, and went to bed at a reasonable hour, and found that, if the sun shone and the sky was cloudless, life need not necessarily be entirely 'bloody'.

In the November of 1902 he had an offer to play in a new piece by Barrie called *The Admirable Crichton* at the Duke of York's, and he accepted. He asked for twenty-five pounds a week, which he received. It was quite a good part, and Harry Irving and Irene Vanbrugh were to be in the company. When rehearsals started, he found that he was to play opposite a young actress called Muriel Beaumont, whom he remembered meeting over a year ago at a tea-party somewhere. She had been acting at the Haymarket, and he had done his usual tricks – imitations of Irving and Tree and Waller. Did she remember him? he asked. Yes, she did. She had been very impressed with his imitations. How nice that they were to be in the same play.

All this said very unaffectedly and simply, without the slightest attempt at flirtation or anything, which surprised him, because she was so terribly pretty that it seemed peculiar not to be aware of it.

Never mind, it meant that there was going to be more to this play than he had first thought – they were to play the juvenile lovers. Naturally he would see a lot of her.

The Admirable Crichton was produced, and became an immediate success. Both the Hon. Ernest and the Lady Agatha were applauded and praised as the young couple who fell in love on the desert island. It was an easy trifle for Mr Walk-About. He had only to be amusing, and cheeky, and very much attracted by Lady Agatha. The latter required little effort, as Muriel Beaumont, aged twenty-six and dressed as befitted a desert island, where conventions were thrown aside, was a thing of beauty that would cause the most blasé and jaded young man of twenty-nine to pause and wonder. It was not only her face. She was easy to talk to, and by this he meant she did not always want to talk herself, but seemed perfectly content to listen to him, which was a great change from any woman he had known before. She had read and adored *Trilby*, and was interested in his childhood and his family, and asked questions about Papa, and asked if it was not terribly lonely for his mother. He told her that he supposed it was, but to tell the truth, he had not thought about it for some time. Then she told him about herself, how she lived with her father and mother in Battersea, and her father was very strict, and had been very much against her going on the stage, but she had, and she enjoyed it very much, and everybody was so nice and jolly together, didn't he think so too? And he said, 'Not always,' and looked bitter and told her that he had learnt much in eight years, and of course he was older and more experienced than she was, but perhaps he would tell her one day. And she said, 'Yes, of course,' and looked very solemn, and nodded her head, and he saw by her eyes that she knew nothing, nothing at all. In spite of being twenty-six and living in the theatre, she was no more than a child enjoying her first party, unaware of flattery, and malice, and the little false loves that last a night and a day. Nothing had come into her world to spoil her or touch her; she was untroubled and serene, like the picture of Mummie when Papa first met her nearly fifty years ago, and the hard core in his heart melted and was gone. Something triumphant, happy, and alive came into being and was part of him, and he knew that he loved her, that she had come to him at last.

It was bewildering and sudden; he had not expected it; he had been prepared for continual disillusion, and a perpetual cheap cynicism, and now his ideas were upset. He must start all over again; have new faith, new ideals, a new purpose in life. If this thing were true, if this thing were lasting, then life was worth living now and for ever; nothing else would matter; it would be a haven from all turmoil and distress, a beacon to warn him and a star to guide him. It would be like believing in God. It would be like being born all over again. Had not Papa found Mummie his good angel, and did not he marry her at twenty-nine, and was she not the light that set his little spark of genius aflame? Success had come to him in his first year of marriage, and he never looked back. Why should not his son do the same? Could not he prove to Mummie and Trixie and Guy that he was not an idle waster, not the idle good-for-nothing they feared, but someone with purpose, and strength, and will, of whom they would be proud, as they had been proud of Papa?

All this passed through his mind as he sat at the back of the stage against the rocks that were part of the scenery in the second act, and Muriel sat by his side, and he talked of everything under the sun and made her laugh, and nobody came near them, and they knew they were happy.

They never met outside the theatre. He would never have dreamt of asking her to a restaurant, and of course she went straight home to Battersea every night. Then there came a day when she told him rather shyly that she had received an invitation to a private dance, and her friends had asked her to bring a partner, and would he be very bored or did he think he might like to come?

Like to? Of course he'd like to; he'd adore to; nothing in the world would please him more. And they went, and they danced together, and they sat out in a conservatory, and he was as young and nervous as though he were a boy of twenty again, and they listened to the music, and he held her hand and asked her to marry him. She smiled and said yes, and they looked at one another and wondered, and both of them were certain that nothing quite like that had ever happened to anyone before.

'I'm going to be married,' said Gerald in triumph, telling everyone he knew. Almost immediately it was in the papers, and they were being congratulated, and the audiences were delighted, and the old wise ones of the stage shook their heads and said it would not last a week.

'It's the real thing,' Gerald told Mummie, and she said, 'Yes, darling, of course,' and sighed and wondered for how long, and wrote a little note asking Muriel to come to dinner. 'Tell Trixie I've pulled myself together,' said Gerald, 'and she'll find no further cause for complaint, and, anyway, few sisters have brothers who are as fond of them as I am, and tell her she will love Muriel.' It was very difficult for the family to be enthusiastic when they first heard the news. Gerald had let them down before, and really these young actresses were all the same – pretty, no doubt, but artificial and shallow and insincere thinking of nothing but themselves.

'I shall love to come and dine with you on Saturday,' wrote Muriel to Mummie, 'for I am looking forward so much to meeting you, although I feel as if I knew you already.' That seemed genuine enough no doubt, but you can't tell by writing alone. Would she be just another Marguerite Sylva or Daphne Barrymore?

The family sat in Portman Mansions waiting for Gerald and Muriel to arrive: Mummie twiddling her hair nervously and frowning; Trixie eagle-eyed and curious, ready to speak her feelings; Sylvia watching

Mummie and praying silently for the best; May talkative and critical, her quick ears the first to hear Gerald's key in the lock.

Gerald hung up his coat in the hall. 'Go on in and meet them,' he whispered. 'I'll follow in a moment.' He knew his family; he knew just how they would be sitting, feeling, and fearing the worst.

The door opened and Muriel came into the room. She looked round her a moment, smiling; and, instead of the powdered little actress she had expected, Mummie saw a tall slim girl, with light brown hair and no paint on her face, dressed simply in good clothes, a girl with wide-apart eyes who looked right amongst the furniture from New Grove House and Kicky's drawings on the wall, and the books and the rugs. As Mummie went to greet her, Muriel ran forward and took her hands and kissed her, and said, 'I am so glad to be here with you all'; then looked a little troubled, and lowered her voice, glancing towards the door, and said, 'I'm in such a way about Gerald, he is starting one of his horrid colds.'

Mummie looked at the girls and smiled, Trixie nodded her head, and Sylvia and May leant back with a sigh of relief.

The ewee lamb was safe in the fold at last.

CHAPTER FOUR

GERALD and Muriel were engaged for only six weeks, and were married on the 11th of April, 1903. He took her to Whitby for their honeymoon. He wanted her to know the old rooms where they used to go every year, and the harbour where Papa had strolled with Chang padding at his heels and the broad-hipped fisherwomen had paused to smile at him, the red roofs and the cobbled stones, the salty, fishy, spray-laden Whitby air, with its tang of cutch and rope yarn, nets and herrings. Here was the place where he had learnt to swim; and there was the grass court where he and May had fought many a heated tennis battle; and there was the spot on the cliff by the Abbey where he had read *The Wreck of the 'Grosvenor'* for the first time; and that was the road that led to the moors, where they had held picnics; and there was the tree beneath which May at eleven had started her immortal and alas! unfinished book, *My Life as a Midshipman*.

He had not returned there since Papa had died and America and the stage had claimed his thoughts. Mummie had taken to going to Ramsgate now, where she had a house for the grandchildren, for Trixie's and Sylvia's boys. But here was his Whitby, unchanged and best-beloved as of old; and the little span of years rolled back and he was a boy again.

It came to an end too soon, and *The Admirable Crichton* called to them once more, and back they went to London and the Duke of York's.

The play ran until the end of August, and they were both very relieved when it came off, as Muriel could now devote herself to the preparations for moving into their new home. Up to the present they had been in rooms, and during the early part of the summer had taken a cottage at Walton-on-Thames, which was a happy refuge from the hot weather. 'When I'm not picking green-fly off rose heads, I'm picking the black fly off dwarf beans,' Gerald gravely wrote to Mummie. 'Everything is doing very well except Japanese iris and parsley. I haven't been outside the estate yet, but Muriel manages both indoor and outdoor servants with marvellous tact, and even the stableboys worship her.' (The cottage really had about three rooms, and a tiny square of garden.) Mummie nodded her head and smiled. Darling Gerald was so funny. And it was a wonderful thing to see him happy like this.

Dear Muriel was obviously taking great care of him. She had not seen him looking so well for years. He had got quite brown, too, not that horrid washed-out colour she was used to. He never took his eyes off Muriel.

'I shall be so glad when we get into our little house,' Muriel was saying. 'I'm making all the silk blinds for every window, and a woman is helping me with the flax ones. I'm going to have white wallpaper in the drawing-room. Don't you think that's the wisest plan? I'm sure I'm going to love the house, and Regent's Park is so close to you, isn't it? I do hope the move won't be too exhausting in this heat; we have so much baggage, and I know it will never get into a one-horse bus; we shall have to have one with two horses.'

'What about giving us some books?' said Gerald, strolling round the room. 'All we possess is last year's Bradshaw and an out-of-date, coverless copy of *The Poultry World*. I feel they are not going to fill our bookshelves. Here, can't we have some of these?' – ramming his hand amongst the standard works.

But Mummie was busy with Muriel and household

matters. 'How will you manage if Bessie is having her holiday?' she was saying.

'Well, I thought of having a caretaker in over the move,' replied Muriel, 'and then of course there will be Kate as well; but, to tell you the truth, I don't find Kate very satisfactory; she came to me the other evening and said she did not want to stop, simply because Gerald had spoken rather sharply to her in the morning about the way the toast was sent up. Did you ever hear such nonsense? I think I shall let her go when her month is up, but it won't be at all convenient.'

Mummie nodded in agreement. 'I will look out for someone for you. I dare say Sylvia might know of a suitable person. And did you enjoy your weekend at the Barries', Gerald darling? Tell me about the new play.'

'H'm. So-so. I dare say it will be all right. I don't rave about it, you know. I just play myself, which doesn't call for much; but then I'm bone idle, as you know. It'll mean dining comfortably at seven and leaving the house at twenty minutes past. Chester Place is going to be jolly convenient for the theatre. I hope Muriel won't find the evenings too dull.'

Muriel shook her head. 'I shan't be dull with all my needlework,' she said. 'You don't realize how much there is to do in a house, and I shall be thankful of the rest after Crichton. Besides, if I do feel lonely I can slip round here to the flat to be with Mummie.'

'We shall come to Sunday supper every week, darling,' said Gerald, 'and don't you go off to Ramsgate for ages and leave us in London alone. Just because I'm married, it doesn't mean that the old cup of tea can go and forget her ewee lamb. I insist on seeing my family as much as ever.'

'Trixie is very anxious to know if she can be of any help,' said Mummie. 'She is longing to see your little house.' And then, when Gerald turned his back to reach for a cigarette, she lowered her voice and whispered in Muriel's ear, 'I hope you don't mind, dear, I had to tell her your news, and we are all so delighted and happy.'

Muriel blushed, and whispered back, 'Of course I don't mind. I shall be only too glad of her advice. Perhaps she could find me a nurse. I don't want anyone too expensive, and those monthly nurses are sometimes so grand, aren't they? Tell her it's not until February.'

'Trixie is always very knowledgeable about that sort of thing,' said Mummie; and then, as Gerald joined them again, she said in a louder tone, 'You must be sure and tell me if there is any little thing you want that I can spare you. Tell me, dear, are you all right for knives and forks?'

'Yes, for God's sake let's have everything like that in order,' broke in Gerald. 'I mean, damn it all, one'll want to ask a fellow in to dine occasionally; and if you have to eat peas off a knife, and drink cold slops, and use cardboard instead of Bromo in the usual offices, it's not going to be too good.'

'Isn't he dreadful?' said Mummie. 'I'm sure Muriel will manage her little house too beautifully. I think I must make out a list of the things Gerald dislikes, dear, in the way of food. He will never touch anything out of a tin, of course, and he will not look at meat that has been cooked twice. And if he gets one of his colds, you must be sure and give him hot food.'

Muriel nodded gravely. 'I believe it was tinned salmon he had the other day which upset him so. He had it at the club. But he is looking well, don't you think? He is being very good about taking his cod-liver oil capsules. I got him another box yesterday.'

Gerald shouted with laughter. 'Oh, Trixie! Oh, Sylvia! Why aren't you here? Did any man have a more adorable wife than this? Don't listen to her, Mummie darling;

she is lying to you. I pour all my capsules down the sink, and there are two tins of Horlicks' Malted Milk unopened in the bathroom cupboard.'

But Mummie went on quite unperturbed: 'He likes a little something when he comes in from the theatre at night, but I expect you know that. I'm glad you'll be dining at seven; that means he won't have to bolt his food. It's so bad for him to do that, and gives him a dreadful colour.'

'Colour be blowed!' said Gerald. 'There's nothing wrong with my colour, old lady, it's my profile that's against me. I've always been plain, but I'm getting plainer every day. Whose fault is that? Not yours, dearest; I'll let you off that. If I had a profile like yours I'd be playing Hamlet now in a falsetto voice, instead of fighting my way as a juvenile at twenty-five pounds a week.'

'I hate you to call yourself plain,' said Muriel indignantly. 'I'm sure you would be very hurt if anyone else called you so.'

'Ah! so she's beginning to find out my weaknesses,' laughed Gerald. 'I wonder if I'm the lucky fellow I thought I was? No, I repeat that I get plainer and lazier every day. I find acting a miserably nervous business, and I wonder why I was ever allowed to go on the stage.'

'What nonsense, darling! You know you couldn't do anything else,' said Mummie comfortably.

'That's a nice way for a mother to talk, I must say. You know you goaded me to it, forced me with whips and scorpions. I had wished for the Church myself, but you were against it. Besides, I never could remember when, and when not, to say words like Sexagesima.'

'Don't pay any attention to him, Muriel; he's making it all up.'

'What I find difficult on the stage is not being able to say what one wants,' said Gerald; 'it's absurd to say to a girl that she is as far above me as heaven from hell instead

84

of merely telling her I love her, and talking about England's national pastime when one means cricket. It's these cursed authors who are the trouble. I always want to rewrite everything myself. It's different with Jimmie Barrie; he can write what he likes and get away with it, but some of these chaps – my hat!' He whistled, and shrugged his shoulders. 'One day Guy and I will write a play together and show 'em how to do it, eh, old 'un?'

Mummie smiled and nodded her head. How cocky he was! How pleased with life and with himself! How gay! How like Kicky had been when they were married first, just forty years ago . . .

She watched them from the window of the flat as they went home, Gerald still talking twenty to the dozen, and pulling faces behind the cabby's back.

The new play, *Little Mary*, was produced in September and ran until the following May. Gerald and Muriel – or Mo, as he now began to call her always – had moved into the little house at Chester Place and were very happy and contented, both rather house-proud and flushed with marriage, and believing, with every other couple under the sun, that no other home was quite as nice as theirs. Mo, waiting for her baby, put her feet up and listened to Trixie's wealth of information on how to bring up children. She engaged a maternity nurse on Trixie's special recommendation, and remembered all the time that Gerald's health was more important than her own, and found time to write a note to Mummie at Ramsgate saying she would be laid up any moment now but she was thankful to say Gerald's cold was much better, as he had stopped indoors all day and she had made him wear a woolly round his head at night.

'It's a little dull waiting about like this,' she added, 'and I don't like to venture out in case anything should happen. Trixie says it would be most unwise. I did go for a drive the other day, but I didn't enjoy it much as the carriage was closed, and as soon as Gerald saw it he went off to the club instead.'

In February Gerald developed diphtheria. Of course, this was much more alarming than having a first baby. He had to be isolated, and couldn't see his first-born, Angela, who arrived three weeks late, anyhow. But when he eventually did see her he was tremendously excited, and exceedingly proud, and the whole family were delighted, as this was the first du Maurier girl to be produced. Trixie had three boys, Sylvia five, and May, alas! childless.

'Papa always wanted a grand-daughter,' said Gerald; 'that endless tale of boys was a great disappointment. If only he were here to see Angela.' And Angela, plain and rather fat, looking like every baby but with an added glint of humour in her eye, blew bubbles, and made rude noises, much to her father's delight.

These were the long days, the peaceful days, and Gerald was profoundly happy.

This morning is one of the most wonderful mornings I remember [he wrote to Mummie in the early summer from a cottage in the country]. The weather-cock is pointing to the east, but there is no wind, and a blazing sun, and a blue sky with white mountains in it. We spent yesterday on the river, I throwing a fly, and Mo making short clothes for Angela, who this morning was looking quite handsome. Dear thing, she has quite a face of her own, but, I'm sorry to say, the back of my head.

The thought of London is so distasteful to me that I feel quite unhappy I have a house there. I'm beginning to know more about birds than I've ever dreamt of, and can distinguish the cry of the female chiff-chaff from that of the spotted fly-catcher. All the young ones are learning to fly, and it's great fun watching them. I play a good deal of tennis and shall be fairly good by the end of the summer, I hope. Mo and I sit in our chairs in the evenings like cups of tea; you'd be amused to see us.

The proofs of my Kodak have come, and there is one of

Angela trying to be funny which is a poem, and shows great promise for her future as a droll. We are all very well and very happy, but it seems ages since I saw any of my beloved family – and if it were not for Mo and her comic baby I could wish I was the ewee lamb again. We send you all our love, dearest, and come down soon and see us, but bring a spencer, as it's cold o' nights.

Your loving son,

GERALD

In December, James Barrie, who was a great friend of the Llewellyn Davieses, and adored Sylvia and her boys, wrote for them his immortal *Peter Pan*, and Gerald played the parts of Captain Hook and Mr Darling. The play was unlike anything that had ever been written before, and nobody expected it to be a success. The word 'stunt' had not yet crossed the Atlantic, but Gerald would have used it had he known it; the play was original, no doubt, very great fun to do, and if it only ran for a few performances, at least it would amuse Jimmie Barrie himself, and entertain Sylvia's boys, who appeared to be responsible for its appearance. Befogged journalists gave inaccurate and premature descriptions of the piece, saying that Mr Barrie had written about an unconventional Fairyland which was inhabited by cuddlesome Eskimos and a quaint little person called Peter, dressed in red leaves, and that Mr du Maurier would play the fierce Pirate King, a melodramatic and romantic individual.

The result became history, as everyone knows. Peter Pan never has and never will grow up; he is not Barrie's property any more, but lives in the minds of all the children that will ever be, a personal belonging, an invention of their own. The play has grown into a tradition that will never die, an annual joy that time cannot dim, a necessary part of childhood, familiar, lovable, and gloriously shabby, and though the boys for whom it was written are men now, and two of them are dead, their possession will remain a memorial to them for all time, and a discovery to the grandchildren whom Sylvia never lived to see. Alas! James Hook, that dark, unhappy man, what pains were endured in his begetting!

Can it be that children are less timid nowadays, that aeroplanes and wireless have made piracy no longer a pastime fit for kings? When Hook first paced his quarter-deck in the year of 1904, children were carried screaming from the stalls, and even big boys of twelve were known to reach for their mother's hand in the friendly shelter of the boxes. How he was hated, with his flourish, his poses, his dreaded diabolical smile! That ashen face, those blood-red lips, the long, dank, greasy curls; the sardonic laugh, the maniacal scream, the appalling courtesy of his gestures; and that above all most terrible of moments when he descended the stairs and with slow, most merciless cunning poured the poison into Peter's glass. There was no peace in those days until the monster was destroyed, and the fight upon the pirate ship was a fight to the death. Gerald *was* Hook; he was no dummy dressed from Simmons' in a Clarkson wig, ranting and roaring about the stage, a grotesque figure whom the modern child finds a little comic. He was a tragic and rather ghastly creation who knew no peace, and whose soul was in torment; a dark shadow; a sinister dream; a bogey of fear who lives perpetually in the grey recesses of every small boy's mind. All boys had their Hooks, as Barrie knew; he was the phantom who came by night and stole his way into their murky dreams. He was the spirit of Stevenson and of Dumas, and he was Father-but-for-the-grace-of-God; a lonely spirit that was terror and inspiration in one. And, because he had imagination and a spark of genius, Gerald made him alive.

Every Christmas now for thirty years James Hook has flown his flag, but he is a ghost of his former self; the magic has fled and the terror has departed. Although he is ours for eternity, he yet remains the peculiar property of the man who first gave him life in 1904.

Acting is like writing, like painting, like any other work that comes from within, and, once Hook had been created, Gerald grew as tired of him as an author wearies of the book he has just written. It became no longer a novelty, but a dreary routine, part of the daily round.

Two performances a day was no joke in a play that lasted nearly four hours; and playing to crowded houses of screaming, excited children was trying to the voice and to the temper. 'There's only one thing I'd rather not be doing,' said Gerald in a fit of irritation, 'and that's sweeping the floors of a mortuary at a shilling a week.'

He cared not a whit for success, and he was already beginning to show signs of boredom when a play ran monotonously well. Once a first night was over he lost interest; the thing was no longer an adventure. It became tedious and dull; the fever and the excitement were lost.

The truth was that failures were unknown to him, and his notices were invariably good. He did not have to endure heartbreak and disappointment; he was never out of a job, never poor, never pressed for money or worried about the future. He did not know what it was to wait at stage doors to interview managers and beg for a part in a new production; he had never experienced that wave of utter thankfulness that comes with the knowledge that for six months, anyway, your salary is secure, and you can pay your rent. He was lucky; and his very luck threatened to spoil him, to weary him of his own talent, to make him become jaded with the success that he had learnt too early and too soon.

Meanwhile his home life continued to be a source of endless content and enjoyment. Mo was acting once more, but after *Crichton* they never played together again, which was a good thing and prevented that little stain of jealousy which occurs too frequently in stage marriages.

The comic, plump Angela was learning to walk, and called 'Daddy' loudly whenever she saw Gerald, which gave him a tremendous thrill, though he realized that every parent had this experience. He was a member of the Garrick Club and was beginning to enjoy it more than the Green Room, although he preferred home and the food Mo provided to either restaurant or club, and already if she left him for as much as two days he was lost and miserable. He felt very ill used when she and her mother took Angela to Felixstowe for a fortnight in July for a breath of sea air. 'The house is dreary and deserted,' he grumbled to his mother, 'and I never go into the place except to sleep. I can't think why Mo wanted to rush off to a stinking hole like Felixstowe.' And Mo, thankful for a rest after a tiring run during the hot season, fretted for Gerald, and wrote to Mummie inquiring after his health, wishing he would stop at the flat with her and be properly looked after; fearing that, left by himself, he would lead a rackety life in town and go to bed at any old hour – 'you know what he is; and perhaps smoke too much and drink more than is good for him, and then go off on that horrid motor-bicycle he has been and bought, which I am sure he will never manage properly.'

Gerald hated being alone. He became at once restless and miserable, and unless he was working he was at a loss to know what to do with himself, bored with his own company, preferring the companionship of almost anybody to solitude and his own thoughts. He had to have people around him. He must talk, he must have his audience, and for preference he would have his own family – Trixie, who made almost as much noise as himself, arguing, laying down the law, going off into great bursts of laughter at his jokes; May, finer, more critical, easily roused to fierce argument and returning thrust for thrust with an equally pointed sting; Sylvia, the peacemaker, soothing and devoted, always tactful at the right moment;

and Mummie herself, nodding and twiddling her hair, disturbed when her children became too heated, frowning at her darling Gerald when he overstepped the mark.

And then Guy, the best-loved, the friend, the ally, the confidant, the guardian of Gerald's youth and his best counsellor, got married, at the age of forty, to Gwen Price, to whom he was devoted; and Gerald, with nearly two years' experience of marriage behind him, was at last in the position to give his senior words of advice, a proceeding he found vastly amusing. Neither of the marriages spoilt the brothers' friendship for one another, and, although Guy was to be much away in India and elsewhere, their affection never weakened, their ways never drifted apart. And the soldier, who prior to Gerald's marriage had always felt responsible for him, was able to leave England with a free conscience, having handed him over to Mo, metaphorically speaking, with supreme belief in her powers of guidance and understanding.

In May 1906, when he had been just over twelve years on the stage, Gerald made his first really big success, becoming at once one of the most popular and best-known actors of the day. He was thirty-three, the same age as Kicky had been when his weekly drawing began to be the most sought-after and favourite page in *Punch*, and, although he was delighted that the play was performed to full houses and caused a terrific sensation, Gerald was no more impressed with his own powers than his father had been.

Raffles was the first crook play to herald the American invasion, and it was an immediate and wild success. It was badly written, poorly constructed, and the love interest was puerile, considered by later standards: but the pace and excitement of it left the 1906 audiences breathless. They were not used to it. They were thrilled at the idea of the hero's being a cricketer and a cracksman at the same time; the ceaseless action and the novelty of the idea kept them on edge from beginning to end.

The part of Raffles was 'actor-proof' as Gerald admitted himself, and it would have been almost impossible to have made a failure of it. For all that, he brought something to it that was personal and unique – a suggestion of extreme tension masked by a casual gaiety – making of Raffles someone highly strung, nervous, and finely drawn, yet fearless and full of a reckless and rather desperate indifference, someone who by the force of his high spirits had developed a kink in his nature.

There was nothing in his Raffles of the present-day hero-crook who, gun in hand, blusters his way through three acts of smoke, bullets, and sudden death with a fresh meaningless gangster oath every other second.

To quote from a critic of the day,

Raffles secures the weapon, and the cold sweat of reaction from intense strain is all that there is to show how great it has been. It sounds ridiculous to write of an actor – who, as one knows, has paint upon his face – showing this by sheer strength of emotion. Nevertheless, it is what Mr du Maurier contrived to convey to those fortunate people who occupied the front row of the stalls on Saturday night. Such acting leaves an impress on the memory as of some scene that has been lived through. To play such a scene as this, slowly but surely working to a tremendous emotional climax, with few words and the difficulty of an assumed calmness which needs much subtlety, is the achievement of a tragedian of uncommon quality.

And yet there were those who believed that because Gerald did not hump his back, cover his face with hair, wear tights, and speak blank verse, he was therefore no actor. How many times, then and afterwards, did people exclaim, 'But du Maurier, he does not act; he is always himself.' To act is to portray an emotion; to show the feelings aroused by some sensation, whether joyous or tragic; to make the man in the audience feel, either uncomfortably or happily, 'That might have been me.' This is what Gerald, who started the so-called naturalistic school of acting, tried to do.

Perhaps he was not always successful; perhaps he permitted himself too much of that inevitable reserve and casualness which is the chief characteristic of the normal Englishman in any circumstance. It may be that the jaded playgoer, wishing to be entertained, demands a more highly tuned atmosphere in exchange for his money, expects a false, exaggerated character in a false, exaggerated situation, does not want to watch someone who might be himself suffering or enduring as he would if the story were his, and the situation his own. It is too 'natural'. It is too much 'like life'. He has been made to feel insecure; his after-dinner complaisance is destroyed. He does not come to the theatre to be reminded of his own little failings, weaknesses, and general behaviour. He wishes, if possible, to be transplanted to another world where men and women do not behave like themselves.

And this type of playgoer Gerald could not please. Their conception of entertainment was not his. They walked in different directions. It was impossible for Gerald to act as this man would have him do. He would have considered it false, untrue; in a word, as bad art.

Whether he was right or wrong does not matter to this story. But in 1906 the natural style of acting came as a welcome change after the extravagances, the grand gestures, and the facial contortions of the last century. It was an inevitable change to come about with the growth of new ideas, freedom, and the modern outlook. It could not have been suppressed any more than motor-cars and aeroplanes; and Gerald appeared on the crest of the wave as leader in his little sphere, most typically and naturally the man of his day.

Raffles ran for a year, though Gerald left it during the

Christmas holiday to play Hook once more in *Peter Pan*. The theatre had shut, of course, in August, and he took his holiday. He went this year to Seaview with Angela and Mo, and later to Scotland with Mo alone. In March they moved from Chester Place and took a larger house quite close in Cumberland Terrace, as Mo was expecting another baby.

'I think we shall like it,' Gerald told Mummie; 'there's a large nursery, and a spare room, and perfect drains! Of course, Lambert is in on the warpath and wants to whitewash everything and everybody. It's a hundred and fifty pounds a year, but we shall be able to manage it.'

Chester Place seemed suddenly very small and cramped, and the new house in Cumberland Terrace quite imposing in comparison, standing back behind an archway, with two storeys and a basement.

Mo, rather fussed with the move, told Mummie she hoped the house would not be difficult to run; they must have another housemaid, and, what with one thing and another, she felt a little fretful. She had read in the paper that someone had caught typhoid from eating oysters, and Gerald had them for lunch every day at the Garrick Club. Wasn't it alarming? But he wouldn't be dissuaded from eating them. And then, poor lamb, he had seen somebody knocked off a bicycle and killed only yesterday; she was afraid it had upset him!

February and March were always his bad months; they seemed to depress him, and he had got very tired straining his voice in *Peter Pan*. And then in April came the first of the family tragedies, and poor Arthur Davies, Sylvia's beloved husband, died after a wretched illness, an operation, and much suffering. She was left with five boys and little money, and herself quite heart-broken and very delicate.

James Barrie, already devoted to them, became the boys' guardian, and relieved her of much responsibility, but she was never the same after Arthur had gone from her. Poor, gentle, gracious Sylvia, by far the sweetest nature of them all; it seemed so cruel and meaningless that she should suffer.

'What's it all for?' asked Gerald, angry and bitter. 'Why should a fellow like Arthur be taken, who never said an unkind word in his life, and what possible good can it do to anyone in the world for darling Sylvia to break her heart?' Death, to his eyes, was not inevitable. It was a malicious and purposeless happening that in its very working denied the existence of God. He blasphemed, and stormed, with tears pouring down his cheeks, like a child that refuses to understand.

He was, alas! to know many deaths, and to have one by one his beloved family taken from him. But to him there was no mercy in their release and no great purpose in their going. He would not acknowledge that they were spared many things – the war, and fear for their sons, and the reactions of a weary country; that had they lived longer they must have suffered greatly, for they would not have belonged, they would have been out of place in a hurried, fevered world; that most especially Sylvia and Arthur, creatures of great peace and tranquillity, would have been hurt, misunderstood; and that they could never have given their boys the upbringing and the security that Barrie was to give them. But to Gerald there was no purpose and no wisdom, he denied God and mocked at eternity; all he cared was that those he loved went from him, and he did not understand.

Raffles came off at last, and the new play, *Brewster's Millions*, was another big success.

Once more [as the critics said] the point of the evening was the fine work of Gerald du Maurier, who, if he did not improve on Raffles, continued the same amazing promise, and on whose shoulders rested the chief weight of the acting. He conveyed the passing joy and despair of the character with extraordinary skill, without any exaggeration or any apparent trick. Coming so soon after his wonderful impersonation as Raffles, it confirmed his reputation as the cleverest comedian on the English stage.

Gerald received a tremendous reception at the end of the play, and was delighted with the success, giving it a year's run.

Actually it ran for three hundred and twenty-one performances, and he was not far out. *Brewster's Millions, What Every Woman Knows, Arsène Lupin,* and *Alias Jimmy Valentine* were the plays that followed one another in slow succession, and in each he scored a big personal triumph. Having created Raffles, he must do it again and again under another name. The public would not let it rest. They wanted nothing else, hence Arsène Lupin, another gentleman crook – only a duke this time, and French into the bargain – and Jimmy Valentine, the safe-opener from Sing-Sing.

Both these plays were poorly written and full of impossible situations, but Gerald invested them with glamour and his audience shouted their delight. If they were nothing else, these plays were good entertainment, and fulfilled their purpose well; and to be popular and liked had never been uncongenial to Gerald. Why should he bother about real plays when these trifles filled the theatre, and he was well paid, and he had only to look over his left shoulder at a dark corner and light a cigarette to ensure a breathless hush amongst the audience? Why make the effort to learn long and exquisitely written speeches by good authors, when 'I love you, damn you!' and 'What about a drink?' succeeded even better amongst the public, and took less time to say? It was pleasant, this business of being charming and rather amusing and making love light-heartedly. Financially it was proving enormously profitable to all concerned, and infinitely more worth while than standing in tights before a dark curtain, protesting to five people in the stalls that all our yesterdays have lighted fools the way to dusty death. Gerald can hardly be blamed, and, if he was sneered at, he was more often envied. Call it luck, call it talent, call it a mixture of both with a spark of genius thrown in, and you are somewhere near the truth.

It requires a very strong personality to get away with many of the things Gerald did, but there is no denying he succeeded.

It does not necessarily follow that what he did was easy; it looked simple, of course, just as skating looks simple, or playing first-class tennis, or painting a picture; but it requires hard work and concentration, coupled with artistic breeding, to do any of these things gracefully and well, as Gerald knew.

It's all over, [he wrote to his mother after the first night of *What Every Woman Knows*] and we're none of us sorry. It was a highly strung, nervous business, and no good to one's internal arrangements. If Angela and Daphne look like following in their parents' footsteps, I shall put them in a convent. It was the biggest success Barrie has had, and you should have heard the applause. I'm told I played my bit well, and everyone was pleased all round, but what an effort it has been. There must be some happy medium in life between a rainy day in the country, with no immediate occupation, and the first night of a long and difficult part

which proves that acting was not the casual walking on for a couple of hours every evening that it might be supposed.

In January 1909 something happened that was far more exciting to Gerald than any little popular success he had gained for himself, and which gave him an infinitely greater satisfaction.

Guy, now out in Africa, had written a play and left it at home for Gerald to read. Gerald saw at once that the play was astonishingly good, and in a class by itself. 'This is the real stuff at last,' he said. 'I knew Guy had it in him, and it was bound to come. He was not born Papa's son for nothing.' Without saying a word to Guy, who, with his wife, was in Natal, Gerald took the play to Frank Curzon at Wyndham's Theatre and produced it under his management. There was no part in the play that he could take himself, and he was still performing in *What Every Woman Knows*; but he put everything he knew into this, his first production, and the result was a triumph that he had not believed possible.

The play had no title as Guy had left it, and Gerald called it *An Englishman's Home*, insisting that the author preferred to remain anonymous and called himself simply 'A Patriot'. Of course, the truth leaked out, as it was bound to do. The wild success of the first night was one of those rare happenings that come only once or twice in a lifetime, and Guy, out in Africa, woke one day to find himself famous. From all over the world telegrams and messages of congratulations poured in to him and Gwen, and in this way they heard of the production for the first time. It was a great and memorable occasion. Guy's name was in every newspaper and on the lips of every man and woman in England. No play quite like it had ever been written before, and it is not an exaggeration to say that the whole of London was obsessed with the idea.

Men like Haldane and Lord Roberts wrote to Guy, when they had seen his play, and said it was the finest piece of propaganda they had ever seen, while little clerks and shopkeepers all over England added their letters to the rest in a frenzy of enthusiasm. The family, of course, from proud, excited Mummie down to the smallest nephew at his preparatory school, sent fevered, incoherent messages to Guy, telling him to leave the army, to return home; his fortune had been made.

I dare say, old chap, [wrote Gerald] that you have been cursing me and thinking the whole thing vulgar, and wishing you had been here yourself, but, believe me, nothing could stand up against this overwhelming success. It has become a national question, and no man has worked harder than I have to keep your name out of the papers. Mummie is afraid that the Army Council and the powers that be will have your decorations stripped from you and your body thrown to the gulls in Hyde Park, but I know you are above that sort of thing! You will make quite a lot of money, I should think, but that also I know you won't care about. God forgive me for lying! Your classic profile is in all the first-class papers from *The Times* to the *Draper's Record,* and there is a large photo of you in a shop in South Molton Street in three colours, and beneath it the pattern of the boot you usually wear; also a little paragraph saying you owe them £3. I thought it as well to pay this. I paid £90 into your bank in advance of royalties. Unless you come home quickly I shall blue everything.

As you may imagine, it has been an anxious time for your little brother, but he has been rewarded by the thought that he has worked a little surprise on one who could make a fortune writing for the stage if he were not so monstrously indifferent, unambitious, or, shall we say, lazy?

Well, good luck, *mon brave.* The governor would have said, 'All of which is very amusing.'

And the three sisters wrote characteristic letters to their suddenly famous and bewildered soldier brother, who sat holding Gwen's hand while the table rocked under the load of Press cuttings and telegrams.

Well, beloved, well! [wrote Trixie, in terrific spirits] imagine the delight and excitement of your family at witnessing the enormous success of your play. You can imagine how I ached to tell you that it was in rehearsal. You dear old thing, how happy I am for you. I feel weak with excitement, and why, oh why, can't you be here for us all to talk it over like we did *Trilby*? It's all so amusing, and I can't sleep for excitement, and I feel a little feeble and 'not quite wise,' as they say in Cornwall, and could talk to you for hours and hours.

My beloved Guy, [wrote Sylvia] the world is writing and talking of nothing else but your play. I am, alas, in bed, and cannot go, but I think of you all day. Darling, I am so pleased. I can hear you and Gwen talking about it, and wish so much I could hear you. Mummie tells people the author's name is a profound secret, but in my heart I know she tells everyone she meets!

And the quick and critical May:

Dearest Guy, it's a huge success. I don't know where to begin. I wish you'd been consulted on one or two points, though. The first act is a little long and could bear cutting, and what about the ending? The acting was capital. The women were the weakest. I suppose Gerald will write you full details, beloved.

It was a wonderful moment for the du Mauriers. It was like *Trilby* all over again, and it proved that Kicky's talent had not died with him in '96, but existed, in some flaming, secret way, in Guy as well.

An Englishman's Home happened twenty-five years ago, and the war that it prophesied has come and gone. So much has happened since, so many things have changed; people have grown old, and have forgotten, and are dead; the realities of the true war were perhaps more terrible than Guy's imagined invasion, and the little play that stirred the whole of England in 1909 may seem inadequate and pathetic today. We have had our *All Quiet on the Western Front*; we have had our *Journey's End*; plays about war by civilians who fought on foreign soil. Twenty-five years is a long way back, and memories are short. But Guy was a soldier, and his play was about civilians who fought in England to defend their homes and their women, and he knew what invasion would mean to us who have never known. *An Englishman's Home* may be forgotten, old-fashioned perhaps, out of date, but the story is ageless, the lessons it tried to teach are still unlearnt; and nationally, for all the succeeding war in

Europe, the situation is still the same. There are Mr Browns all over England like Guy's Mr Brown, living their little lives day by day, ordinary, monotonous, heedless of wars and rumours of wars, content with their homes, their newspapers, and football. And suddenly, without warning, even as it might happen today and in our time, the country is invaded. Mr Brown is awakened from his apathy too late, too ruinously late; his home crashes about his ears, and he and his family are killed. This is what one newspaper said about the play in 1909:

Reduced to its central idea, this brilliantly conceived and constructed play is simply the story of the tragic fate of Mr Brown, shot by foreign soldiers without trial because he is seized bearing arms without military uniform in defence of his scattered home in Essex.

Each of the three acts is alive with incident, but the evolution of Mr Brown is the main theme and the supreme attraction. We see him change from the garrulous middle-class country-villa resident with a weakness for diabolo to the frantic, desperate, grief-maddened patriot who meets death proudly at the invaders' hands after a last foolish broken-hearted display of heroism with the rifle he handles for the first and last time in his life.

Mr Charles Rock, the creator of the part, became world famous in a week. When he is left alone in the last act, and the audience has neither wit nor satire to distract it, the play becomes a tragedy of thrilling intensity, and for several minutes Mr Brown holds breathless every man and woman in the theatre. The enemy – not necessarily Germans – are advancing to the attack. The British are in retreat. Mr Brown has obstinately refused to leave his home. In impotent rage he seizes a rifle lying on the ground and fumbles with it vainly. At last, by accident, he fires the last cartridge it contains. He learns the trick of loading it. He gropes on the floor for unused cartridges and fires from the window, taking cover instinctively from the advancing enemy. He kills a man, and is convulsed with triumph. Two foreign soldiers enter by the window. One fires at him and misses. The other scrambles over the blockading piano and charges with his bayonet. Mr Brown is surrounded, challenged by an officer, condemned, and led out to be shot.

Two minutes later his daughter, who crawls in to seek him, hears the volley that means his death.

'What is it in *An Englishman's Home* that has created such a furore of enthusiasm in all who have seen it?' asked someone. The entrances at Wyndham's Theatre are besieged for hours before every performance. And after each of the three acts the audiences applaud and cheer with a unanimity and vehemence without parallel in the history of the British stage.

The answer was that *An Englishman's Home* touched a chord in the heart of every man and woman who saw it. They knew that this was their play, and perhaps their story, and the question arose in their minds, 'Supposing it should happen to us?' Mr Brown was one of themselves, and died in the way they too would die. The wave of patriotism, quite distinct from aggressive jingoism, that swept the country at this time was largely due to the influence of Guy's play, and the popular newspapers, seizing their chance, fanned the flame and started an agitation appealing for compulsory military training for all able-bodied youths between the ages of eighteen and twenty-one. People everywhere became alive to the problem of national defence; it seemed imperative that every man should be prepared to defend his home should the occasion arise, and there was a remarkable increase in the ranks of the Territorials. And then, like all bubbles that swell triumphantly for a day, eclipsing everything else in their vicinity, the bubble burst, evaporated, and was lost; the excitement died down; the Press lost interest; the men returned to their football and the women to their fashion articles. *An Englishman's Home* became no more than one other crumpled manuscript in a dusty drawer, and Guy soldiered in South Africa as though it had never been written.

It was, however, decidedly the most impressive thing

that had ever happened to the du Maurier family, and, though *Trilby* and *Peter Ibbetson* are read today and Guy's play has been forgotten, his message was a national one and not an individual fragment. There is some measure of glory in the knowledge that his words must have inspired many of those Englishmen who, five years later, laboured amidst carnage and terror in a foreign land to save their precious homes from the disaster he had so fearfully foreseen.

In 1909, however, there were no wars or rumours of wars, and the du Maurier family, like every other family in England, lived without fear of the future, happy in the security they believed to be enduring. No. 24 Cumberland Terrace was a great success, and Gerald had developed into a true home-lover. The days when he had sneaked into New Grove House as the sun came over the hill seemed very long ago. No late nights now, no poker-playing at the Green Room or the Garrick, but straight back to the house after the evening performance, with Mo preparing a little supper in readiness – some of his favourite cold beef, perhaps, with the inevitable radish and cos lettuce. They began to entertain; it was easier here than it had been at Chester Place, and friends would drop in for lunch and tea on Sundays, while the evening, of course, was always reserved for supper with Mummie at the flat. In the week-days when there was no matinée, Gerald played golf with four companions, coming home about six, all of them very rowdy, and healthy, and happy. And Gerald would lead the way up to the nursery to see the children – Angela talkative, rather advanced for her age, and not a scrap shy; Daphne inclined to hide her head with strangers, biting her thumb, looking another way. Gerald was something of a clown in the nursery, a funmaker; he could always be relied upon to put up a performance, either by imitating somebody the children knew or drawing upon his imagination. As they grew from babies into children, and occasionally the little nursery storms came to his ears, he would settle disputes in strange, amusing ways, turning a scolding into a game. There was the famous time when Daphne pulled Angela's hair and trod on her face, Angela replying with her peculiar death-grip like a bear's hug. The joint shrieks of rage reaching Gerald in the drawing-room, he had them brought downstairs, and, dressing up as a judge, staged a court of law with the children as prisoners at the bar and witnesses in one. It lasted until past bedtime, and, when the nurse came to fetch them, the original quarrel had long been forgotten. He also tried to teach them manners by making them shake hands with cupboards and chairs, solemnly introducing them as guests. In parenthood, as in everything, he was original!

The following year, in 1910, Gerald was faced with a big decision, and had arrived at one of the most important moments in his career. The question was whether he should continue under Frohman, earning a salary, and, though doing undoubtedly well, yet have no definite voice in productions and little responsibility, or go into management at Wyndham's Theatre with Frank Curzon as partner, choose his own plays and produce them, and, besides a large salary, take twenty-five per cent of the profits.

The latter idea was definitely an attractive proposition. But Gerald was not conceited, nor was he a fool, and he knew that it was quite possible for the venture to fail. Suppose his judgement were faulty, suppose the plays he produced were dismal failures and Curzon lost all his money? It would be a big undertaking, whatever happened, and would necessarily mean much strain, hard work, great responsibility, and complete sacrifice of personal freedom. The old lazy days would go for ever; the light-hearted shrug of the shoulder, the careless 'Let 'em all come' attitude, could be his no more. He had reached the parting of the ways.

'I have got to settle soon about my future,' he told Mummie, 'and it's rather a knotty proposition. Frohman acknowledges he cannot do for me what he would like, as he hasn't a theatre. Curzon has Wyndham's, and I could choose my own play, company – everything, in fact. Three thousand a year, and twenty-five per cent of the profits. Curzon would merely supply the money, and give advice when I asked for it. It would mean finishing first the run of *Jimmy Valentine*, which is playing to enormous business. I know of a play I could start with, and perhaps Barrie would let me have one later on. What about it, old lady? I have the du Maurier timidity and unventuresomeness, but I feel that the time has come.'

He was thirty-seven; he stood by common consent, said a critic, in the very front rank of his profession, while enjoying a corresponding degree of popularity, and by going into management he would be sure of every encouragement on the part of his public. Had he the necessary energy, concentration, and staying power to go right ahead and climb to the top of the tree? Gerald thought, and wondered, and looked into himself. He knew Mummie would be proud of him and Mo delighted. He knew that everybody expected it of him, and that it would be cowardly and weak to refuse. Youth lay behind him, and the old careless days; there would be little fishing with Harry Esmond now, and fewer days of golf with Laurie Grossmith and Marsh Allen. If he undertook this thing, then it would mean being serious at last. However much he laughed and jested and pretended that nothing mattered, deep down would be anxiety, strain, a determination to succeed and to achieve something of value; not for his own sake, not because of Gerald, but because this very trade he had chosen must develop and prosper, must not be degraded or cast down, and because slackness and indifference were a confession of failure, a betrayal of Guy and Papa, who had not failed.

He shut his eyes, and said, 'Now then, Papa, what do you think?' and looked at the photograph on the mantelpiece, and into his mind flashed the Breton motto that the governor had always used in his moments of stress: *Abret-ag-Araog* — First and Foremost — and it seemed to him that Papa winked at him with his blind eye and murmured, '*Allons, mon petit, pourquoi pas? La vie n'est pas si dure que ca!*' And Gerald answered, 'All right, let's have a go at it.' With that he went to see Frank Curzon and accepted his offer, and opened at Wyndham's Theatre with *Nobody's Daughter* on the third of September to an audience who cheered and shouted their approval, whilst he smiled and bowed his acknowledgement.

The success was quite wasted, however, and his heart was aching, for Gerald was thinking only of Sylvia, the wistful, the gentle, who had died exactly a week before.

CHAPTER FIVE

IT was a wretched and miserable beginning to his first year as manager, and to Gerald's superstitious mind it seemed a bad augury for the future. It was as though someone – God, or Fate; call it what you will – said to him that he must pay for his success in certain ways; that to become famous he must surrender what he loved the most. He soon found, as he had expected, that being manager of a theatre, and responsible for the cast and the production, required much more concentration and work than the happy-go-lucky playing to a salary had done, and, as a natural consequence, something of his youthful carelessness was lost to him now for ever. He could never relax quite in the same way again. There was no shifting of responsibility, no going back in his tracks. He had made his decision, and must carry his burden to the end of the road.

As a man of thirty-eight he had commitments both in the theatre and at home. He must call rehearsals, arrange meetings, discuss the present and the future with Curzon, pick up the telephone and ask Tom Vaughan, his business manager, for advice; see young actors and actresses about parts for new productions; talk about salaries; see to it that every member of his little community, from the leading lady to the call-boy, were satisfied and not disgruntled; and to do all this needed tact, understanding, and an unfailing good temper.

Duties began to accumulate, small items that seemed of no great importance but which he could never have tackled ten years ago: taking the chair at the Green

Room, making speeches, arranging matinées for charity, giving his opinion on theatrical matters, on productions, and on plays.

At home, another baby was on the way; there appeared to be more servants in the house – an under-nurse, second housemaid; there was a chauffeur for the car and Mo had a groom to look after the pony. They took houses in the country for the summer because of the children, at the same time keeping open No. 24; and in little quiet, insignificant ways life was becoming more of an undertaking every day. It was not the simple thing it once had been.

Darling, a wave of remorse has broken over me – I never write to you. It is not from want of love, filial duty, thought, all those things that go to make up the perfect son (which I do not pretend to be). It is brain fag, mental apathy, anaemia – May has it to a certain extent; it's a form of not behaving like your true self, unless you are under the influence of a drug or very well in health. Darling, I cannot speak to you, unless I see you. Scrawling lines on paper, and putting a penny stamp on the outside, is no medium for me. I want to see my audience, my friend, my mother – *this* takes too long. Writing is a taught thing, it's not natural, animals don't write; they bellow, or frolic, or make sounds expressing what they feel.

Mo is doing this at the present moment, and I don't blame her, as it's half past one, and I have to be up at eight! Come and stop with us, come and talk to me, why don't we all meet more often? I don't see enough of my beloved family.

So Gerald wrote to Mummie from Croxley Green during the hot summer of 1911. *Mr Jarvis* had been tried and failed, and *Passers By* filled Wyndham's in its stead. Another baby had been born, a girl once more ('Thank heaven', Mo was reported to have said, when told), and wife, daughters, maids, and dog, including the fifth-hand Rolls Royce that broke down at every hill, made the country their headquarters for the summer. Even Polly the mare, who dragged the pony-cart behind her, was driven down in state from Regent's Park, and distinguished herself by producing a foal the following day. 'I suppose trotting all those miles hurried it on,' said Mo rather seriously, and Gerald had to stuff a handkerchief in his mouth and look out of the window. Was there any other woman in the world like this? How impossible to be married to anyone else!

It was good to be in the country after the dust and noise of London, and he wandered about with a book on birds in one hand and a book on wild flowers in the other, dressed in shabby tweeds, with a spy-glass round his neck and Angela and Daphne trotting at his heels.

He was beginning to love these summers in the country. He had been doubtful about Denham at first, but this place at Croxley Green was more attractive, and later the Elizabethan house at Cobham was a positive joy, with the River Mole at the bottom of the garden, and rapids to shoot in a cranky boat, and snakes in the long grass, and a ghost on the staircase, and in the trees and the hedges every conceivable form of bird.

On a long day in which to idle, with the hot sun above, and a sky the colour it ought to be, there was nothing better than this. But let it rain, let a cloud appear as small as the back of your hand, let the trees sob in a wind and something appear for lunch that was not underdone roast beef and cos lettuce, then somehow – difficult to explain, but the charm would be gone, a sense of desolation would come upon him, the house seemed cramped and dark and strangely uninhabited, and he would begin to fret for London.

'I'm a Cockney,' he used to say. 'It's no use getting away from it. A day or two in the country is all very well, but not for ever; it's too slack. I find trees depressing after a while, and I can't relax. It's no good, one is either born like that or one isn't. It's something in the blood.'

The truth was that he possessed the type of mind that

cannot find peace in relaxation. After working hard in the theatre, whether producing a play or acting during a long run, he could not put a brake on himself in any way, he could not rest naturally. He was not content to lounge with a book, to close his eyes. He made no attempt to find companionship and quiet within himself. No, he must be distracted; he must be amused; he must never at any cost be left alone. Above all let there be people, let the one day in the week, Sunday, on which he should relax, sound from morning till night with the chatter and laughter of friends. If friends could not always be found, then acquaintances would do – any fellow he had met once and who seemed vaguely amusing, any girl with a pretty face who said she could play tennis. It did not matter a scrap who came so long as the lunch-table was full, and everyone talked, and when they were all gone he could fall into a chair exhausted in mind and body. This was later, of course, when he lived at Hampstead, and was no longer young; in the Croxley and Cobham days people were not yet an obsession, nor could he afford to entertain so lavishly. But even then he was restless; he was not really content unless he was doing something; he must have golf on his Sundays, or tennis, or one or two close friends down to spend the day. For all his fondness for birds, he did not watch them hour upon hour, but after a certain time would stretch himself, and yawn, and wander into the house for a drink and a cigarette, and glance at Mo, happy in her gardening or needlework, and moon for a few minutes and say, glancing at the telephone, 'What about getting old Basil over for golf, and Laurie and Coralie to stop over Sunday?'

He said it was in the blood; that Papa had been the same; but Kicky, though hospitable and devoted to his friends, had rested contentedly with his own family, had sat back in his chair while Pem read to him in the evenings, and had no thought of distraction. It was the century that had changed, and Gerald belonged to it. He was in advance of his time, and a forerunner of the restless age. He declared himself an enemy to progress, a hater of motor-cars and speed, but even as he protested his love for quiet, for the days of carriages, and dignity, and grace, his feet were beating to a jazz *tempo* and his hands reached out for the cocktail-shaker.

The future and the past were at conflict within him, and they dragged him different ways. He possessed the sentimentality of the one and the cynicism of the other; the moral conventions of the Victorians and the unscrupulous shrug of the twentieth century; the high standards of 1880, and the shallow weaknesses of 1920.

He fell between two periods and was a product of neither. He hummed the songs of Maud Valerie White and danced to American crooners. He bemoaned the simplicity of his childhood's home yet swore at tepid bathwater and cold plates. He deplored the passing of the old traditions yet was himself an instigator of freedom. He would have fought duels for friends who were only slightly insulted; carried vendettas into succeeding generations; yet would whip the same friends with some stinging personal observation and a modern unforgivable inquiry into their private lives.

He was old-fashioned and advanced; strict and lacking all discipline; more ribald than the poets of the Restoration and as easily shocked as the author of *The Daisy Chain*. He would have liked women to be shingled and wear crinolines; to be innocent yet appreciate his jokes; to have the grace and dignity of the women in Papa's drawings but be accessible and familiar like the moderns. He demanded the impossible, and life defeated him, worried and bewildered him. He was constantly at war with himself and his own beliefs. There were no rules set down that he could follow. He had to follow his instinct, and his instinct was made up of too many adverse strings. Weakness and strength, shallowness and depth, nobility and poverty, intelligence and stupidity – all these qualities were his, and were at variance with one another, struggling for a supremacy none of them attained, making him a creature of great promise, baffling, lovable, but for ever unfulfilled.

'I wish Gerald was not quite so fond of Dieppe,' said Mo after the August holiday in 1911, and Mummie nodded her head and agreed.

'Always that old casino and gambling, and too many cocktails,' Mo went on. 'It wouldn't matter if it wasn't for the fact that he needed a rest, and then he does away with all the good of the sea air by staying up to all hours in those stuffy rooms. He goes back to London to rehearse the new play looking just as washed out as when we went away.'

'It's no use, Muriel dearest,' sighed Mummie. 'Gerald has always been the same, and nothing will ever change him. He cannot and will not rest. You may as well go stand upon the beach and bid the tide – you know what I mean; it comes in Shakespeare – as persuade Gerald to do what is good for him.'

And Gerald, having worn himself out during the day playing countless sets of tennis in a tournament, followed by high diving and showing off before the French beach crowds, finishing up with baccarat in the casino until two in the morning, wondered why he felt jaded in September and not quite so enthusiastic over the next play.

They had tried Dinard one year for a change, but he had loathed it. The casino was dull, and he complained that there was nothing to do in the evenings, and he did not like playing tennis with people he did not know. They all had to come back, although it was the middle of August, and the children were packed off to Ramsgate instead. Another year they took a house at Mullion, hoping that Cornwall would amuse him, but this was an even worse failure. It poured with rain, and the sitting-room was poky, he said, and there was nothing whatever to do except climb rocks and cliffs, of which he at once chose the most impossible and dangerous, with his nephew Geoffrey for companion. When this palled, he declared himself finished with the place, and off he went to Dieppe with Mo once more, leaving the children in Mullion; and, mixing with the crowds and the clatter and the bustle, he believed himself happy again.

'Wait till you come to forty year,' Papa had said, and in 1913 Gerald was beginning to realize what he had meant. It seemed a long way back now to the quiet studio at New Grove House, the curtain blowing at the open window, and Chang snoring on his sofa in the corner. The governor was blessed in his generation, and if he suffered fears of blindness, and was depressed about his work, he surely did not know this terrible fear of boredom, this craving for excitement, for amusement, for being entertained by men and women; this horror of being left alone for one moment. He could not know the anxiety and worry that went with the managing of a theatre – the pettiness of details, the search for the right play, the necessary tact he must have in all his dealings, the fatal ease with which one could take a false step and be landed in some impossible position. 'Wait till you come to forty year.' Why had Papa said that? What had he guessed of him? Did he too know this odd little demon of restlessness, this occasional emptiness, this fretful discontent? Had he lived with Papa all those years and never guessed? Was there something in the blood that made them both long for the infinite and be for ever unappeased?

Oh, well, forget it, cast it aside; above all, don't think, because in thinking lay danger; and Gerald would go off to the Garrick Club or the theatre and shake everyone with his rollicking spirits and his youth and vitality, his sense of fun, his wit, his gaiety, much as Kicky had done at the *Punch* dinners forty years before.

They were alike, these du Mauriers, with their terrific spirits, their sudden depths of depression, their bursts of laughter, and their quick anger. They had the same little sadnesses, the same vivid, eager curiosity, the same passion for their children mingled with jealousy and pride. They had a certain youthfulness inbred in them – a look of eye, a tone of voice – that proved they would never grow old; and for all their love of life, and the world they lived in, they made haste to leave it.

Sylvia had been the first to go, in the August of 1910 – not reluctantly, perhaps, not with any great wish to linger. Arthur had left her, and the light had gone, and, for all the five boys she adored, she would not stay. The ill health he left her had been a burden which she carried, and it had grown too heavy and must be cast aside. She was like a phantom of herself, a wraith of the Sylvia that had been, and almost the only thing of her that remained was her crooked, wistful smile. Day by day she grew weaker; she had to be carried from room to room, and finally she did not leave her bed. The boys knew that she must leave them, from George, the eldest, to Nicolas, the youngest, who was only seven. They laughed and joked beside her bed, pretending not to notice she had changed. She was only forty-four when she died, and she was buried beside Arthur in the Hampstead churchyard, close to Kicky's grave.

Three years later Trixie died, aged forty-nine; warmhearted, eager, irresistible Trixie, who demanded so much of life – more than it ever gave her; whose sense of humour triumphed over sorrow; who would not be cast down. Adored by her family and by her friends, she was fierce in her love for her sons. Trixie the generous, the curious, with her great bursts of ribald laughter, her exaggerated statements, her domineering, critical frown,

Trixie, whose very voice proclaimed her youth and energy, never knew how ill she was, and laughed even as she died. She was buried at Berkhampstead beside the baby she had lost nearly twenty years before.

The deaths of Sylvia and Trixie were a terrible shock to the du Mauriers. Mummie became tremulous and shaky; she could not bear to be away long from the children that remained. The illnesses of her two eldest had been a great strain on her nerves, and she had not spared herself in the nursing. She had been so proud of her daughters, so concerned for their welfare and their happiness; and now they were gone, and would come to the flat no more, and she felt herself to be very weary, very tired, with a pain beneath her heart that she did not understand.

She clung to Guy, and to Gerald, and to May, who had always been the thin and delicate one, and had survived her sisters; she begged them to stay near her and not venture far away. She was happy too in Trixie's and Sylvia's boys, giving them all the love and the generosity in her heart, remembering their anniversaries, their little likes and dislikes. Whatever they demanded, she was only too happy, too pathetically happy, to grant.

'Don't do too much, darling, that's what I'm afraid of,' said Gerald, 'and you must not be too strenuous with all these various grandchildren, having them to meals every day, and letting them spill things and overeat. Send mine back when you are tired of them, because I can't bear being without them, but I know they love being with you and it does them so much good. And I wish you'd take a glass of claret or a little champagne with your food; you would never have that pain of yours then, and it would feed your blessèd old heart. I should die of nerves if I had no stimulant, as you know.'

He could not believe at first that Trixie was gone. Sylvia somehow had seemed fated, for he felt that she would not long survive Arthur. Her illness, too, had prepared him. But not Trixie, not his gay, light-hearted Trixie, who never spoke of illness and should have lived for ever.

All his tears and his bitterness could not bring them back. He had no faith and no belief. He knew they were dust and he would never see them again, and he put them from him and plunged into his own life that seemed so futile sometimes, so very unworth-while, good only for the very work it entailed, giving him some sense of achievement, however paltry, however small.

'Thank God for one's luck, and for being repaid for trying one's best,' he said after the first night of *Diplomacy* – an enormous success – in March 1913, which utterance was surely a denial of atheism in itself, but Gerald was always inconsequent. He had worked hard at this production, taking infinite pains with his two young leads, Owen Nares and Gladys Cooper, who thus made their first real success together; and, though *Diplomacy* was an old play well known to the majority of playgoers, the revival this time was a notable one in every respect. Sir Squire Bancroft, who owned the rights of *Diplomacy*, gave valuable help over the production, and was himself very much impressed with Gerald's methods and technique.

A friend of Kicky's, and his contemporary, he now became a great admirer and counsellor of the son. 'Poor du Maurier,' he said, 'I wish he had lived to see how his son Gerald adorns the stage he so greatly loved himself.'

Although it was forty years since its first appearance, *Diplomacy* had not dated. The story was as exciting as ever, and the situations as tense. The play had really been revived as a stop-gap after *Doormats,* but its success was overwhelming, and it ran for a year.

Henry Beauclerc was not a big acting part, but it needed the usual du Maurier ease and grace, and if clumsily handled would have marred the piece. It was a good part for a producer, and Gerald was able to take it in his stride without any great effort of mind and concentrate on the other members of the already excellent and dependable cast.

He was already far more interested in producing than in his own performance, and was perhaps, then and later, too apt to allow himself a secondary part, involving little strain, and making the production itself of paramount importance. His judgement of plays, from the point of view of entertainment, was nearly always sound, and he made few mistakes; but, reckoned as works of art of a literary and permanent value, they were often poor enough in material and with little to recommend them, succeeding only because of his own peculiar personality, his uncanny *flair* for finding unknown talent amongst his company, and for the polish and grace with which they were produced. He was too much inclined to look for plays with what he called a 'good plot' and forget those with greater depth and greater meaning; he believed action to be essential, and disliked scenes of continuous talk. He often described himself as being 'lowest of the low-brows' when that unfortunate word came into general use. And a certain caution, unlike everything else in his character, prevented him from throwing grand gestures of adventure and risk, the consequences of which might have been appalling or tremendous, but which would at least have made theatre history. He played for safety; his bump of ambition was not highly enough developed, and he was curiously self-conscious about his own talent, which he under-estimated continually. It was his charm and his personality that brought people to his theatre, and not the plays, or the expectation of a great and memorable performance.

It was deplorable that he was so often restricted by the poverty of his plays, which, though financially successful, tethered him by their mediocrity. But for this handicap he might have risen to heights reached by no member of his profession except Irving, and possibly Tree. Both worked by different methods of approach, and, like artists in the grand manner, boldly painted scenes of pageantry on a huge canvas, while Gerald, faultlessly and gracefully, like his own father, drew drawing-room figures in black and white. Of course, there were, sprinkled here and there amongst the others, plays of value by famous authors, and it is significant that his best performances took place in these, and most especially in the plays of J. M. Barrie. He was made for these parts, as no one else can ever hope to be. He brought a delicate, pristine quality into his interpretation of those characters so peculiarly and lovably original; a note from the woods and the wild places – something wistful, something gay, a faun-like carelessness, a happy-go-lucky shrug of the shoulder. It will be impossible to forget his tragic, haunting performance as the embittered, drink-sodden Harry Dearth in *Dear Brutus*, with a world of promise unfulfilled behind his weary eyes; and the sudden transformation into the care-free, youthful fellow with a song on his lips and a boyish daughter for a playmate, shouting with laughter and whistling to the moon. It is the fashion amongst some to laugh at Barrie plays; they have been unkindly parodied, and, because of their very delicacy and originality, they lend themselves to ridicule, but it is an irreparable calamity to the English stage that since 1921 we have waited in vain for the author to break his silence. As Dearth in *Dear Brutus*, as the Prince and the Policeman in *A Kiss for Cinderella*, as John Shand in *What Every Woman Knows*, Gerald was incomparable. His acting in these plays was in a class by itself.

His art was rare and difficult to define, it was as though he walked on tiptoe, his finger to his lips, elusive and slightly mocking, abandoned at one moment and detached the next, following a tune beyond the hills that none but

118

himself could hear, and then becoming suddenly human – too human, too embarrassingly personal and alive, a faun with a cloven hoof.

Whatever may be said of his acting in other and more worthless plays, his rendering of Barrie's genius was unequalled for depth, sensibility, and charm.

His methods of producing were ingenious and typical. He became every character in the play in turn, man or woman, and walked, talked, and behaved as he believed they would behave in natural circumstances. 'Don't force it, don't be self-conscious,' he would say. 'Do what you generally do any day of your life when you come into a room. Bite your nails, yawn, lie down on a sofa and read a book – do anything or nothing, but don't look dramatically at the audience and speak with one eye on the right-hand box. If you must look in front of you, stare right at the back of the pit as though nobody was there.' He pulled fun at his company continually, mimicking light-heartedly, and entirely without malice, their little faults and mannerisms. 'Don't walk across the room as though you were a mannequin in a crowded ballroom, darling; it's unnatural; it's affected. Look, this is what you did'; and he would mince from one end of the stage to the other, his hips swaying, his eyes rolling, his hand patting an imaginary strand of hair into place, while the company and the girl he was imitating roared with laughter. 'Try and remember it's your own drawing-room, and there's no one there but yourself, and you're tired after a long day, and all you want is a drink and a couple of aspirins. Perhaps I'm entirely wrong, but what about trying something like this?' And he went off the stage and came back through an imaginary door, and was not the producer any more but the character he intended to convey, jaded, obviously tired, and smothering a yawn, glancing at the table to see if there were any letters, throwing an imaginary pair of gloves on a chair with an imaginary hat, standing in the middle of the room for a moment, weary, bored, humming no sort of tune under his breath, and then calling over his shoulder for the maid in the imaginary hall to bring an iced drink. 'Don't necessarily do that,' he said afterwards, 'but something like it. Do you see what I mean?'

Constantly tactless and continually thoughtless in private life, when producing he was particularly careful never to offend anyone or to hurt feelings.

'Marvellous, old chap,' he would say, 'that's just exactly what I meant. Half a minute, though; I'll tell you what; I believe it would be almost better from your point of view if instead of having a fit, you merely turned your back and looked out of the window. Do you see what I mean? It would look tremendously impressive from the front, and it's just the way this fellow would behave after hearing the news. Guitry did it in *Le Tribun*, you know, and of course what he did you can do identically. Do you see what I mean? I can't help feeling that the fit and rolling on the floor – which you did marvellously, my dear chap, and better than anyone else could possibly have done – is perhaps a little wasted in this situation. I believe what I suggest will touch the audience even more than the fit, and you will then make it the most important moment in the play. Do you see what I mean?' And the other, having just given an appalling display of shy-making emotion in the middle of the stage, would nod in agreement, tremendously self-impressed, and proceed to give the simple, quiet little exhibition that was required of him, believing that he was Irving over again and that his name would be in headlines in the daily papers.

Ardent love-making on the stage Gerald considered very bad theatre. He did not attempt it himself, and strongly discouraged it in others. 'Must you kiss her as though you were having steak and onions for lunch?' he would say. 'It may be what you feel, but it's damned unattractive from the front row of the stalls. Can't you just say, "I love you," and yawn, and light a cigarette and walk away? Unfortunately, nobody was able to do this quite as he did it himself. He had methods of his own. He seldom kissed women on the stage, unless it was on the back of the neck or the top of the head, and then he would generally slap them on the face afterwards, and say, 'You old funny, with your ugly mug,' and walk away talking of something else as though he did not care. It was effective enough, anyway, if box-office returns were anything to go by, and, though unorthodox and original, was certainly less embarrassing than the steak-and-onions form of love-making.

The nearest he ever got to this was when he played André le Briquet in *The Prude's Fall*, and had to be French in speech and gesture; the result was not perhaps steak as we know it in England, but it was decidedly *entre-côte minute,* and rather overdone at that.

Although Gerald was against this sort of thing on the stage on principle, he was equally scornful of shyness; he would not let actors and actresses who were playing a love scene be stiff and awkward with one another. The man must hold the girl naturally, and not as though she were a cactus-bush, and the girl must cling to him affectionately, ruffle his hair if she liked, and put her cheek against his.

'Be playful, be like puppies, be fond of one another,' he said, 'but don't go to the extremes, either one way or the other. Strike some sort of medium between afternoon tea in a cathedral town and supper in a flat in Paris, for Gawd's sake!'

His criticisms were always taken in good part by the company, and there was never any ill feeling or discontent amongst them.

People were extraordinarily happy under his management, because he never worried them, he never nagged;

he had a laugh and a friendly word for all of them, and there was an atmosphere of freedom and contentment in his theatre that was different from any other. Trouble was rare, and, if it did occur, had for cause this very good nature of which it was unfortunately easy to take advantage. Perhaps a woman, her head turned by success, and imagining from his nod and his smile, his 'Darlings' and his easy familiarity that was the same to man, woman, child, and dog, that he was seriously attracted by her, would worry and bore him with little parades of jealousy and stupid and undignified scenes that she considered important. And because he was weak, because he had not strength of will enough to say 'Go to hell,' he would find himself embroiled against his better judgement, mixed up in a sort of fifth-form intrigue when he ought to have known better, all starting from a chance phrase like, 'I love the way your hair grows,' followed by lunch somewhere and two cinemas. It was so easy to be kind and to give presents, and so pleasant to be liked, and then, before one was aware of it, people clung to one, made protestations, became over-affectionate, and threatened suicide. It all developed from a gallant, light-hearted business into something unattractive, unnecessarily dramatic, and beyond everything a bore.

He would return home moody and disgruntled, pour himself out a drink on the sideboard, and swear aloud, and then go in to Mo and pour out the whole story with a wealth of detail, very injured and ill used, complaining much as a child complains when the fire burns him.

And Mo would listen patiently, secretly rather bored and rather scornful of the little troubles he brought upon himself, and she would tell him, very much as Mummie had done when he was younger, that it was his own fault for encouraging people in the beginning, and he was too susceptible to a pretty face and too cowardly to admit when he was bored, and of course women took advantage of him; he was easy money; and why not have a nice rest and forget all about it? And there was some of his favourite underdone cold beef for dinner, with a little cos lettuce and radishes. And he would be humoured and coaxed back to contentment, and begin to laugh at himself, and in five minutes would begin imitating the unfortunate cause of the trouble, to hoots of laughter from the children, who had appeared on the scene and who mocked at him invariably for his passages at arms and his favourites that lasted a day.

'The stable' was the children's somewhat indelicate name for Gerald's little gallery of favourites. 'Who's the latest in the stable?' they would jeer, 'and what's the form this week? I'm not going to back —— much longer.' And they would begin to discuss likely winners for the future suggesting names for his pleasure, while Mo carved the beef and mixed the salad, and Gerald, with his mouth full, joined in the crowd of suggestions, highly amused and indifferent to the fact that the luckless ladies, whose names were bandied so freely amongst his mordant and precocious children, were probably at this moment preparing for the grand finale, seeing themselves as heroines in a tremendous drama, and playing Cleopatra to his Antony.

It was as well for the unfortunates that they did not realize the eccentricities of his household, where discretion was flung to the winds and everything was discussed with a blatancy comparable to that of the days of later Rome and the early Regency, or they might have felt even bigger fools than they discovered themselves ultimately to be.

But it was not all intrigue. The theatre was generally a very happy, light-hearted community, where people did as they pleased, and nobody was hurt, and there was ragging and practical joking more suggestive of the kindergarten than the intense and feverish intrigues of the fifth form.

The fifteen years at Wyndham's were the most successful in his career; financially and professionally he was at the top of his form, and his best work was done and performed in that theatre. He had Curzon behind him in case of difficulty, and his backing in every enterprise; and he had the dependable, cautious Tom Vaughan as business manager. His staff adored him and were men of trust. He was at the height of his popularity, his physical health was never better, and his mental powers were at their most brilliant. His brain worked very quickly then, his judgement was sound, and it seemed as though he could do nothing wrong. He was lucky, of course. He was born lucky. But he knew how to use his luck to the advantage of everyone concerned, which required genius in its own way. He had never for an instant looked back, from the day he had come to his decision in 1910; and, though he had one or two failures, they did not count; they were as nothing among the triumphs.

The public associated him with Wyndham's as they did Tree with His Majesty's and Alexander with St James's; those were the happy days of the big actor-managers who had real theatre sense and theatre understanding, who knew from long experience what their public demanded, who had something of dignity about them, something fine. Managing a theatre was a position of trust, demanding delicacy and tact. The actor-manager was looked up to and respected like the head of any other community. He worked hard that the company should be happy and contented.

Gerald belonged to Wyndham's; he was as much a part of it as the boards, the curtain, the heavy swing door, the row of stalls shrouded in their white and grimy covers, the cat in the dress circle, the backcloth and the false movable walls that were not walls, the dust in the passages, the intimate, indescribable, musty, fusty smell that was the back of the stage and the dressing-rooms and the front of the house in one.

Much of his personality is embedded in those walls. His laughter is still in the passage, his footstep on the stairs, and his voice calling for Tommy Lovell when the curtain falls. For all their passing away and the coming of other sounds – new voices, new laughter, other men and other memories – something of himself remains for ever amidst the dust and silence of that theatre; a breath, a whisper, the echo of a song.

CHAPTER SIX

IN July 1914 Gerald, Mo, and the children, and a gathering of friends and relatives, spent the annual holiday in the wilds of North Wales, at a house called Plas Gwinfryn at Llanbedr. What with themselves, other people's nurses and children, and a few intimates, they numbered about twenty in all at one time. Mo and Gerald had motored down from London. Gerald was tired after the season's run of *The Clever Ones*. It was a relief to get away from responsibilities and the theatre to a quiet spot where nobody talked shop or discussed London productions, and no one had certainly ever heard of or seen Gerald du Maurier. In those days a famous actor-manager was a person to cause excitement when seen about London; people turned round when he passed and nudged each other, pointing and whispering, and it was almost embarrassing to walk about the streets or to enter a restaurant. It was like being a minor royalty, or a Test Match cricketer, or the co-respondent in a modern divorce case. Autographs were demanded when Gerald was stepping from one cab to another, and the luckless favourite could not call his soul his own.

This form of publicity became tiring after a time, and Gerald grew sick of the sound of his name. Wales would surely be a refuge from the pointing finger and the goggling eye. On the way down they lunched at a place called Nuneaton, at a dismal, ill-kept hotel. There was one seedy stranger in the room, who, upon their entering, immediately rose to his feet and said, 'You don't remember me, Mr du Maurier. We met in Liverpool on tour several years ago.' This was somewhat chastening to begin with, and, after they had eaten their mutton to the accompaniment of the seedy stranger's reviving memories, they took their departure and fled westward, stopping the night on the Welsh border, only to be accosted by a cotton-spinner from Chester, who seized Gerald by the hand and said, 'My son will never forgive me if I don't say "How d'you do?" to Arsène Lupin.' It was not an auspicious beginning to a quiet holiday, but such was the price of popularity, and the jaded public favourite arrived at Llanbedr the following day in a torrent of rain and a thick mist that obscured everything from a radius of five yards onwards. The house was discovered to be some distance from the sea, and accessible only by a long narrow stony path. When the beach was ultimately reached, it was found to be dreary and uninviting and inhabited by numberless cows.

It looked as though the daily journeys to the beach were going to be a nightmare, as Jeanne had to be carried down the stony path, and at the age of three was not light. Daphne was a wet blanket where water and bathing was concerned, and Angela showed considerable timidity, like her mother, in the presence of horned animals. Up at the house, the view was charming when not concealed by mist. The garden was a wilderness and a joy, but fruit, ice, and fish were impossible to procure unless sent by rail. Meals, in consequence, involved much labour and forethought. Gerald looked at the rain and the mountain in front of the house, and began to think about Dieppe.

The holiday depression must be dispelled at all costs, and friends were hastily summoned to relieve the gloom. Nephew Geoffrey, the best of companions, with the same sense of fun, and his wife and baby, arrived and they were followed by reinforcements in the form of Mallaby-Deeley, the Ernest Thurstons, and various blood relatives of Mo's. Harlech (good bathing and golf) was found to be within motoring distance. There was also a sprinkling of friends from London – the Pollocks and the Granets – and with the feverish help of all concerned Gerald's boredom was kept at bay. One of his diversions, then and always, was the staging of elaborate and somewhat dangerous practical jokes, and Geoffrey was an ardent fellow-conspirator. The pair worked at high pressure, and brought off many a successful *coup* together, the other members of the party being the victims. It was a good way of passing the time, and nobody was much the worse for it. But rumours of war had a sobering effect, and, when things began to look really serious, this became the sole topic of conversation. News was hard to get in Wales, and Gerald, brought back to realities with a jerk, wrote to Mummie for confirmation.

Still no news of anything definite, [he said] but amazing rumours reach us from time to time. Do you know anything? Every morning, however beautiful it may be, one wakes up with a heavy pain over one's heart. *War*. It will be too terribly wicked if England is dragged into the business just because the heir to Austria was killed by a lunatic. We are living in amazing times, and here we are all conscious that we ought to be doing something, but we don't know what. It's all damnable, but at the same time we ought to help somehow. Take care of yourself, dearest; you are one of the old ones.

Mummie, away at Seaford with May, could give little information, and the party in Wales had to rely upon their newspapers. Nobody felt like playing practical jokes once war was declared, and Gerald forgot his boredom. They all returned to London the last week in August.

These are super-strenuous times, [Gerald wrote to Mummie, still at Seaford] in London, in club-lands, fools are greater fools, wise people are wiser, and it is difficult to keep a sober outlook. Armchair soldiers, pessimists, jingoists – and, worst of all, those people who've just seen somebody who *knows* – telling one the truth. You will see in the paper that the *Highflyer* has been sinking a German cruiser. Good luck to it, whether nephew Guy is in it or not. One takes a snobbish pride in being related to anybody who has the chance of being mutilated, or mutilating others. If one has nobody one loves likely to be killed, one is out of it. People under the influence of drink – in their cups, as it is called – are supposed to show their true selves, but in times of *war* you get them absolutely under a microscope.

Anybody who says a sweet, pleasant, sensible thing at the present moment deserves a Victoria Cross. Nobody that I have come across has earned one yet. May we sup with you when you return, next Sunday, and meet May and Coley, who I am sure, is a godsend in these times? The children are back, and wish they weren't, and say so forcibly, especially Jeanne! But one wants all one's family close at the present moment.

It was obvious that the war would have an adverse effect on the theatres, and the new play at Wyndham's on the 1st of September – *Outcast* – ran only until December. It needed an ingenious brain to discover the right sort of play to appeal to a war-obsessed audience; amongst them would be soldiers on leave and others about to become soldiers, and wounded men, and nurses, young and old people with one thought uppermost in their minds, unable to concentrate on the old serious type of play, with its love problems or life problems that now seemed so paltry in comparison with the big world problem of the moment. The time appeared ripe for a revival of *Raffles,* and this was accordingly produced the day before Christmas Eve. The choice was justified, and it was almost as great a success as before. The pace and the excitement appealed to those who were themselves being hustled and disturbed by the great unrest. They were able to relieve their pent-up emotions in a frenzy of applause, and they followed the adventures of the amateur cracksman with an almost pitiful intensity.

It was ironical that the play in which Gerald had made his first outstanding success, and which was the original cause of his great popularity, should be for ever more associated in his mind with the saddest period in his life, so that in later years he could only recall *Raffles* with bitterness and loathing. Mummie had been in failing health for some time, and the war had come as a great shock to her. She thought continually of Guy, who was out in France commanding his battalion, and of her grand-children – the elder ones who were old enough to fight – and it seemed to her that the peaceful, gentle world she had loved and understood was becoming a place of treachery and horror. She suffered from her old pain under the heart – 'Mummie's pain', they had come to call it – which had come and gone intermittently for years. But now it redoubled its intensity, and she became tired and very weak. It was plain to everyone that she was seriously ill, and, lying in bed at the flat in Portman Mansions, she looked very fragile and pathetic, her hands plucking at the sheets and her eyes following May and Gerald about the room. Guy returned on leave from France to see her, and this brought to her some measure of comfort, but Christmas and the New Year held little promise for any of them, and her children could only wait with fear in their hearts, and look in one another's eyes, and wonder. It was decided, though not without bitter argument and misgiving, that she must undergo an operation, and that she would stand a fairer chance of recovery in a nursing-home, with nurses and doctors at hand, than in her own flat. Poor Mummie did not want to go; she was afraid of operations and she was deeply attached to her own home – her furniture, her little be-longings, the things that she and Kicky had shared and loved. She did not want to be parted from them, and begged to be allowed to stay. But her children believed it to be for the best, and were firm, promising that she should not remain at the nursing-home a day longer than was necessary.

Mummie, however, fretted in the nursing-home. She longed for her lost comforts, her maid Julia, and the food she had been accustomed to. The operation was performed, and she was not strong enough to stand it, as her sons had feared. She died with her arms around them both, on the anniversary of her wedding to Kicky just fifty-one years before.

She was buried beside him in the grave in the Hampstead churchyard.

Men were falling every minute of the day and night over in France, and death was a familiar figure in almost every home those days, but these tragedies could not reconcile the devoted family to the loss of their beloved mother. The worst of it was that they felt that it could have been avoided, that the operation was not necessary, and but for it and the hasty removal to the nursing-home she would have been with them still. Life without Mummie seemed impossible. She was part of their daily lives, and it meant a breaking up of the ties that bound them. The flat must be sold, and her belongings distributed amongst them. She had been so great a comforter, so widely and deeply loved; her generosity, so peculiarly her own, embraced every member of her children's household. There was a present at Christmas-time for all of them – for each grandchild, each nurse, each kitchen-maid; and clothes, and hampers, and little treats and discoveries; whatever was demanded or not demanded of her she gave willingly, from pages out of her cheque-book to the blankets off her bed. She lived for her children, and her children's children, and she left empty a place that no one else would ever fill.

May, with Coley at the War Office all day, must have felt her loss the most at first. Alone in her little house in Chelsea, without a child even to comfort her, she had been Mummie's constant companion and friend.

But between Mummie and her sons there was a link almost visible in its intensity. She kept every letter they ever wrote to her, from the first little scraps at seven years old to the last ones she received from them as men of fifty and forty-two. Guy wrote to her every day of his life when he was away from England, page upon page of closely written manuscript, telling her his thoughts and his actions, his hopes and his fears. Every one of them she docketed and numbered.

Gerald, her ewee lamb, her spoilt darling, wrote less because he saw her more often, and because he was never very willing with his pen; but his letters too she kept and treasured, even to little notes and ancient long-paid bills. These things her sons had touched and breathed upon, had held in their hands. They had been some small, infinitesimal part of them: therefore they were precious and must never be destroyed.

She went from them, and something her sons had always possessed went with her; that first feeling of security and trust, that dependence born with childhood, the faith that she would never fail them. Now this was shattered; it had dissolved into nothingness with her voice and her smile; and there was no longer any certainty in life, and no foundation.

'Take this, O, one never knows, and it was always meant for you,' said Guy to his brother before he went back to France, and he gave Gerald the signet-ring on his little finger. 'Good luck, and *Abret-ag-Araog*,' said Gerald. Guy went back to France with a heavy heart and a new loneliness, wondering what lay in waiting for this poor world so torn and shaken, and whether from the great bleeding heart of it would come a new heaven and a new earth that he and Gwen would share together. Gerald returned to play *Raffles* at Wyndham's to shouts of hysterical applause from his fevered, unhappy audience, and there was foreboding in his heart, and a sense of loss, of ultimate despair.

Sylvia's eldest boy, George, was killed in the spring, at the age of twenty-one. He was gallant and debonair, eager for life and somehow glorious, like every one of that blessed and tragic generation, and his death was an added bitterness and a fresh realization of terrible futility. '*Raffles* is unlucky to my family,' said Gerald hopelessly, blaming himself in some obscure and frightful fashion for the calamities that had come upon them all, and which no power on earth could ever have avoided. He remembered how Arthur, Sylvia's husband, had died during that first successful run, and Sylvia herself had caught infection, and to his complicated, superstitious mind there came the belief that *Raffles* was accursed, and in its apparent good fortune had brought nothing but disaster. February passed – February, which Gerald always called his fatal month and hated – and March came, and night after night he went down to the theatre from Cumberland Terrace dreading the very sight of the word '*Raffles*' written in huge letters above the doors of Wyndham's.

'Wait till you come to forty year,' Papa had said. In a fortnight's time he would be forty-two, and his soul was sick with a fear and a horror that Papa had never known, and he felt tired, and used, and immeasurably old. He was in his dressing-room at the theatre when the telegram came to tell him that Guy had been killed.

CHAPTER SEVEN

In a sense it was an added bitterness that those war years should be amongst his most successful. It was as though an unholy pact had been agreed to by some fearful God, who said, 'Yes, I will give you fame and prosperity if you give me your family instead.' Mummie, Trixie, Sylvia, and Guy, they had all gone now, and only he and May were left, out of that group Papa had drawn at Hampstead forty years ago. The train was broken, the carriages destroyed; all that survived was the third-class carriage and the truck, holding on to each other as they had done in the picture. They were wise who had broken the line. There was little fun and glory in continuing the struggle in a world grown old and weary with fighting, a world where there was no security and no likelihood of peace to come, a world in which men were changing, and women were changing, and the whole business of living was becoming more difficult, more involved; the old simplicity gone, and a sort of haggard restlessness taking its place.

Standards were sinking, and values were out of proportion, and there were no foundations to cling to, no roots to hold; the whole was swept away out of hand in this universal catastrophe that seemed to be changing the very face of the earth. This would have shattered Sylvia and Trixie, thought Gerald, as it shattered Mummie. It was different for May; she had no children, and Coley was over-age. But Trixie's gaiety would have been silenced, with two boys in France and one on the North Sea, and Sylvia's tender heart would have broken like those of all the other mothers whose eldest sons were killed. Mummie,

Trixie, and Sylvia; he could hardly wish them back to this; but Guy ... Guy should have escaped; he should not have gone. There was so much for him to do, so many words of comfort that he had left unspoken, and oh! the things they had not said to one another that would never now be said, the plays unwritten, the questions unasked, the jests they had not shared. How was it going to be possible to endure life without Guy, without his sense, his wisdom, without his help and his smile? How could he go, leaving no message of farewell, no last blessed word of comfort?

He had taken Guy too much for granted; he had not written to him enough; he had not spent the hours with him he could have done, precious minutes and seconds that were perished and gone; they mounted now in his mind to a wild and extravagant total, reproaching him for his thoughtlessness and his neglect. He looked at his signet-ring and thought, 'Guy held this in his hands. It was part of him. That's why he gave it to me at the station. He knew – Guy knew that he wasn't coming back.' And he wondered what message this ring contained, what whispered word that Guy had never spoken.

'I mustn't give way,' Gerald said. 'Whatever happens, I mustn't give way. Guy would despise me, and it's undignified and not like a du Maurier, not like Papa. I've just got to go on, and go through with things, for Mo and the children, and never look as though I minded, or cared. I've just got to go on with the job and do my best, however bloody, damnable, and tiring it may become, because Guy believed in me.'

And he swore an oath on the ring that he would not be defeated, and then he went back to Mo like a lost child to be comforted and loved.

There was much outside his own theatre for him to do, now that he stood so high in his profession, and he began to work hard for theatrical charities, organizing performances for various funds and societies, never sparing himself any work of this kind for one moment, so that soon, whenever a matinée had to be arranged for any purpose, people said, 'Get Gerald to do it,' knowing that he would give all his time and make the scheme a tremendous success.

He had been made President of the Actors' Orphanage in 1914, and this became the dearest and most-loved of his charities. Because of his efforts, the garden-party in aid of the orphanage became a great annual function in the London season, a social festivity attended by everyone who was interested in the theatre, and who gave willingly. It is only of very recent years that this has deteriorated into an undignified, bawling scramble, where a gaping public pay to see certain actors and actresses as they pay to see prize dogs at the Crystal Palace. There was nothing Gerald would not do for the sake of the orphanage, and he worked untiringly that it should prosper. This orphanage was unlike any other institution of its kind. The children lived in a charming old country house surrounded by a large garden and fields, as comfortable and as happy as children in a private school; they were the sons and daughters of dead or desperately poor members of the profession, and, when they came of an age to leave, every chance was given them that they should succeed in their little sphere of life.

'Let's always be kind to people when they're down on their luck,' said Gerald as Harry Dearth in *Dear Brutus*, and it became a catchword of his own, so that it was part of his life from now on to help men and women in his profession who had not had his chances, his luck, his slice of talent – people whose lives ran neither smoothly nor well. He had never cared much for personal success, and now he cared even less; but in future he would take his position as head of the stage with some measure of gravity, because, in doing so, poor fellows who were never sure of their bread and butter might gather a few crumbs for themselves, might catch a glimpse of other things than the gutter, and with his help find a remnant of hope for their future and a reprieve from utter damnation.

The years of 1915 and 1916 were taken up with three productions that bore no resemblance to one another and were all successes. The first two were typical of Gerald's plays at their best, with a striking individual part for him in each of them, characteristic of his talent and his personality, yet so totally unlike in his treatment of them that they were another denial of that worn, repeated statement, 'Du Maurier is always the same.' A person's judgement would be warped, and his eye abnormal, who professed to see likeness between Hubert Ware, the extravagant, unprincipled, cold-blooded, yet oddly likeable, murderer of his wife's brother, and Prince Charming, the flamboyant, fantastic, debonair fairy tale creation straight out of a child's story-book. Psychologically there may be a resemblance, though on the surface one would say that George Bancroft and J. M. Barrie had little in common. But the accusation cannot hold good when it comes to an analysis of acting, and if Gerald had given an easy, walk-about performance as Hubert Ware the play would never have become the classic that it did.

It was, unquestionably, excellent entertainment; it was almost impossible not to follow with interest the story of Hubert Ware's fight for life; and in spite of the evidence against him, in spite of his ruthlessness and his cruelty, of which the audience were well aware, there was something ingenious about the fellow, something irresponsible and strangely truthful, that made them ask themselves, 'Could he have done it? No, we don't believe it.'

It needed more than an easy manner and a charming

way of lighting a cigarette to convince the audience that the jury were right in giving a verdict of 'Not Guilty'; and it required much more again when it came to showing the man in the final act, hysterical, crazy, his nerve gone after the weeks of strain, screaming, in a horrible mixture of pride and remorse, that he was guilty all the time.

It was an appalling, rather beastly anti-climax, but it was successful from a dramatic point of view, and the audience could go home to bed feeling that they had been exquisitely cheated by their darling Gerald; he had given them the creeps most unpleasantly, but anyway they had had full value for their money. For all the crude touches of melodrama and the somewhat novelettish *dénouement,* it was undoubtedly good theatre; and Gerald as Hubert Ware was not the exaggerated creation of fiction he might have been, but an unforgettable figure tragic in his very abnormality; a personality become inhuman because of one kink somewhere in his mental make-up, making a dangerous criminal out of a happy-go-lucky, impecunious idler.

The Ware Case was faultlessly produced and acted throughout, and there was never a moment when it dragged. Since its first appearance there have been many trial scenes in other plays, and the idea has now become somewhat wearisome and laboured. But in 1915 it was original and extremely compelling, and the audience listened in a silence tense and breathless that they could not keep to-day.

A Kiss for Cinderella was Barrie at his most Barriesque, and must have come as a relief after the nerves and storms of *The Ware Case.* Here was Wendy all over again, without her Peter, wanting another Never Never Land, and living with babies in cages all around her walls, and whispering her dreams to the stolid, clumsy policeman, and then being transferred suddenly to her fairy palace like the Cinderella of the story, with the policeman changed into the prince. To Barrie-haters it was definitely a piece of nauseous sentiment that ought to be suppressed, but, to those who liked to swallow their Barrie whole and unadulterated, it was undoubtedly a gem.

They had had their fill of realism in *The Ware Case*, and with Hubert Ware had taken an overdose. But here was fantasy pure and simple, a land of make-believe, a land of dreams, and if it was all impossible and absurd it was extraordinarily attractive. The scene in the Dream Palace was an incredible *mélange* of Edmund Dulac and Watteau and *Alice in Wonderland*, none of whom were at variance with one another. Hilda Trevelyan as the Wendy-ish Cinderella and Gerald as the policeman and the prince in turn, made the Barrie-lovers laugh and cry just in the right places, so that they were able to think of their own dreams and their own fantasies while watching this evasive, delicate bubble that could hardly be called a play. And they could thereby forget for a few hours the casualties in France. Once more Gerald possessed the genius to produce the right play at the right time. The break from *The Ware Case* had been timed to perfection, and *A Kiss for Cinderella* was a happy interlude and a subtle distraction from the anguish of the day.

The play which succeeded this in September, called *The Old Country*, was not such a successful venture, and ran for only three months, but it was followed by yet another triumph for Gerald and Wyndham's Theatre in the name of *London Pride*. Christmas was approaching, and the war had now become a horror of over two years' duration. It was becoming increasingly difficult to forget its existence even during a few hours' relaxation at the theatre, and it was only possible to do so there when an exquisite extravaganza, like *A Kiss for Cinderella*, floated like a butterfly before the tired eyes of the London audiences. But Barrie did not write plays every day, and the problem was to find a story capable of holding the attention and real interest of the public for the two and a half hours they demanded. The old love-stories would not do; the domestic triangles, the little reconciliations, the wiles of burglars and crooks, seemed paltry in comparison with modern warfare, and nobody cared what happened to these stuffed figures who had never existed. Love was a bird of passage in those days; a flame of a day and a night, regretted in the train from Victoria, forgotten in the whine of a shell, and lost for ever in mud and barbed wire. It would not be very easy to make two and a half hours' entertainment out of that. And if somebody else's husband passed the night with somebody else's wife, it really did not matter very much, because both men would probably be killed, anyhow. This only left the crooks, and the crooks had all joined up and had become heroes or good Flanders earth: it would have been tactless and a little unkind to bring them back to Wyndham's Theatre.

Therefore, as nobody could get away from the war, it seemed imperative that the war should be harnessed, too, as means of entertainment, and it was at this very crucial moment that Gerald produced *London Pride*..

It was one of the most popular moves he ever made, and the play ran for nine months. It was essentially a play of 1917, and belonged to that short period of time that was so long and so unending a travail of hardship and disaster, when enthusiasm had waned and despair was ready to take the place, and it was no longer a question of fit and able men swelling an army but the relentless and necessary drive of a herd to the slaughter.

London Pride was a clever piece of propaganda, and was received with enthusiasm by every class of the public. 'Three cheers for Cuthbert Tunks', shrieked the little crowd on the stage when the cheerful, graceless costermonger arrived home to find he had won the Victoria

Cross instead of being shot for desertion – a curious paradox; and 'Three cheers for Cuthbert Tunks', shouted the audience, stung to the quick by Cockney gallantry and the picture that had been painted for them of the rebellious conscript who stole his dead friend's identity disc so that he could take his forbidden leave home to see his girl. This discreditable performance was glossed over by Cuthbert's carrying the same friend on his back under heavy fire; and, after many vicissitudes, such as an unexpected wound in the leg and a still more unexpected encounter with the girl, who had blossomed into a V.A.D. at the crucial moment, the brave Cuthbert returned to Whitechapel, on crutches and beribboned, to the frenzied cheers of gallery and stall.

Somehow in 1917 all this seemed quite possible, and it was felt, by the London audiences who had not been there, that there must be hundreds of Cuthberts at the front, all behaving in an identically romantic fashion, and getting away with it. They found the scenes convincing, from the black dugout where Cuthbert railed against his cancelled leave, to the café behind the line where a body on a stretcher was borne past the open door, and thence to the hospital haunted by an impossible lady visitor, back to the East End and the Pearlie King and Queen. *London Pride* would not bear revival; it is as dated as the cartoons of Kaiser Bill and Little Willie, as alien as the sentiment:

> We don't want to lose you,
>   But we feel you ought to go,
> For your king and your country
>   Both need you so.

It is as antiquated and as buried as the words 'Blighty', 'Hun', and 'Tommy' that lie stored away in the dusty places of men's minds. But in 1917 the play at Wyndham's Theatre was accepted as a genuine, rather splendid piece of pageantry, sincere and very much alive, voicing the spirit of the time; and it helped in a not inglorious fashion to foster some measure of hope and belief in the hearts of those who saw it. It is easy – too pathetically easy – to laugh and deride the sentiments of seventeen years ago, as we laugh and point at the photographs in the family album. But we temper our laughter with humility, with reverence, with a great thankfulness that in that fashion, and with those sentiments, men and women were moulded and born, for without them our inheritance would be barren.

The seventeen years that have come and gone appear again from the dusty bookshelf, with Gerald as Cuthbert Tunks in ill-fitting khaki and a Whitechapel accent, his tongue in his cheek, his eye roving, his hat tilted over one brow – an exquisite picture of a genuine Cockney, with a laugh and a curse in one breath, kissing his girl one moment and cuffing her the next, ready to fight anyone at the slightest grievance and forget it over a pint and a fag the moment after. No drawing-room Gerald here, no polished, easy man-of-the-world, with cigarette-case in hip pocket, wandering languidly towards the sideboard for the whiskey and soda, throwing a careless 'I adore you, funny face', over his right shoulder. He *was* Cuthbert Tunks. He had the slow and rather clumsy movements, the awkward hands, the bold, hard stare, the droop of the lower lip, the arrogant, defensive manner.

''Ere, wot 'jer mean?' he would say, with mouth half open; hands hanging anyhow, eyes glancing swiftly from right to left, and then a laugh – a real broad, good-humoured Cockney laugh – a suck of the teeth, a wink, a jerk of the head; 'What abaht it, kid?' For all his pseudo-hero trappings and his unlikely wartime triumphs, there was something permanent and eternal about Cuthbert Tunks. *London Pride* survived the air-raids and ran for two hundred and eighty performances. *A Pair of Spectacles* was revived for a month, in which John Hare played his original part under Gerald's management, twenty-two years after he had given Gerald a small part at the Garrick in the same play. Hare was now seventy-three and his pupil forty-four, and they played Benjamin Goldfinch and nephew Dick respectively, to the delight of those who remembered the original production and to the indifference of those who did not. It gave way in October to the immortal *Dear Brutus*, the last and the greatest of Gerald's wartime successes before he left Wyndham's to join the army in 1918. Today people are a little tired of *Dear Brutus*; they have seen too many poor revivals, and a revival is often a shabby, spiritless affair, lacking the first flush of youth, and in its very appearance a confession of defeat. It is like the sequel to a much-loved novel; the same characters are drawn for us, but they are changed in some dim, rather wistful fashion; they have grown older, worn; their messages lack fire, and all the old dash and splendour that we remember and expect has gone from them; they are become tame figures of fiction between the leaves of a book, and no longer living creatures of flesh and blood.

Dear Brutus in 1917 was a masterpiece, and so it is today – on paper; but indifferent acting and a certain carelessness in production that crept into it on later occasions have spoilt the playing of it. Harry Dearth was essentially a Gerald part, and Gerald at his best, as he was in 1917. Like all familiar things, he took the part for granted in later years. It became a stop-gap and a means of marking time; the divine spark had gone out of it, and he lost his fervour. Sam Sothern and Maude Millet died, and so did Arthur Hatherton. Faith Celli could not for ever be expected to look sixteen. And there is something about an original cast – a sense of creation, a spirit of *camaraderie*, a first knowledge and a certain awareness,

'We are these people; it belongs to us' – that can never be replaced.

The 1917 cast of *Dear Brutus* could not be bettered; they were right; they fitted the atmosphere; the play possessed them, and they were part of it.

No one was out of step, no one was out of tune; it was as if they were reality bewitched by the spirit of the wood, and trod softly because of it, bathed in magic. Out of the original cast of eleven, all are now dead save three, so that there is something haunting about it now, something sad. Their voices are lost, and yet they echo in the wood. They have no existence, but their footsteps brush the beech-nuts and the moss. The wood is gone, but somewhere in the silence of Wyndham's the trees form like shadows and the branches stir, and Lob stands in the centre of the dusky stage, his finger to his lips.

When Gerald rehearsed as Will Dearth originally, he made up with grey hair and a beard for the second act – the wood scene – and looked exactly like Kicky. It was almost uncanny. But the company would not let him wear it. 'It isn't Gerald; the public will hate it,' they said, and so Dearth remained clean-shaven throughout. But, even so, something of Kicky crept into the part, and the enchanted Dearth of the wood sang his songs in French, and used the almost forgotten du Maurier slang, and blinked at his easel and chaffed his daughter as Kicky had once chaffed May.

Barrie conceived *Dear Brutus* and the artist who had his second chance, the artist who chose to be poor and unknown, and a tramp, with a daughter for çompanion. But Dearth himself, with his change from jaded bitterness to irresponsible content, came alive through Gerald. He spoke to his dream-daughter in the way he spoke to his own children, in the way Kicky had spoken to May, and how Kicky as Barty Jocelyn in *The Martian* had spoken to his daughter; subconsciously these memories dwelt within him and became identified with Dearth; they breathed upon Barrie's artist and gave him a significance of peculiar intensity, unforgettable and strange, as though Gerald, not fully understanding what had happened, pointed a finger to his own shadow and whispered, 'There, but for the grace of God . . .'

Those who watched Gerald as Will Dearth in 1917 saw, not a performance of an imaginary character, but the revelation of a living man, his hopes, his fears, his little ghosts and dreams, what he might have been, what he might yet become, a challenge and a confession in one.

Because he was successful, because he lacked nothing, because he had a wife he adored, and three daughters who were not built of dreams, he made a scapegoat of Will Dearth, a whipping-boy, a scourge for his inner self. Will Dearth was a safeguard, a defence; when he looked up with agony in his eyes and learnt that Lob had deceived him, the wood had been bewitched, and his daughter had never been born, it was Gerald who suffered, Gerald whose soul was tormented, Gerald who whispered behind his double, 'This might have been me.'

It was very moving and very terrible; he concealed nothing, and laid himself bare to the gaze of the world with a ruthless disregard of his own privacy, putting himself in the pillory, to be looked upon by the curious as though in some sudden and desperate need of salvation.

What was really happening at the back of his mind it is impossible to tell. He was certainly unhappy at that time. The war had got on his nerves. He missed Guy and Mummie terribly. He felt lost and hopelessly forsaken, and even Mo could not help him. His performance as Will Dearth was a revelation of the inner man, of whose existence even he himself was not fully aware, and he stabbed himself as he did it, stabbed his heart, and his senses, and his memory, stabbed his family when they came to see the play – so much so that Daphne, aged ten, had to be led sobbing from the box; and, while the play was one of the biggest successes that Wyndham's ever had, and the people whispered to one another, 'How wonderful du Maurier is; not a bit like himself this time,' they felt uncomfortable in their minds, undecided in their hearts, and they wept with Will Dearth as they had never wept before.

CHAPTER EIGHT

IT was surely a mistake to go to Whitby for a holiday; he might have realized that every corner held a ghost, and every twist and turning of the narrow cobbled streets was haunted by memories. There was an echo in the cry of the gulls, and other footsteps followed his upon the quay.

The skies were grey, and the sea wind-blown and cold; the waves broke upon the beach and against the pier with a shudder and a cry of lament.

There were shadows everywhere, and voices from another world, voices from the past now dead and gone; they whispered when the wind blew, and clamoured when the air was still, and down the streets ran the phantoms of children who had played there long ago. Papa walked with Chang in the fish-market; if Gerald listened carefully he could hear the echo of his song around the corner:

> *J'ai tout quitté pour l'ingrate Sylvie,*
> *Elle me laisse pour prendre un autre amant.*
> *Plaisir d'amour ne dure qu'un moment,*
> *Chagrin d'amour dure toute la vie;*

and there was a pause as Papa lit his cigarette, and threw away the match; and then away went his footsteps once more tap-tap with his stick, echoing down the street until it was lost in the shout of some passer-by and the high, thin cry of the fisherwomen, 'A-ny fresh herrings'. Papa was gone, vanished with his song, and, however quickly Gerald walked to the corner, he could not find him.

When he passed the house in St Hilda's Terrace and glanced up instinctively at the window, he saw Mummie outlined for a moment against the blind; she waved and beckoned, and called out something that he could not hear; and then she was gone, as though she had never been, and there was no figure by the open window, only a blind that swung backwards and forwards in the north wind. But as he turned and went away, not daring to glance over his shoulder again, the sound of Trixie's great pealing laugh followed him to the end of the street.

He must never come here again, never, never. There were too many voices, and sometimes they called so loud that he had to stand quite still, wherever he was – in the street, on the pier, in a shop – and put his hands over his eyes and stand and tremble, and hold on to Mo or one of the children, whoever should be there, and wait until the terror and fear and loneliness were gone – banished to the unknown places, if only for a few hours.

He had been drinking too much, of course. He knew that. This was all the result of it, and he had only himself to blame; but it did not entirely explain away the misery of the whispers that he could not reach, the hands that touched him and were gone, the memories that rose and stifled him, beating him and wounding him, reminding him with every echo and every cry that he was alone, alone, alone . . .

'Oh, Guy, help me! Don't leave me! Stay near to me!' he said, and somewhere from within came a little message of comfort, a whisper of reassurance, a warm, live sensation of well-being, as though Guy had touched his shoulder and was standing by his side, and had laughed quietly, and had said, 'All right, G, I'm here; I'll always be here if you want me.' He felt stronger then, more himself again, easier in mind and body; and it did not require much effort to go back to the hotel and have lunch, and to chat as though nothing had happened, and discuss the afternoon's plans with Mo.

'How are you feeling, darling heart?' she would say. 'I can't bear to see you like you were this morning. If only I could do something!' But he would answer: 'I'm all right. Too may whiskeys and sodas, that's my trouble. They give me the horrors.'

He would laugh, and tell her not to worry; that he was difficult, hopeless, an appalling person to be married to; that she was a saint to put up with him, and if it had not been for her he would have blown his brains out long ago. She would shake her head at him. 'Why say such dreadful things,' she used to tell him. 'Why are you so bitter sometimes about life, when you have everything you want, and no really bad worries? You used to not to be like this, lamb.' He would shrug his shoulders, and look out of the window, and see the rain come down to spoil the afternoon – a wisping slanting rain, with a wind from the east behind it, and in the distance the surf thundering on the shore. 'I don't know,' he would say. 'I don't know.' He would look at her helplessly, like a child demanding comfort, as though she must hold the riddle of his universe in her hands, and she would love him and console him as Mummie had consoled the ewee lamb of thirty years before. But she could not purge his blood of loneliness; she could not give back to him the security and peace of a vanished childhood and a lost kingdom.

In 1916 they had moved from Cumberland Terrace up to Hampstead, which was another venture on Gerald's part to retrace his steps into the past. It was one of his subconscious precautionary measures to protect himself from disillusion. Inwardly he said to himself, 'I was happy and safe here as a child, therefore I will be happy and safe here again.'

He would have liked to have taken New Grove House,

but this did not prove feasible, and after one or two vain quests he found Cannon Hall, which was about five minutes' walk from his old home. He loved it at once. He loved the garden and the view, and the rambling plan of the house – the lofty rooms, the old staircase, and especially the view from his bedroom window. He felt like a wanderer returned to the land of his birth. He knew that here, anyway, he had roots. He had security. He would never want to move from Hampstead again. He would be a fixture now and for ever, part of the soil. And May must come up to lunch on Sundays with Coley, as Trixie and Sylvia had done at New Grove House after they were married; and the various nephews too; and there would be some feeling that the family were not wholly lost or scattered. He would stage reunions at Hampstead and a gathering of the clans. On Sundays he would take the children for Papa's walk – down across the Heath from the White Stone Pond towards the fir-trees and the old plague pits above the Bull and Bush, or along the Spaniards Road to the tree at the end by the Stedalls' old house, and tap the tree with his stick, and turn, as Papa had done. On the anniversaries of their births and deaths he must take wreaths and flowers to the grave in Church Row – spring flowers for Mummie and Papa, and bulbs for Sylvia, and a wreath with the Fusilier ribbon on Guy's tablet. It would be a little ritual he would always remember, and then back home up the hill past New Grove House, with a wave at the studio window. His bedroom at Cannon Hall became a gallery of the past, with his school groups of Harrow round the walls, and on the mantelpiece and above it the photographs of his dead family. In front of them stood a silver cross. He kissed these photographs every night, and had a word with each of them. He did not understand that this fetish was identical with the prayers of men and women who knelt beside their bed or folded their hands in church, a superstitious yet primeval declaration of faith in himself and in mankind.

Hampstead made him very conscious of his family. He felt nearer to them now than he had been since they had died, and this proximity gave him a little sense of importance and of duty. He began to look upon Hampstead much as a squire, whose forebears have owned property for generations, looks upon his personal domain. His French ancestry did not really excite him as it did May, he professed to feel alien towards France and her people; and, although it pleased him to have the original glass blown by his great-grandfather in Anjou on the dining-room table at Cannon Hall, he would much rather it had been blown in Hampstead under his present roof.

It was rather unfortunate that his beloved Hampstead was a suburb which developed and extended every year as a greater London. He would have appreciated the picturesque traditions of a big estate, where the mistress of the house carries conserves to the poor and the rheumatic, and the squire is heralded with a curtsey and a doffing of the hat.

As it was, he could only be acknowledged by the milkman, whose firm had supplied necessities to New Grove House in the 'eighties, and by the chemist who had done the same, and, although the crossing-sweeper soon took to greeting him with a cheery nod, Gerald could not quite feel that he was entitled to inquire after the wife and the little ones as he would have done had he been really squire of Hampstead!

To be pointed at and recognized as Gerald du Maurier lacked the flavour it might have had if the pointer, clad suitably in smock and gaiters, had exclaimed, 'You be the livin' image of your great-grand'fer who fought alongside mine, sir, at Waterloo.'

Meanwhile the children were beginning to grow up

and to become companions of a sort. It was fun to take Angela out to lunch. She never suffered from shyness, but laughed and chatted with everybody, and was already something of a hostess. It was fun, too, to play cricket on the lawn with Daphne and Jeanne, who, in jerseys and knickers, dreamed and thought as boys, calling each other by imaginary surnames and performing tremendous deeds of valour for the sake of a school that did not exist except in their own imagination. Gerald liked teaching them to bowl over-arm in orthodox fashion, and to play a straight bat; he bought them boxing-gloves and made them tap each other's noses; he discussed *Treasure Island*, and *The Count of Monte Cristo*, battles of the Mohicans, and mutinies on ships. He took Daphne down to Harrow and showed her the fourth-form room, and his old house, the Grove Ducker and Speecher, and they listened to the school songs. He had not thought about Harrow for years, and now he began to remember and be glad, and it was one of the proudest moments in his life when he was cheered coming down the steps on Speech Day by the whole school assembled in the yard below, an old custom that was reserved for great celebrities, and which the idle, happy-go-lucky Gerald of the old days had never dreamt would come to him. Later, when the war was over and the matches at Lord's were resumed, he was one of the most faithful of Harrow supporters, sitting hour after hour with his eyes glued to the pitch, an enormous corn-flower in his buttonhole, and the children by his side, shouting 'H A R R O-O-O-O-W' at the top of his voice with all the enthusiasm of the lower third.

It would have been amusing to have had a son there, like many of his contemporaries, but, strangely enough, he never wanted to turn his daughters into boys.

'Daughters are the thing,' said Harry Dearth in *Dear Brutus*, and Gerald said the same. It was fun to trace their likeness to the sisters he remembered — a reminder of

Sylvia in Angela when she laughed or sang, or turned her head suddenly; a resemblance between Daphne's nose and forehead and Papa's, but a chin that was identical to May's; and, although Jeanne at the moment was a pocket edition of Mo, there was something of Trixie in her upper lip and in her brow. It seemed to him a tragedy that Papa and Mummie were not living at New Grove House, where the children could wander in and out at will, and poke about the studio as he had done, while the governor put them into *Punch*, and chuckled, and whistled a French song under his breath. He read *Peter Ibbetson* and *Trilby* and *The Martian* again. He looked through all Papa's drawings that were in his possession. He tried to soak himself in the old atmosphere of things he had known once and were now gone from him, and he wondered why being hasty and impulsive and young should have made him indifferent to these treasures at the time when they might have helped him most. It seemed to him sometimes that there had been much of his life misspent and wasted. He had idled, he had lazed, he had too often taken the easiest way. It was so simple to be selfish, to be indulgent with oneself, to be careless about other people's feelings, to hurt their sense of values. Generations never understood one another. That was one of the tragedies of life. He had loved and respected Papa, been proud of his talent and his success, but they had never been companions. They had talked different languages. He had been restless, and excited, with no time for anything but his personal enjoyment, his stage fun, his little loves; and Papa at sixty had appeared to his narrow judgement immeasurably old, rather fussy per- haps, rather stingy about small expenses, content to sit back in the studio of an evening and listen to Mummie reading aloud from some dreary classic. Gerald had been impatient with them sometimes, wondering how they stuck the boredom of it, the monotony, when he himself was going to sit up half the night playing cards with the boys in the Green Room Club.

How little he had known of Papa's inner self, his little hopes and fears, his problems never mentioned, his dreams unspoken save in his books. They had never been companions, and now that he wanted his friendship it was too late. He felt very alien to that self of twenty years ago, that careless, carefree self, who ran through the woods chasing his own shadow. How obstinate he had been, how unwilling to listen, how pig-headed and weak and superficial, and yet – and yet, with all his faults of over-enthusiasm and impulsiveness, they had been the good days, the lively days; the days when getting up in the morning had been an adventure because of the unknown lurking round the corner, not the effort that it was today.

He could not remember the morning when it had ceased to be an adventure. But somehow the day must have dawned with a pallid sky, and a cold wind with the rain behind it. Perhaps he had been late the night before, had too much to drink, smoked too many cigarettes, and, sleep not coming as easily as it once had done, had lain awake and watched the curtains blow and the stars vanish. And then he had wondered upon his little purpose in the world – how small and insignificant a thing he was, how lacking in value, how useless in mind and body, and he had asked himself why did he, night after night, play his part upon the stage with painted face to people who had dined too well and did not care?

There were men who built bridges, he reflected, and men who fought disease, and men who flung beauty upon canvas for tired eyes; men who cared for sick animals and children; men who grew plants and cultivated flowers; men who prepared food for the body's need, who were clever with their hands, made furniture, made electric bulbs, mended broken things; and there were men who thought of music for the jaded and men who wrote poems for the weary.

And he was nothing but a mummer, a trickster, playing antics in some disguise before a crowd. All he had won was a cheap popularity, and what good was that to him or to the world? The right plays were not always written; successes would not always come; friends proved themselves not true friends; families died or were broken up, and always ahead would be the thought of growing older, growing more weary, more worn, less inclined to struggle and care. And why, why, to what end, with what endeavour – oh, God, to what salvation? He must have fallen asleep as the shadows grew longer and the light grew paler; there were little lines beneath his eyes and round the corners of his mouth, and when he woke again the day had come, but the adventure had vanished with the morning star – for ever.

It was possibly a combination of these feelings that led Gerald to join the army in the summer of 1918. There was really no necessity for him to do so. He was forty-five, with a family and responsibilities, and, whatever his private thoughts about the stage as a career, he held a prominent position in public life. He was hopelessly unfitted for a soldier's duties. He had no idea of discipline or experience of hard living, and had never so much as killed a wasp. Had he been younger, the training would have probably done him a power of good, like any other civilian; but the actual facing of war in all its dreariness and squalor would have given him an acute neurosis and a bitter sense of the injustice and futility of it all, as it did so many other men whose natures were individualistic and hypersensitive. Gerald in a trench would have been hopelessly inefficient. He was clumsy with his hands. He could never have handled weapons of any sort, and his inability to concentrate would have made him useless in an attack. His only chance would have come had he lost his temper. The sight of a friend being killed beside him would have had the immediate effect, and it is easy to imagine him very white in the face, blaspheming and cursing, ready in an instant to tear the guts out of the unknown killer.

But these moments are not frequent in war, and, although Gerald would have made a ribald and incredibly funny companion behind the line, the squalor, the discomfort, the ugliness, and the appalling monotony of it all would have brought him to despair.

As it happened, the war ended in November, and Gerald had only a few months' soldiering as a cadet in the Irish Guards at Bushey, which was a different matter altogether! Nevertheless, he had joined the army and was prepared to risk his life. In a way it was a gesture to his profession, of which he was undoubtedly the head, and a declaration that he took this position seriously – so seriously that he was determined to set an example. Fellow-members of his own age were not so particular, however; the gesture, as such, was wasted on them, and the general opinion was that Gerald had done a foolish thing. What did he want to join the army for, with *Dear Brutus* playing to packed houses at Wyndham's Theatre, and money being made, and a lovely home in Hampstead and a fond family? Why chuck it all away just when he was at the top of his form? There were plenty of younger people who could go. So argued the wise ones, who clung to their security, and then they shrugged their shoulders. 'If Gerald likes to mess up his life, let him, but it does not mean that we are going to do the same. After all, one can always get up concerts for the wounded and arrange matinées for the blind. That's doing much more good to the country than scrubbing floors as a cadet.'

This was one way – and rather a good way – of tackling

the problem. It was not Gerald's way, though. He had arranged numerous benefit performances to help the services and the wounded and the blind. He had done all that. He had worked hard in these ways during the four years, and he was not satisfied. He did not want to help as Gerald du Maurier, but as the man in the street, the man next door, the man on the office stool and the man in the ploughed field. They gave up their trade and their little security. They did not take refuge behind charity performances. Everywhere, in every branch of life, older men were going now – responsible men, men with families and business ties – and it was up to Gerald to do likewise.

If other men faced discomfort and misery, he could do the same. Besides, surely Guy would have expected it of him. He would have taken his gesture for granted. He would have smiled at him, his head a little on one side: 'Well, G, what about it?'

And, after all, what the hell did one's personal life matter beside the countless thousand lives that were sacrificed every day and asked no question? So Gerald left *Dear Brutus* and Wyndham's Theatre in the hands of his old friend, Harry Esmond, and, after an attempt to get a commission and other vicissitudes which proved to him that joining the army was not altogether a simple matter unless you were prepared to serve in the ranks, he found himself a cadet in the Brigade of Guards Training Corps at Bushey.

Poor Mummie, how miserable she would have been had she lived to see her spoilt ewe lamb in his drab plus fours and puttees, with the hard military cap, the whole outfit giving him a rather shrunken pallid appearance that was not consistent with the polished, debonair du Maurier of Wyndham's Theatre.

What anguish would have been hers had she know the hour her darling was obliged to get up in the morning, and the food he was to eat, and the buttons he must polish, and the passages he must clean, and, on top of it all, forced to go out on a raw morning, when the ground was wet with dew, to dig a trench! What hampers she would have sent him, what countless instructions about underclothes and socks; what bottles of cod-liver oil would have found their way to him packed amongst jams and sardines and Cadbury's chocolate. But Mo, of course, was Mummie all over again, so that Fortnum's was ransacked for stores and provisions to supplement Gerald's daily fare; and Beale & Inman's was searched for vests and woollies to keep him warm; and Cannon Hall was shut up and the staff dismissed, and a humble dwelling on the main road some five or six minutes from the Bushey gates harboured Mo and the children, so that Gerald need not feel too lonely, and might even go home to his tea. What teas, too, for a man who had never looked at the meal for twenty years; sardines, bread and paste, bread and honey, ginger cake, plum cake, and perhaps even a poached egg on toast, and three or four large cups of tea to wash them down. It was Harrow all over again, with Gerald, at forty-five, wolfing ginger cake and chocolate at a tremendous pace, talking with his mouth full to a handful of fellow-cadets who had just left their public school and were barely eighteen. Although he professed to loathe every moment of his time at Bushey, it was an incredibly funny interlude in his life, and he was better in health and spirits than he had been for years. He got thinner, perhaps, and he slept badly, but he grew fit and hard, and the very simplicity of his diet and his daily life acted like a tonic on his system. He learned nothing, of course; when the Armistice was signed and he was free once more for civilian life, he knew no more about the art of war than he had known when he joined. A map was an incomprehensible mass of lines and figures, and a Lewis gun was a piece of mechanism whose utility he preferred to take for granted. He had gone right back to the fourth form, and craned to look over the shoulder of his nearest companion, a lad straight from Eton, and to copy his notes in a frantic hope that they would be accepted as his own. The brain-work was beyond him. The man who had produced *Dear Brutus* had not an idea in his head about trench warfare, and the questions put to him, that the young cadets from school found simple enough to answer, were insurmountable problems to the manager of Wyndham's Theatre.

It was impossible to teach him; he would not concentrate, and, as he had done at Harrow thirty years before, he was inclined to shrug his shoulders at authority and make humorous remarks at serious moments. The instructors found it easier to ignore him than to waste precious time in expounding theories which obviously meant nothing to him at all, and which he did not attempt to grasp. On the other hand, Cadet du Maurier took infinite pains with his personal appearance. There was no button that shone brighter than his, no belt more polished, no uniform more carefully brushed, and the room which he shared with Cadet Burghard, the only other man of his own age, was a model for cleanliness and order. That the board under Cadet du Maurier's bed was loose, and made an excellent store for port and whiskey, escaped the vigilant eyes of those in command. Nor did they know that the occupier of the bed held little celebrations with his companion after lights were out much in the manner of the hero of *Teddy Lester's Schooldays.*

All the old cunning of the fourth form came back to him, and every morning, before the general summons to rise went forth, a thin, lithe figure performed cat-burglar antics from window to window until he had reached his objective, namely, the bathrooms allotted to the officers and forbidden to the cadets, who washed in a fraternal manner in company. And, while his superiors and his equals slept the sleep of the just, Cadet du Maurier splashed in a steaming hot bath, holding a metaphorical finger to the nose.

His deceptions were a source of great satisfaction to him, and he boasted of his little exploits to Mo and the children when he came in to tea as though he were really and truly the Leader of the Lower School.

He went about with a gathering of cronies – boys who were contemporaries of his own younger nephews – and the small sitting-room in Mo's little house would be crammed at tea-time with Gerald and the boys, all eating as though they were starving, shouting with laughter, and talking twenty to the dozen, with Gerald of course as ringleader.

If it pained Mo to see their joint lives so interrupted, with Gerald leading practically a prison existence, with active service ahead of him, she made no complaint, and was thankful for the half-hour in the day when she might see him. The children, naturally, were delighted. A small furnished house was a novelty, and the cadets were fun, and there was a new sense of freedom that was wholly delightful in this departure from the normal humdrum way of living. Gerald had little sense of superiority or importance as a father, and he did not feel humbled before the eyes of his children when they peered through a barbed fence during the afternoon walk and laughed at him as he shovelled earth with a spade in an endeavour to dig a trench for the safety of his platoon. On parade he was not quite so happy. Drill he detested, and he was apt to get the giggles from sheer nerves. The N.C.O.s had some difficulty with the pronunciation of his name, and he became anything from Demure to Demerara. He incurred the animosity of one gentleman with a very loud voice and harsher tongue, who was swollen with self-importance, and who made a set at him from the start. He had a shrewd suspicion that Cadet Demerara did not take him or his duties seriously, and he was determined to put him in his place. The climax came when the insubordinate Gerald, having committed some misdeed and being reprimanded for it, looked solemnly straight in front of him, and the sensitive sergeant, red in the face and bristling with importance, lashed out in a voice of thunder, 'What are you staring at me for? I'm not Gladys Cooper.' The position was too much for Cadet Demerara. He crumpled up weakly and gave at the knees, but whether he was marched off parade under escort is not, so far as can be ascertained, on record.

On one occasion Gerald tried to justify himself in the eyes of his companions, and to prove that he might be of possible use in some branch of the service, such as the Intelligence Department. A war game of sorts was in progress for the edification of the cadets, and Gerald, in the home forces, was given the opportunity to break through to the enemy if he could and bring back information. Childishly excited, he got into touch with Mo and told her to hire a car, and to pick him up at a certain crossroads, bringing with her properties from Watford in the form of a false beard and spectacles, an overcoat, and a hat. Heavily disguised, they prepared to tour the enemy country, but, alas for his plans, whether he over-acted or gave the first really bad performance of his career it was never decided, but the fact remained that the car was stopped at the first outpost, and he was immediately recognized and taken prisoner amidst derisive enemy cheers. Cadet du Maurier had failed again.

His chance finally came when, towards the end of his time at Bushey, a performance was staged, by the cadets, of the play *Vice Versa* by Anstey Guthrie, and here Gerald came into his own as producer. It was all a great lark, and thoroughly appreciated by everyone, and no schoolboy could be more triumphant than Gerald when to his delight it was arranged that the Adjutant should play a prominent part in the play, and must therefore obey Gerald's orders as producer. He felt as though the enemy had been delivered into his hands. The cadets gave a fine performance under his tuition, and the formidable Adjutant ate out of his hand for the first and last time. It was a memorable occasion for Cadet du Maurier.

He knew his place, though, and did not presume beyond his authority, for there was another time when Lily Elsie and some members of the profession came down to Bushey to sing at a concert, sponsored, naturally, by Gerald. As she went into the mess for lunch, conducted by the Commandant, she caught sight of a well-known figure standing very humbly in the background. 'There is darling Gerald,' she exclaimed delightedly, and would have flung herself upon him but for the cautionary arm of the Commandant. 'That's all right,' the great man explained; 'you'll be seeing him later; we are going in to feed first.' Lily Elsie looked very bewildered.

'But surely Gerald is joining us for lunch?' she said.

The Commandant murmured something in her ear to the effect that the cadets took their food at a separate table, and the indignant and shocked Lily Elsie was dragged into the mess protesting loudly, whilst Cadet du Maurier, abashed and ill at ease as a schoolboy who has been dragged into foolish prominence by the tactless stupidity of a visiting relative, stumbled over his feet and tried to efface himself behind a six-foot-six companion.

He looked a very different Gerald from the idol of Wyndham's Theatre; he could not even fumble in his pocket for the inevitable cigarette to help him out of his difficulty.

Like the little miseries of youth, which appear so insignificant and funny in after years, the restrictions of army life seemed very hard and important at the time. Gerald wondered what it was like to be free and command his own soul. It was almost impossible to think that once he had been manager at Wyndham's and head of his profession, and that men of the age of his superior officers used to come to him and beg for a job. War was a great leveller. It smoothed out the furrows between men; it proved the futility of snobbism and the comparative unimportance of position and prominence when faced with a universal problem. The Armistice came in time to prevent Gerald from seeing the ugliness and horror of war from personal fighting experience, but those months at Bushey shook him to a certain extent, and acted as a splendid antidote to self-importance. The temporary loss of his position could not hurt him, and could only do him good, though it was rather late in life to be treated all over again as a schoolboy, with only schoolboys for companions.

CHAPTER NINE

THE aftermath of war. Peace, with its promises unfulfilled, brought the bewilderment that comes of tension
relaxed; effort was no longer necessary and strain had
suddenly slackened. Sacrifices were quickly forgotten.
There was no call to courage; or, rather, a new brand of
courage was required to face the reconstruction of the old
life on a fresh basis. It could never be the old life, that
was the difficulty; the values and the standards had gone
up in smoke and were irrevocably lost; it meant creation
of a new order handled with a fine sense of balance, and
nobody had any equilibrium left. People were too tired,
too utterly worn in mind and body, and theirs was the
nervous fatigue that will not be healed by rest and
quietude, but demands a stimulation and a fresh impetus
to excitement. It was a jaded world, a restless yet a shattered world, never to be quite certain of itself or of the
problematical future, never to be secure again. Men and
women could not depend upon one another in the old
way. They were no longer able to say, 'We shall be
doing this in ten years' time,' because their existence had
too long become a thing of chance; even their moods
were temporary, and a smile today would be a yawn
tomorrow.

The hackneyed proverb that held some significance
during the war, 'Eat, drink, and be merry,' held the new
qualification of 'for tomorrow, alas! we do not die.' There
was the unaccustomed monotony of living now to be endured, living in boredom without the sting of danger,
only too open to doubts and to fears and to an insur-

mountable apathy that murmurs, 'Has it all been worth while? Did we endure for this?'

All over Europe men were asking themselves this question, and the reaction was experienced by everyone who possessed too much imagination and too little fortitude, too great sensibility and not enough control.

A certain quality in their nature had been fed by the underlying spirit of high tension and excitement that belonged to war. They had given the best of themselves, and now it was over, finished, and they had neither the strength of will nor the fixity of purpose to adjust themselves to the new order and the demands of peace.

Gerald was a typical product of his time, unsettled in mind and body, uncertain of himself and of his wishes, aware that the war had broken the old traditions and the order of living, that even in his little sphere changes must be admitted and recognized. The theatre of the twenties would be radically opposed to the theatre that Tree and Alexander had so lately known. The days of the great actor-managers had gone for ever, and a new financial spirit had come into being.

The theatre was invulnerable no longer; outside influences bore down upon it, and the little sacred world of drama and comedy became a pit for profiteers and a juggling game for clumsy amateurs.

To make money, more money, and yet more money, was the only goal in mind, and those who refused to be exploited, and to their sense degraded, must fall by the way. The American invasion began, and the English stage was swamped with American plays and American actors and actresses. The managers and businessmen followed in the wake. American methods were introduced, and their influence was felt in every quarter; box-office returns were of sole importance in this trade that was no longer an art or a profession. If English plays lay dusty and unread in drawers, and English actors and actresses were out of work, it did not matter so long as there was a queue outside the pit and the non-acting manager could drive past in an enormous car with a cigar in his face and say to an admiring companion, 'Seen my little show? It's the biggest thing in town. I'll get you a box for tomorrow night.'

At the stage doors where Irving and Tree had stood, where Wyndham, Alexander, and Hare had stopped to say good evening to the doorkeeper and to nod a friendly smile, new owners swayed past like swollen turkey-cocks, hats on the back of their heads, knowing none of the employees by sight, and calling every woman by her Christian name. The theatres had no more individuality about them than a counting-house, and the actors and actresses dashed in to work and out again like clerks and typists. Profits increased, and so did salaries; the novice who would have been paid two pounds a week in the old days now sniffed at eight; because of this easy money, idlers and profit-seekers were drawn to the stage from sheer financial interest. Often they possessed neither ability nor experience, and flooded the market by their presence, very often obtaining a job through influence or other tactics.

Any girl who left school and did not know what to do with herself, who wanted to make pocket-money and to amuse herself, decided to go on the stage; any young man too idle to do anything else, and possessing some sort of an appearance, was certain that an actor's life would be ideal.

The theatres were besieged by these amateurs, who drifted on and off the stage as the spirit moved them, cluttered the passages and the dressing-rooms with their undesirable friends, poked fun at the rest of the company or at anyone older than themselves who had experience, cared nothing for the building that had known tradition and dignity, and gibed at the very profession that so mistakenly fostered them. Their influence was pernicious.

The intensity of the earnest tragedian, who talked and lived for art, and believed only in disguise and the melancholy of blank verse, was vastly preferable to the indifference and the shoddy superficiality of the newcomer. In the heyday of Alexander and Tree the personality of the actor had been invested with some glamour; he was a distinguished and romantic figure whose private life was unknown, and whose actions and thoughts behind the barrier of the curtain were believed to be mysterious and strange. It was exciting and almost unbelievable to see him in plain clothes in the street, divested of his make-up, and the curious would speculate upon his way of living and his home, wondering in incredulous fashion whether he had any other life but the one they had seen with their own eyes upon the stage. Now this mystery was a mystery no longer; actors and actresses were to be seen in all the most popular restaurants and at every party; they insisted on knowing social as well as theatrical success, and a new, rather false atmosphere was apparent, over-intimate, over familiar; a gush of insincerity, mingled with too obvious flattery, filled the air in place of the old, easy comradeship and mutual respect.

It was the dawn of the superlative age and the vogue of the emphasized adjective; the word 'darling' rose too easily to the lips, and 'marvellous', 'wonderful', and 'divine' described the colour of a new lipstick or the texture of a silk stocking. 'Do you know So-and-So? I worship him,' would be said about some individual met for the first time; or, if he had proved unpleasing, 'My dear, he is complete and utter torture.'

People did not tell the truth or speak with any sincerity, and, when they allowed themselves to be plain-spoken, they went to the other extreme and became insulting and offensive. Men and women became the pitiful representatives of an unattractive age. Although the guns were silenced and peace had apparently enveloped the earth, there was no quietude. Dance mania was the new fever, and the air was poisoned by the braying of the saxophone, the whine of love songs, and the stamping rhythm of the cotton-fields. There was a sense of desperate expectation in the dreary monotony of night-clubs, a hope that in a new face would come salvation in added excitement; and if the cocktail-shaker produced a pleasant haze it also softened the judgement to a comfortable extent.

People who had hitherto been furtive about sex, and unhealthily self-conscious, now became brazen and unnecessarily boring, sniggering and bold like the small boys who chalk rude words on the garden gate. Life was not worth living unless somebody was 'having an affair' with somebody else – an expression which conjured up untidy sofas, trodden bracken, and the cramped rear seats of cars. It was easier to go through a little heated, fumbling performance than to make polite conversation; and, if the companion was somebody else's husband or somebody else's wife, the very action became a sort of substitute for a jeer, and a plume in the hat at the same time. Society had become a magnified lower fifth, grown sideways out of all proportion, where little passions and little storms raged and blew to the accompaniment of jazz bands, and man did everything to his neighbour but love him as himself.

The arts suffered from this bounding reaction, this modern version of anti-climax, and none worse than the theatre. It was a somewhat degraded and unattractive profession of which Gerald found he was the head in the early twenties, and nobody realized it more than himself. He belonged to the past and to the present – to the Victorians, the Edwardians, and to the post-war Georgians – and the very interbreeding of these qualities was enough to cause confusion and misunderstanding within him. He deplored the passing of tradition, of ceremony, of respect; yet he led the way to familiarity and easy-going tolerance

168

with his careless 'darling', his shrug of the shoulder, his desire to be liked by his fellows. He allowed anyone to call him by name, to drink his whiskey, and to borrow his money. Yet he was distressed by bad manners, by effrontery, and by ingratitude. He protested against the 'social' development of the actors and actresses, yet he was one of the worst offenders in giving parts to men who wore the school tie and to girls who were daughters of his old friends. He complained of publicity and vulgarity, but he lunched at a restaurant every day of his life with a pretty woman, if he could find one, even if he took the unique measure of asking Mo to ring up and make the appointment for him.

He lamented the fact that bad plays were written and that the material sent him was poor. But he made no very great effort to read plays himself or to go out of his way to find good ones.

He believed in being a citizen, in doing his duty and upholding tradition. But, for all the red tape of Bushey, he did not impose discipline upon himself or upon those who worked under him, and, in spite of his declared abhorrence of the post-war men and women, he was the first to fall under their influence and to be caught up in the silly, superficial mesh of intrigue.

He dramatized incidents and the parts he took in them. He swore vows of fidelity and oaths of revenge. He staged tremendous quarrels with his friends about nothing at all, and followed them up with grand scenes of reconciliation.

He was inconsistent in all he did and in all he thought. In many ways he was a child never come to maturity, shutting his eyes to the real treasures of life that lay within his grasp and living in a world of his own fantasy, bright yet tortuous with pretended pageantry.

Although the spirit of the theatre was changing, and he was unsettled in himself and in his ideas, it seemed on the surface that things had not greatly altered, and Gerald followed up his wartime successes with others equally triumphant in the years that immediately followed the peace.

He returned to Wyndham's in 1919 with *The Choice*, a play by Alfred Sutro, which ran for nearly a year, and in which he played the strong, masterful, if not altogether silent John Cordways, who glowered at his secretary and commanded him to pick up a pen in a voice of thunder, and then showed his affection for the woman he loved by smacking her on the jaw and turning his back.

It was a true du Maurier part, and Gerald excelled himself.

Always, with the parts he played, some of the characteristics of the figure he portrayed slipped half consciously into his behaviour in ordinary life. When acting a gloomy part, he did not always leave the gloom behind him when he passed out of the swing doors of the theatre, and when playing a gay, irresponsible ruffian he would bring his gaiety and his good nature home with him. He was exceptionally light-hearted during the run of *Bulldog Drummond*, because the irrepressible Hugh could never be depressed under any circumstances. He was sad and full of foreboding during *Dear Brutus*, because Harry Dearth had made a failure of his life in spite of worldly success. Lord Arthur Dilling shrugged his shoulders and lit his cigarette with blasé self assurance, amused and tolerant of life and himself and Mrs Cheyney, and Gerald did the same when he came home to dinner. But poor Paolo Gheradidi in *Fame* became paralysed in the second act, and lived in rooms at the seaside, where it rained all day, and from Gerald's behaviour while the play lasted it was obvious that he still stood by the lodgings window and watched the surf beat upon the shore at Pegwell Bay.

In *The Choice*, John Cordways was a gloomy fellow

who appeared to carry the troubles of the world upon his shoulders, and sat in heavy silence until it became necessary to speak, when he would answer a question with a curt monosyllable. At home Gerald did the same, and it was with a feeling of relief that the family saw him to the end of the run and watched him rehearse the slightly caddish, debonair, but, thank heaven, definitely light-hearted André Le Briquet who in a foreign and unscrupulous manner was to bring about *The Prude's Fall*.

He had never played two characters consecutively who were so utterly opposed in temperament and in manner, and it was a significant example of his many-sided nature that he was able to do so. Cordways was banished to the limbo of forgotten things, and was only resurrected when the bathwater was cold or the beef was overdone; and in his place walked the dashing Le Briquet, very flippant and French, who made love ardently and successfully to every woman he met. And if the ladies who came to lunch at Hampstead on Sundays were overwhelmed by the unexpected charm of their host, it was at least a delightful and fluttering experience, and appeared to go extraordinarily well with his grinning and uncomfortably precocious family.

'The stable' was filled to capacity during the influence of André Le Briquet, and stakes were high and betting furious as to who should win first, second, and third places, and in what length of stride.

It was a common sport in the evenings, while Gerald ate his cold beef and Mo mixed the salad, for the children to wander in from cricket in the garden and expound their views. 'You are awful, Gerald; you shouldn't encourage them,' Mo would say, half-shocked and half amused, placing a plate of exquisitely carved underdone roast beef, complete with cos lettuce and radishes, before the spoilt child who, as André Le Briquet, continued to weave his web of enchantment. And it would be decided that Viola Tree, who was as yet a little strange to them and forbidding, and had not yet settled down into being the dear, absurd, maddening, and adorable clown of their maturer years, was leading by a short head from the last favourite, but that she would have to run fast to keep the lead, and that the dark and sombre Hilda Moore, who had been well up at the start, was proving a non-stayer and had almost dropped out of the running altogether.

As for the beloved Gladys, who by rights should have won in a canter, and would have done could the children manage the race themselves, she had refused at the start and turned her back on the whole proceedings, and was looking another way when the pistol was fired.

The field ran in a bunch some way behind the leaders, and never looked threatening at any time, though now and again the head of an outsider could be distinguished from the crowd and seem prominent for a moment or so, only to drop behind when the pace increased.

It was a strange, unorthodox game, it could only be played amongst children who had Gerald for a father. It was little wonder that they grew up with distorted values and a warped sense of humour, and that they startled him in later years with ideas whose foundation he had laid himself. For Gerald was inconsequent in fatherhood as he was in everything else. He was immeasurably shocked when the daughter of fifteen, to whom he had recounted in detail an episode of his youth the night before over a whiskey and soda, came to him the next morning rocking with laughter and appreciation over one of the most cynical and sordid of Mr Somerset Maugham's short stories.

He was astounded when the child before whom everything was discussed, and who had met neurotics in the theatre as a matter of course, asked him whether it was true that boys kissed one another at public schools, and how very amusing it must be. He gazed at her in horror and had no answer. Men and women who were not married, but were living together happily in spite of deserted husbands and wives, came to family lunch on Sunday almost every week of the year, and Gerald was grieved and startled when his own daughters declared that they did not believe in marriage, and if they ever fell in love they would prefer to do without the help of the Church, and lead independent lives. He joked with them of how, in the old days, he had crept into New Grove House when the milk arrived at the door, and went in to breakfast to kiss his mother as though he had just come down from his room, but he would watch in the passage for his own daughter to return, and question her hysterically, like one demented, if the hands of the stable clock stood at half past two. In '21, however, the children were still children, and André Le Briquet had no grown-up daughters who returned with their latch-keys in the small hours; and after six months' protestation in broken English to his Prude he went the same way as Cordways and Hubert Ware and Harry Dearth, and was supplanted by that aggressive, ruthless, let-'em-all-come-and-be-damned, hilarious, and unnaturally competent roughneck, Bulldog Drummond.

For four hundred and thirty performances he smashed his way into the private if illicit concerns of the bullying Peterson and the sinister Dr Lakington, breaking their electric light bulbs, kidnapping their imaginary patient, a glass of beer in one hand and a revolver in the other, and finally killing the miserable doctor with his own hands by cracking his spine on a sofa, while his Phyllis watched him in mingled terror and admiration from a safe corner. *Bulldog* was a glorious riot, a sort of super *Raffles*, and about twenty times as exciting. It was nonsense, of course, impossible and absurd, but nobody minded; all that mattered was that Hughie Drummond and his priceless friends should smash up the Peterson gang in the most hair-raising and bloodiest fashion possible.

Not a moment dragged from beginning to end, and every curtain fell on a revolver shot or a scream. The fight in Lakington's laboratory was, from the point of view of entertainment, one of the best things ever staged. It was horribly realistic, with very little fake about it, and it was a nightly miracle that neither Gerald nor Bertie Hare was injured.

The scene was incredibly well produced; it had been carefully and untiringly rehearsed, and on the opening night it startled the fashionable first-night audience out of their usual apathy into a frenzy of approval. The stalls got up and cheered, dropping gloves and handbags with this unaccustomed applause, and the gallery and pit shrieked their delight in a scream that topped the opening bars of the National Anthem.

Bulldog Drummond had come to stay, to the enthusiasm of the London public in general and to the disgust of those who preferred to take their entertainment in the form of a soliloquy before one black curtain. Whatever were the literary merits of Sapper's masterpiece, it was undoubtedly entertainment of the highest order, and Gerald held that the primary function of an actor was to entertain. He had succeeded in his own inimitable way, and many people of every condition left the theatre happy and well content with themselves because of him.

Whether it is justifiable to reward the man who entertains in the same way and in the same degree as the bridge-builder or the colonist is neither here nor there, and does not matter to the story. But Gerald had worked hard in his sphere, and done much for the members of his profession, and it was thought fit to honour him with a knighthood in the January of '22. He received it with mixed feelings, and was aware of the same hesitation and doubt he had experienced twelve years earlier when faced with the prospect of going into management. It meant added responsibilities, a position to be maintained, and a prestige to be upheld. It meant that he was now officially recognized as leader of his profession, and must take his leadership in all seriousness and keep the standard high accordingly. It was an honour, and must be treated as an honour. It was a strange stepping-stone in the career of the boy who had sung 'The Whistling Coon' at Whitby, and had caused his mother sleepless nights because he made his father laugh with his imitations of Irving on the studio floor.

Mummie would have been very proud of her ewee lamb, and Papa delighted, and brother Guy would have nodded his head and smiled a gentle mocking smile, while the words, 'You haven't done so bad for yourself after all, young 'un,' would have meant that he felt for his brother, and understood. But Papa and Mummie and Guy were not there, and he would have to face congratulations that were not entirely sincere, and handshakes that were overhearty, and smiles that were a little strained, and silences that were eloquent and spoke for themselves.

And Mo would be dragged on to committees, and the servants would become snobbish, and waiters would be obsequious in restaurants instead of friendly, and a trades-man here and there would add columns to the weekly books, and old schoolfellows would appear from the Far East and ask for sustenance, and costers on the Heath at Bank Holiday would spit on the ground, and women waiting for buses at Camden Town would scowl as he drove past in the car, and men who had hit him on the back before would avoid his eye, and above everything there was a pompous, ugly, rather false phonetic sound about the very words Sir Gerald, when du Maurier alone had been a thing of grace.

So he went to Buckingham Palace in silk stockings and

knee-breeches, yearning in his romantic soul for a peri-wig and a sword and a plum-coloured satin coat, and pretended he did not hear when the chauffeur, rosy with embarrassment and a sort of desperate pride, called him Sir Gerald for the first time.

He settled down to knighthood as he had settled to management, to marriage, to popularity, and to everything else, and it was not long before his handle became a thing of habit that he scarcely noticed, and the children stopped blushing when Mo was termed 'my lady'. It was a pity, when he came to think of it, that they had not created him a peer – Baron Hampstead had a good, full-sounding flavour that was not to be despised – but he must make up for it by distributing largesse amongst the poor of the village. And so it was that his pockets these days became more than ever easier of access, with half-sovereigns and pieces of silver appearing like magic from his old-fashioned purse at the sight of anyone bent or pale of feature who had the good fortune to stumble in his path. It was a pose of his, when paying a bill, to pay in sovereigns, never in notes, and then to say, with a shrug of his shoulder and a smile, 'All right, you can keep the change,' no matter what the sum.

People thought him a millionaire, or a wizard in finance, and it was like a game to him to keep up this pretence – to talk casually in terms of thousands just for the amusement of watching expressions on people's faces. The bluff gave him tremendous satisfaction for no particular reason, and it was little wonder that in later years, when he was really pressed for money, nobody believed him. It was one of his forms of practical joking that nobody could understand but himself, and where exactly the joke came in he could never quite explain. At this time, however, he had certainly reached his most affluent period, and money came easily to the hand. His plays were both theatrical and financial successes, and he was king of his particular world.

What triumphs they were, those opening nights at Wyndham's, with a play tuned to the highest pitch of perfection by diligent rehearsing, every member of the cast on his toes and at the top of his form, ready, like athletes in the pink of condition, to break records! They were nervous, of course – that was to be expected – and Gerald, coming home to an early dinner before the play, would show the strain by eating very little, by forcing his laughter, by humming just a shade too loudly the bars of a song.

Mo and the children, dressed in their best for the occasion, sat with flushed faces and wet hands, looking forward to the evening with mixed feelings, for by now they knew every line of the play as well as Gerald did himself; they knew just where it dragged, just where it was loose, and if somebody forgot his lines it would be greater agony than the dentist's chair. They drove down to the theatre in the car, and already a crowd had assembled on the pavement to watch the audience arrive. There was a whisper that turned into a shout when Gerald got out of the car – 'There he is – there he goes' – and high-pitched exclamations as the family followed – 'There she is – look, there are the children – oh, isn't she sweet – look at that one' – and the du Maurier offspring followed their parents along the narrow alley-way that led to the stage door, scarlet with embarrassment, hiding their faces in their party cloaks. A wave of excitement met them as they entered the theatre; the very atmosphere was pregnant with emotion, and Tommy Lovell, the stage manager smiled nervously, swallowing as though he had a bone in his throat, and rather bright about the eyes. Gerald's dressing-room was filled with flowers – from great monstrous emblems that topped the ceiling from acquaintances he had met at lunch, to the children's pot of heather on his dressing-table, and all manner of bulbs and pots and baskets, while telegrams fell from the table and slopped on to the floor. In the passage the call-boy shouted, 'Overture and beginners, please'; a haunting, fearful proclamation, a definite statement that escape was impossible and that the evening must be endured; and in a minute the first scrapings of the fiddles and the tap-tap of the conductor's stick could be heard, through the muffled barrier of the safety curtain, beyond the stage.

'You'd better get along to the box,' Gerald would say casually, as he put on his dressing-jacket and sat down before the mirror. The children would disappear, Mo hovering a moment to kiss him and wish him luck, and soon they had found their way to the box and were gazing down to the audience below, a great hum of excited chatter, laughter, and voices coming up to the box with a throbbing, unforgettable sound. Mo always sat well back screened by the curtain of the box from curious eyes, and Angela, the religious one of the party, was obviously praying in her corner, lips pressed together, hands tightly clasped. Daphne glowered sullenly at the stalls, hating everyone on sight, her eyes lighting for a second at the sight of her beloved Gladys; while Jeanne, newly promoted to the first-night status, beamed in appreciation upon the world in general, and waved a plump hand to the embarrassed staff from Cannon Hall, who returned the salutation meekly from the front row of the upper circle.

The orchestra blared its way to a conclusion, the programmes rustled, the doors were closed, the lights dimmed, the curtain rose suddenly with a swift and terrifying motion, and the play, for better, for worse, had begun.

Back in the dressing-room, Gerald was dressing for his part. He whistled softly between his teeth or hummed a little song. It was going to be all right, he knew that. His judgement had not played him false. They had a real winner this time. But even with this belief there was an element of danger, a spark of uncertainty, that made the whole thing an adventure, an unbeatable thrill. One could never be entirely sure, and a first-night audience was a temperamental crowd, an unknown quantity. His heart beat a little more swiftly than usual, and his hands trembled as he lit his cigarette. 'Sir Gerald, please,' came the sing-song voice of the call-boy.

In less than three hours it would be over. The clapping would have died away, 'The King' would have been played, his speech of thanks delivered, the crowd of friends from the stalls would be flocking round to the buffet at the back of the stage, and he would be receiving congratulations from fifty people at a time, a glass of champagne in one hand and a sandwich in the other, while Tom Vaughan and Frank Curzon rubbed their hands in satisfaction and murmured in his ear, 'All right, Gerald, old man, you've done it again.' But now he was alone; this was his moment; this was his one little spark of adventure, the one time when he enjoyed acting, when it thrilled him, when, in spite of the nervousness and the strain, it meant anything at all.

'Now then, Guy,' he whispered, 'a little help, please. *Abret-ag-Araog*. Come on, do your best.' He stood in the middle of the room, sensitive, aware, on tiptoe with excitement, his ears pricked like a fawn.

'Sir Gerald, please', said the call-boy for the last time.

He went quickly on to the stage, whistling, the light of battle in his eyes . . .

CHAPTER TEN

THESE were the years of the big holidays – Algiers, Cannes, Monte Carlo, and later a villa in Italy. *Bulldog* made money, and what was money for but to spend? And it would not be Gerald and Mo alone, but the three girls as well; and Sybil, Mo's sister, who was also his secretary; and Ronnie Squire for companion, and Harry Esmond in addition, and a whole complement of Innovation trunks and Revelation suitcases, hat-boxes, dressing-cases, and mysterious paper parcels; cigarettes to be smuggled through the customs, and parcels of books never read; mackintoshes, tweed coats, and field-glasses to be carried loose, and three or four hats to be changed *en voyage*; every magazine ever published, from *Country Life* to the *London Mail*, walking-sticks for impossible occasions, packs of cards to alleviate boredom, and games of skill or chance bought hastily and at random at the last minute. It was travelling in the grand manner with Gerald, and an experience not to be lightly undertaken. Couriers must await him on every platform, cabins must be reserved, railway carriages locked after him, and largesse distributed liberally and without hesitation to every official encountered from the gentlemen covered in braid to the menial who taps the wheels. The little covey of porters would trail along the platform at Victoria, staggering under golf-clubs, tennis-rackets, dispatch-cases, pillows, and rugs, with two more of Gerald's inevitable hats balanced precariously on top of eight daily newspapers. Mo would follow laden with fruit, packages from Fortnum's, a case of wine, and six library books; and Sybil, her hands shaking with the appalling responsibility of pass-ports, tickets, reservations, declarations, registrations; and the three children, laden in their manner and already suffering from Channel nerves, an undigested breakfast, and a stomach warning. Gerald himself would appear from quite a different end of the platform, vague and rather uncertain, having changed his hat again and bought three more magazines and a toy that would not work. As soon as he caught sight of his family he would act a part, bending suddenly, his hand to his heart, and coughing and groaning as one in the last stages of a malignant disease, feigning conversation with an un-known old lady whose back was mercifully turned, and who did not perceive the maniac who gibed at her with trembling finger and incredible grimace. And as the little party crawled into the Pullman carriage, and seated them-selves amidst incredible confusion, the racks, the tables, the chairs, and even the floor and passage strewn with their innumerable goods and chattels, Gerald would sigh suddenly, press a pound note into the hand of an astonished passing porter who had nothing to do with them, and, fumbling in his pocket for a match, would discover that he had left fifty boxes on the dining-room table at home; and he would ask Sybil, who was already sitting with closed eyes, clutching a bottle of smelling-salts, to get on the telephone immediately to Cannon Hall and have someone sent down in a taxi with the parcel, bringing at the same time a cap that was hanging on a nail behind some old boxes in the cupboard below the stairs. It was not until the door had been closed, the engine had whistled, and the guard had waved his flag, that Gerald, looking out of the window and perceiving a spot of rain on the glass, would remark in a genuine and rather wist-ful voice, 'Don't let's go after all. I'd much rather stop at home.'

On the boat he took sole charge, banishing the frail

females of his party to their cabins, and, in a different overcoat and hat, he paced the deck in the teeth of the wind and spray, his pockets bulging with passports retrieved from the stricken Sybil, who, eyes bright with various sea-sick remedies, moved in another world. Mo, her cabin black as a pit, with the curtains tightly drawn, murmured faintly through the aroma of eau-de-Cologne and aspirin that she did hope he would be careful and not go too close to the side of the boat where there was nothing to prevent him falling but some horrid ropes. And the children, sick as cats, looked up at him with resentful eyes and prayed for death. Calais was reached in a lurch and a twist of the malignant vessel, a sickening shudder and groan, and Gerald blew once more into the cabin, unbearably healthy and his face wet with spray, speaking exquisite and suspiciously fluent French, that was far too good to last, to a mob of hysterical porters, who with ruthless hands and garlic breath poured over the luggage in a frenzy of expectation.

The customs was a nightmare of mislaid keys and unravellable knots; of burst locks and broken string; of wine and cigarettes passed by unscrutinized and overcoats searched with zeal, only to reveal sheet upon sheet of Bromo. There was the usual misunderstanding over reservations in the *wagon-lit* – sleepers that had been booked for the following day instead of the day in question; tongues that moved like a two edged sword and hands that spread outward to the four winds. Sybil still in a dream, and faint for want of the food she refused to take, fumbled in a monstrous handbag with sheaf upon sheaf of typescript, caught up with rubber bands and bearing the stamp of the travel agency, while Gerald, his French becoming moment by moment faster and more improbable, looked round from the tail of his eye for the despised interpreter, and, irritated almost beyond endurance by the hitch in the hitherto royal progress, pressed *mille* notes into the outstretched palm of the wavering conductor.

The magic worked, accommodation was found, and the du Mauriers took possession with all the triumph and aggression of a conquering tribe, unpacking suitcases and clothing as though they were making settlements for life.

Gerald was not one of your placid travellers who curl up in a corner, with overcoat buttoned to the chin, and compose themselves for sleep; his sleeping-berth must be as like as possible to his bedroom at home, the wash-basin arranged with endless mysterious bottles and lotions, toothpastes and powders, sponges and loofahs, suits hanging against the door, pyjamas and dressing-gown upon the bed; while the carriage next door must be fitted up as a sitting-room – drink and fruit and cigarettes on the folding table, books, papers, and cushions on the seats, and some sort of arrangement of suitcases so that Gerald and one of the girls could play bezique.

Eldest sons of the nobility who made the Grand Tour in past centuries could not have made greater preparations for their comfort, for all their carriages and coaches, their band of followers, their team of horses. Gerald would have been a typical scion of the eighteenth century, arriving at wayside inns with a flourish and clatter, filling the stables with his horses and the guest-rooms with his friends, strewing the sanded floor with wet cloaks and muddied boots, calling loudly for ale and chucking the pretty daughter of the landlord under the chin with a 'God's blood, and damme!' There was nothing very romantic about a first-class sleeper *en route* for Monte Carlo, unless you could imagine yourself a diplomat with secret papers in a portfolio that might possibly be stolen from you by a mysterious lady in a dark veil, the only clue to whose identity was a lace handkerchief, heavily scented, dropped in the corridor with the monogram 'A' in the right-hand corner. Gerald possessed a fertile imagination, and although, alas! the days were gone when Daphne and Jeanne could play Edward Royle and Duckling to his Captain Coxen without feeling self-conscious, walking the poop of the full-rigged ship *Grosvenor* with oaths and scowls, discussing molasses and ship's biscuits in bitterness, hands ready to reach for marline-spikes and belaying-pins at the slightest provocation, they could at least appreciate the possibilities of the occasion, and invent with him incredible stories about their fellow-travellers, observed in the dining-car in the next compartment.

Once arrived at their destination, whether Monte Carlo, Cannes, or the heights of Mustapha, they would find suites awaiting them, bedrooms, bathrooms, and a sitting-room, which at first sight might not always please because the outlook would be north-east instead of south-west, or because it looked out upon a road and not a garden. And the manager would be questioned at once as to whether he would change them, and by the time they were settled in different rooms, and the atmosphere had become less alien, packs of cards and library books and newspapers and knitting on the chairs, and the familiar table of bottles and soda-syphons in the corner, Gerald would say that he did not think he was going to like the place and could not they all go on somewhere else? One place would be too crowded, another place too empty. There was always too much wind beside the sea, and in the mountains it did nothing but rain. Here the beds were hard and the food impossible, and there the heat was tiring and gave him a stomach-ache. And whose idea was it, anyway, to go abroad to a filthy, stinking country when they had a charming and comfortable home where he could always be sure of getting cold roast beef and radishes?

The big holidays were not, then, always the joyous, carefree things they might have been; there would be an undercurrent of anxiety to spoil the best moments; a strain of nervous expectation on the part of family, friends, and children that 'Gerald was going to be bored.'

The pity of it was that he could be the best and most adorable of companions when he chose, the greatest laughter-maker of them all, original, absurd, eager for adventure, ready to explore, and keen to make discovery, keeping the party, by the force of his personality, at a high pitch of enjoyment and enthusiasm. And then he would wake one morning to a grey sky, or with a pain inside him, or having slept badly the night before, and the whole atmosphere would be changed at once – gloomy, spiritless, and flat; conversation at the lunch-table would falter, laughter would seem stale and out of place, and no one would have the courage or the desire to prepare for any undertaking.

Too many excuses are made for the 'artistic temperament', too much latitude allowed to those unconscious tyrants who move in a world of their own moods and whims. From a tiny child Gerald had been spoilt and indulged. Mummie had given in to him, and Mo was Mummie all over again. He had three daughters and no sons. He was the god and the flame of his little household of women, and no man in the world could withstand such an onslaught and remain unspoilt. It spoke well for his inner nature and his true personality that his character was not objectionable and impossible.

If Guy had not lived so much abroad, if Guy had not been killed ... but, then, suppositions are useless, unsatisfactory methods of solving problems. It is all too late now, and Gerald's particular problem will never be solved. The seed of discontent was born in infancy, nurtured through childhood, and cultivated in manhood. It grew in the soil best suited to it, and was tended and cherished by the very hands most necessary to its development. Its roots were too strong in the ground, too thick and too tenacious, for the core to be destroyed in full maturity.

Since Guy had died Gerald had lived without the company, the true understanding, and the equality of a deep and genuine male friendship. He possessed friends, of course. There were plenty who slapped him on the back and called him 'dear old Gerald', with whom he played cards, golf, and tennis, who laughed at his jokes and his fund of stories, who respected his position and valued his work, who acted with him in the theatre or came up to Sunday lunch at Cannon Hall. But he had no really great friend who was superior to himself from any point of view, whose opinion and whose advice were valuable for their worth, sincerity, and sympathy. There was no man who could turn to him and say with his whole heart and brain, 'Do this,' or 'Do that,' 'Don't be a damn' fool, Gerald.' He needed the friendship of such a man more than most people. He needed the stimulating company of an intellectual superior who was at the same time well balanced and tolerant, forceful and sympathetic, fired with energy and enthusiasm, but harsh with all the severity of an elder brother who cannot and will not flatter, who squashes 'temperament', self-pity, and self-indulgence with that straight-from-the-shoulder form of truth-telling that Gerald above all men appreciated.

There was no such friend, and Gerald lived alone amidst his little court of women, having the monopoly of attention in his small world, without the slightest competition from anyone and with no interference.

It was all too late now, anyway. When you are approaching fifty you dislike advice almost as much as you do when you are fifteen. You are equally intolerant, equally sensitive about little personal things such as your appearance, your popularity, and what people are saying about you behind your back. You are often more bitter about disappointments, more readily angered and wounded, and the man or woman who tells you of your faults is at once an enemy, a traitor within the gates. It is discouraging to find the first grey hairs, to feel the first rheumatic pains, to wake in the mornings with an aching back and then be obliged to read the newspaper with the aid of spectacles.

It is something of a shock to wander into the Garrick and glance at your contemporaries, and to realize that half of them are bald and half of them have paunches. The boys with whom you were at school, and who were perhaps your juniors, are definitely elderly men with squeaky voices, slow of step and ponderous of brain, with married sons and daughters, telling interminable stories of no particular point after one glass of port.

It is baffling and rather disturbing to take a woman out to lunch and in the course of conversation discover that she is, after all, only a few years older than your own eldest daughter, and that when you were a gay young man-about-town she was not even born. These things do not make for peace of mind. You ask yourself silently the question, 'Am I being a bore? Do people already yawn when I come into a room? Is this man being false? Is this woman being insincere?' And, with a sort of desperate belief that you are touching wood for safety, you turn with abandon to those friends who praise you most, who laugh longer than the rest, who hang upon your words, who wait upon your will, who are happy at a smile and beaten by a frown, who by their very subjection to your personality prove that your power is not shaken and your pedestal of glory still stands firm. There was a definite feminine strain in Gerald's nature, and because of it he preferred the company of women to that of men. Feminine but not effeminate, he laid too great a stress on a woman's values. He had a woman's eager curiosity about other people's private lives, a woman's tortuous and

187

roundabout methods of getting to a certain point, a woman's appreciation of gossip, a woman's love of intrigue and drama, a woman's delight and absorption in little mysterious flirtations that last a day. He would have made an ideal courtier to a Valois prince, toying with poisoned glove in the presence of Catherine de Medici, toasting the beauty of his choice with a careless laugh, splintering the stem of his glass into a thousand fragments. The average male is a little bored with the company of a woman for long unless he is in love with her. He would rather be working, or playing golf, or catching a fish. Even your hearty profligate is dumb and tongue-tied when he is out of the bedroom; but Gerald, with his feminine strain, could sit for hours over coffee and cigarettes after lunch at a restaurant and listen with genuine interest to the recital of somebody else's love-affair. The woman who was unhappily married, the girl who sighed for a lover abroad, the lady who could not make up her mind between two people, the unfortunate who became entangled with the husband of a friend – these were all problems of rapture to his curious ears. He made suggestions; he gave advice; he watched the progress and the fulfilment of his prophecies with an almost fiendish satisfaction. And he rubbed his hands like Mephistopheles when people 'went off the deep end', as he expressed it, and landed themselves in an emotional mess. Nor was he gifted with discretion regarding his little mysteries. It was almost impossible for him to keep a secret or to guard a confidence. Without malice, he found himself urged by some strange necessity, like an excited child, to spread his stories abroad, to embroider them with his own fancies until they became veritable works of art.

This intense interest in other people's lives gradually became his one hobby and relaxation. The old days of golf in the country with four light-hearted, congenial companions belonged to the past. Tennis was reserved for

Sundays, and when he was not actually working for his profession – acting, producing, or arranging a matinée for charity – he would spend long hours in the company of the more discouraged of his friends and newly discovered acquaintances. They were nearly always women with not enough to do in life, who liked nothing better than to talk about themselves.

It was a futile waste of nervous energy, a poor substitute for relaxation, and one of the strongest allies of that creeping paralysis, boredom, which year by year now threatened to cloud the bright pattern of his life. The ordinary hobbies of the ordinary man could not hold his concentration. His love for birds was not really strong enough to permit him more than an occasional day in the country. He would proceed there in comfort in a car, with a companion and a picnic basket containing the right food; he would not go alone. The country for longer than a week-end he found depressing. He loathed walking and gardening. Fishing was monotonous and stupid when you could buy fish at the fishmonger's. Blood sports were cruel and useless. Bathing induced chills on the liver. Boats were a nuisance to moor and hard to the seat. And his clumsiness of hands prevented him from quickness with sails or engines. He read little. Occasionally a well-written novel would engage him to the final chapter, but more often he would start a book with a yawn already on his lips and leave it unfinished. He needed some terrific stimulation to awake him from the slow descent to a state of apathy, and the stimulation was not forthcoming. His brain and his entire nervous system, which cried out for work and yet more work of an intensive kind, became stagnant and discouraged for the want of it; he frittered his powers away on unimportant things and on unimportant people. He did not understand that because of this a profound dissatisfaction with life, and an appalling sense of emptiness, should be part of him, that he would reach an *impasse* that would close in upon him and from which he would seek in vain the light of the day.

He had one friend, who, with real perception, saw that he could master his boredom if he chose, could harness his brain and his spark of brilliance to the command of his own will, and, by flinging caution, idleness, and self-depreciation to the winds, could stretch out his hands to the sky and work miracles. But, for all her almost masculine intelligence and great intuition, Viola Tree was, alas! a woman. Had she been a man she would have been perhaps the perfect friend, the wise counsellor, the good companion. But the very fact of her sex made the equality of friendship impossible. She was a woman, a wife, a mother; she was also a schoolgirl who had never grown up, a flapper with open mouth who knelt before her hero, anxious to please, hungry for praise, cowed at a gesture or an unkind word. She was quick-tempered, easily roused to wrath; she died a hundred deaths and jumped into a hundred mental rivers after some heated argument; she saw herself being romantic and picturesque when she was in reality incredibly funny. She plunged and struggled in hopeless confusion when she imagined she was straightening some entanglement. She was often dunderheaded, tactless, obstinate, a mule.

She was a Lewis Carroll creation, a character from *Alice*, a child and a clown, with a perfect, almost unbelievable sense of humour; adorable alone, dressed in an old skirt with odd stockings, munching an apple and discussing Charles the First with her mouth full of pips; ill at ease at a smart party, talking too loudly, perhaps being 'clever', praising a modern picture, damning a book because it was fashionable to damn it.

Sometimes insincere in little things, emotional and forced, she had a great and generous heart, a deep and tigerish affection for her friends, and a wise understanding of the big problems of life. She was not her father's daughter for nothing. She had great theatre sense. She was cultured, artistic, extremely intelligent, and, if she had had only the necessary force of character to give her the superiority in her friendship with Gerald, she might have fired him with some of her own tremendous enthusiasm and energy; jogged him into making great theatrical gestures as her father had done, and prodded his brain into the activity it demanded, so that it should not waste itself in petty interests. But no true harmony can exist between a man and a woman. They rub on each other's nerves. They do not work in tune. So it was that the great plays remained unwritten, the dramas unproduced; the stories and the books lay still and unbegotten, and Viola and Gerald went their separate ways as friends and not collaborators, both temperamental, both individualists, incapable of merging their separate personalities. And Gerald, whose very soul cried out for a goal in life and an ultimate purpose, was still without his creed and without his leader.

That they were capable of working together and producing a play for the theatre was proved when, in 1923, they wrote *The Dancers*, a novelettish piece which, if it could not be called great literature, was, to say the least, grand theatrical entertainment, dramatic and full of incident, and acclaimed by all the critics as a splendid piece of work. It ran at Wyndham's for very nearly a year.

The authors kept their identity secret until the first night, the name on the programme appearing as Hubert Parsons, but the truth could not remain hidden for long, especially in Gerald's keeping. The triumphant success on the opening night called for an announcement, and, once known, the popularity of the play was even more ensured.

The Dancers was something in the nature of a 'stunt', and as a 'stunt' it succeeded. Two young actresses made enormous personal successes, Tallulah Bankhead as the American Maxine and Audry Carten as the pathetic, attractive, and strangely bewildered post-war product Una, a character more or less built upon herself.

Gerald allowed himself an orgy of satisfaction as the Earl of Chievely, who was discovered in the first act, in an open shirt and riding-breeches, giving out drinks behind a bar in the Wild West, with an adoring Maxine at his side, and was then summoned to England by the news that his relatives had met with an accident and he had come into the title. This first act was a riotous piece of pageantry, colourful and attractive for all its resemblance to magazine fiction, and the audience were naturally enough escorted back to London, where the new earl discovered a childhood playmate in the nervy, dance-mad Una, who, in a panic, accepted his offer of marriage and allowed him to fall deeply in love with her while hiding the fact that she was expecting a baby, the result of 'a moment's lapse' with a youthful and irresponsible dancing-partner.

The best acted and most dramatic scene in this play of surprises was the wedding dinner at the hotel. After some exquisite comedy by Gerald, as Chievely, trying to speak French to the waiter, and many minutes of quick and easy dialogue, the unhappy Una, left alone with her conscience, realized that she could not go through with her deception, and in a sudden frenzy poisoned herself, to be discovered dead a few minutes later by Chievely.

Recounted in cold blood, the story screams of the cheap editions on the top shelves of libraries or thrust upon the traveller's eye at a station bookstall for the sum of sixpence, complete with glaring wrapper. But acted by Gerald and Audry Carten with a wonderful sense of delicacy, restraint, and sincerity, these two characters lived and were human, were painfully, agonizingly human, playing upon the emotions of the audience in a fashion that could be vouched for by wet handkerchiefs and swollen eyes.

Analysed, *The Dancers* falls to pieces. It was one of those plays that must be seen to be appreciated; a play that by good acting and equally good producing became in itself a play of value, but without these things could never have survived. The fourth act was an anti-climax. Maxine came upon the scene once more, having apparently taken the world by storm as a ballerina, was visited by an older and wiser Chievely, and the curtain fell with the assumption that these two would find happiness together, and that the generous, warm-hearted Maxine would help Chievely to forget the wretched past and the ghost of Una. It was one of those pseudo-happy endings that dramatists, with an eye to the box-office, feel themselves obliged to give the public, who do not care for tragedy; and that the fourth act did not kill the play is proved by the three hundred and forty-four performances to which the curtain rose and fell. The acting alone at Wyndham's would have kept the theatre full, and it was not surprising that after the two hundred and fiftieth night the newspapers were again full of 'the best acting in London' and 'the magnetic force of Gerald du Maurier, Audry Carten, and Tallulah Bankhead, all three who give brilliant and intensively moving performances in that capital melodrama, *The Dancers*.'

If Gerald and Viola could do this once, they could have done it again; and with what improvements and with what added judgement; what new endeavour, what matured understanding – Gerald with his sense of drama, Viola with her sense of culture; Gerald with his eye for effect, Viola with her literary restraint; Gerald with his flair for public taste, Viola with her intellectual grasp of what is good and what is bad in art.

But *The Dancers* remained an isolated achievement, alone in its melodramatic and rather highly coloured glory, returning, when the year was ended, to that limbo of forgotten plays, side by side with the old novels and the faded portraits, lost fashions and dead tunes.

It was the last of the Wyndham's big successes, and, when it was withdrawn the following year, four plays appeared in quick succession, two of which were failures, one of which did moderately well, and one a stop-gap in the form of a revival. It looked as though the du Maurier luck had turned at last. For nearly fifteen years Gerald had reigned at Wyndham's Theatre unchallenged and undisputed, his word as law, his judgement unquestioned. Frank Curzon, his financial partner, seldom if ever interfered. Gerald was responsible for the choice of plays, for the production, for the selection of the company. During the fifteen years many actors and actresses had played under his tuition and had made the first successes of their careers, passing out of the theatre to find fame on their own account and to become in turn favourites of the public. Gladys Cooper, who had made her name as Dora in *Diplomacy* in 1913, was, ten years later, under her own management at the Playhouse, and the most popular actress on the London stage. Owen Nares, also a graduate from *Diplomacy*, was in management, and suffered, as did Gerald, from that unfortunate appellation 'matinée idol.' Ronald Squire, the butt of Bulldog Drummond, was rapidly rising to public favour, and had been compared with Charles Hawtrey. These were only three out of a countless number who learned their trade with Gerald at Wyndham's Theatre.

In 1925 *A Man with a Heart*, a poor play by Alfred Sutro, petered out into failure. Gerald was tired and low in spirits. There appeared to be no play in sight. He needed a holiday. He was bored. He was fed up with the theatre.

He was also worried about May, who was desperately ill and not likely to recover. He realized that she was fated to follow Trixie and Sylvia, and that he would soon be alone, without one member of the du Maurier family left.

At times they had had fierce arguments, he and May; she was quick-tempered, critical; she knew his faults and did not mind describing them to his face. He was the younger brother she had bossed as a little girl, and she was not afraid of him. She was passionately devoted to her family, and because of this devotion she wished to watch over them as Mummie had done; to advise the nephews, to criticize their wives, to have, as it were, a finger in the family pie. She had, with the exception of Guy, more brains than the rest of the family put together, more culture, and an intuition and a sense of humour that were entirely French. But she had not the same sense of sociability that her brothers and sisters had possessed. She disliked meeting people and being entertained. She detested anything that was 'smart' or 'society', and she disapproved of the stage atmosphere. Nothing would drag her behind the scenes to Gerald's dressing-room, to meet his friends; anything in the form of gush or flattery, the endearments and the 'darlings', were like red flags to a bull. She was happiest in her little house in Chelsea, lean, and brown, and boyish, dressed in an old jersey and skirt, alone with her husband, her dogs, and a handful of cronies, poring over the most difficult of the Sunday acrostics, with books scattered about the floor. And now May, the companion of his childhood and much beloved for all the little criticisms and disagreements, was to lie with the others in the Hampstead churchyard, and there would be no one left to remember with Gerald the old contented days.

It was about this time that Freddie Lonsdale came up to dinner at Cannon Hall with the manuscript of his new play under his arm. He was in great spirits, excited about his play, which he hoped would be produced by Gerald at

Wyndham's. It may be that Mo provided too good a dinner, it may be that the port was too old a vintage and too strong for a man who was worried, and depressed, and overtired. It may be that it was just an unfortunate example, hitherto unknown, of damn' bad manners, but the fact remained that when Freddie, seated before the fire in the library, looked up from his manuscript in eager anticipation, it was to discover a comatose Gerald with his head on a cushion and his feet up, not only sound asleep, but snoring! Poor Freddie, smitten in his soul, leapt to his feet in a towering passion and rushed from the building, followed by an expostulating and highly embarrassed Mo, who begged him to be calm and not to break his and Gerald's old friendship of so many years' standing. But Freddie would not listen; he was really angry, and the situation, as the politicians say, threatened to become serious.

The solution of the problem was achieved by rather roundabout means. The play was offered to Gladys, who accepted it, and arranged to present it at the St James's Theatre in conjunction with Gilbert Miller. The leading part and the production positively screamed for Gerald's treatment, and the upshot of it was that Gerald and Freddie, like preparatory schoolboys, shook hands and were friends. Gerald finished his period of management with Curzon and left Wyndham's, for better, for worse, going to the St James's in a sort of co-management with Gladys and Gilbert Miller.

His forty winks had cost him a small fortune, though, for he was now receiving a salary instead of a percentage of the profits, and, as Lonsdale's play ran for a year, the realization that it might have been at Wyndham's but for that one evening's lapse was not the happiest of truths. It was one of those stupid, unnecessary incidents that need never have occurred. If Gerald had exercised a little self-control and Freddie had not permitted his sense of humour to die on him, the old association at Wyndham's would possibly never have terminated.

Actually Frank Curzon was a sick man, and he died two years later. But the profits that Gerald would have made out of *The Last of Mrs Cheyney*, had he produced the play at Wyndham's, should have been a safe guarantee for other ventures, and his friendship with Edgar Wallace, which began about this time, would almost assuredly have brought about a partnership that could have achieved great things had the association been possible.

As it happened, he had reached the summit of his little mountain; he was fifty-two, and life and the theatre were not the great adventures they once had been. He was to know one or two more triumphs, and in one play, called *Interference*, he gave a piece of silent acting that could scarcely have been bettered on any stage; but henceforth living and acting were not always to be effortless or easy. Financial worries lay ahead, and, with two exceptions, the days of the long runs and the great successes were gone for ever.

CHAPTER ELEVEN

WHEN Gerald appeared as Arthur Dilling in *The Last of Mrs Cheyney,* on the opening night he received a tremendous ovation. He had been absent from the stage for six months – since the last Sutro failure, in fact – and the public were naturally not aware of the vicissitudes through which the Lonsdale play had triumphantly emerged. The play was a fashionable, amusing piece of nonsense, light as air and sprinkled with titles; nearly every line was witty, and calculated to bring a smile to the most blasé of playgoers, and the cast was positively brilliant. It was the sort of piece that kept you at a high pitch of entertainment for the two and a half hours of its duration, and that you forgot as soon as you left the theatre.

No thinking or concentration upon the part of the audience was required, and there was never a boring or heavy moment. It was essentially an 'after-dinner play', and immensely popular with those members of society, all white ties and sequins, who drop into the stalls rather late when the curtain has risen, whispering loudly and trampling over other people's toes, demanding to be pleasantly shocked and not too energetically amused for a few hours before congregating once more in an over-heated supper-club.

It had been a rather doleful year at Wyndham's. It was followed by a holiday in Italy which, when the rain came down from the mountains, threatened the usual boredom, and which even the high spirits of nephew Geoffrey and the indefatigable Viola, to say nothing of the anxious ministrations of wife and family, could not entirely assuage. This holiday was followed in its turn by May's death. And it was a relief and a welcome change to be once more in a popular success, with a real friend like Gladys and a company that was unanimously light-hearted and content.

Gladys was probably the only woman in the world who had never flattered Gerald at any time, and, though deeply appreciative of his genius, she never made any attempt to blind herself to his faults.

She met him on her own ground, as an equal, the most feminine of women with a face like Danaë and eyes that will never be surpassed in our lifetime. She gave him what was probably the only genuine platonic friendship of his career. No wiles from her, no tantrums, no lamentations, no probings and interferings into his private life, no fifth-form jealousies, no undignified intrigues. Every matinée during the run of *Cheyney* they met for lunch, like two men at a club, silent, shoulder to shoulder, Gerald with his cold beef and Gladys with a chop; now and then discussing the affairs of the day, brief and matter-of-fact, or comparing notes about each other's children.

No lingering over coffee for her, no long stories, no confessions, no declarations of private misery, no mysterious revelations.

No hammering broke down her great reserve; no indirect questioning, no sudden suggestion, penetrated the wall she had so wisely built around herself. What lay at the back of her mind, what remembrances, what plans, what past endeavours and what future goals, only God and Gladys ever knew.

Possessing great physical and moral courage herself, she had little sympathy for the weak or temperamental, no patience with moods, no psychological insight. With her firm chin and wide nostrils, she strode through life brushing obstacles from her path, her eyes on the horizon, an intolerant and rather gallant figure. Her common sense and her abrupt, matter-of-fact manners made her a very good companion for Gerald; she had the effect on him that a practical, thoroughly normal nursery governess has on a spoilt and pampered child. He knew she would never stand for nonsense, and would scorn a display of nerves or temperament, and, like all spoilt children, he was able to respect someone who treated him for what he was worth and made no claim upon him. Although she did not possess one half of Viola's imagination or intuition, the very lack of it made her, possibly, if not a better friend, at least a better influence. Viola made herself a slave, a whipping-boy; she was too sensitive to his changes of mood; she let him ride rough-shod over her feelings; she had for him an almost dog-like devotion which he accepted without question and took an almost sadistic pleasure in testing. How often he would return home in the evening, after a day in the country with Viola, and relate with genuine childish delight to his wife and children how he had had 'a hell of a row with the old mug', and had sent her home in the depths of despair.

Then, after relating the little episode with glee to his, let it be confessed, not always entirely attentive family, who murmured with a yawn, 'Poor old Viola! God knows why she stands for it!' he would wander off to his rest before leaving for the theatre, still chuckling to himself over the grand *coup* of his day. And when his twenty-minute sleep had mellowed his mood and he was struggling into his overcoat in the hall, he would call out to Mo to 'ring up the old fool and tell her Gerald says he takes back all he said.' And the curious dissertation would follow of Mo getting through to Viola on the telephone and saying in indignant tones, 'Don't let him bully you. You're far too patient with him. Now, what about our game of golf on Friday? I think it would be best if you had a little lunch with me here first.' At the other end of the line Viola would blare an incoherent message of thanks, speaking anywhere but into the mouthpiece, one hand clutching pencil and paper on which a thousand-word article had to be written by midnight and the other still grimy from a saucepan with which she had the vague idea of boiling an egg for her husband, who, stretched on a divan with a rug over his knees, called out, 'Why don't you give me the sort of food that Muriel gives Gerald?'

Perhaps the most typical Viola-ism ever known was the time she fell into Fowey harbour from the launch, missing her foothold on to the quay from the boat, and dressed all wrong in a narrow satin skirt that clung to her ankles and a large picture hat on her head, she swam round in circles calling out, 'Lovely, lovely', and emerged at last a dripping, curious figure, picture hat a little askew, and satin skirt covered in straw and mackerel scales.

That she caught a chill, and a few weeks later nearly died of peritonitis, was the even more typical sequel.

It is impossible to imagine any of these incidents happening to Gladys. She would be far too capable ever to fall out of a boat, or would only do so with deliberate intent, when, dressed for the part and glowing with health, she might strike out for the opposite shore, shouting over her shoulder for 'slackers' to follow her, like an imperious and popular games mistress. For all her incredible beauty, there was something essentially boyish about Gladys. Gerald would never have dared vent his temperament on her as he did on Viola. She would have shrugged her shoulders in contempt, and said 'Fool' in a voice that above all others could be peculiarly icy when it chose, and walked out of the room whistling between her teeth.

He had a terrific admiration, affection, and respect for Gladys. He would have fought duels and gone to the scaffold in her name. But she was the one woman in the world who made him feel less than his usual height, and he had a delightful and wholesome fear in her presence.

Meanwhile *The Last of Mrs Cheyney* played to full houses, and Gerald was more contented than he had been for some time. The atmosphere at the St James's Theatre was thoroughly healthy and normal. There were no bickerings, no jealousies, no silly little affairs to break in upon the good humour of the company. It was a welcome relief after the strained, rather wrought-up closing few years at Wyndham's. Gerald's love for practical jokes found full expression during this time, and he rarely entered the theatre without a toy of some sort in his pocket, or a nonsensical packet of tricks from Hamley's, and these would be produced at the breakfast-table in the last act, screened from view of the audience by coffee-pots and toast-racks, but fully exposed to the luckless eyes of the unfortunate company, who were expected to keep a straight face while clockwork mice hopped about the tablecloth. It became quite a regular ritual during this scene for some sort of little private display to take place, and there was eager competition as to who should 'darc' furthest. The slightest incident can appear hysterically funny to performers on the stage, much as it must do to choirboys in church. They know for the sake of their souls that they must under no circumstance whatever laugh aloud, and the strain can sometimes be complete agony.

Nobody on the stage was ever safe when Gerald was present; he would go to the most appalling lengths, and take infinite time and trouble with his experiments. Nothing pleased him more than a successful joke, and, back in his dressing-room, he would rock with laughter until the tears ran down his cheeks, while he told the story of one of his latest shock discoveries. He would invent strange contraptions with string, and place them under the tablecloth, then press some sort of bulb and the plates and cups and saucers would jump about in undignified fashion before their respective owners, who were trying to look as if they were really eating eggs and bacon; there were rolls filled with cotton wool, bananas made of soap, and apples that squeaked a protest when moved; there were cushions that uttered significant and unmistakable sounds when sat upon, collapsible knives and forks that crumpled in the hand, tumblers that melted at the first drop of liquid.

He even once went to the trouble of staging that well-known Chinese torture of the drip of water (though this was in a later play than *Cheyney*), and made scientific arrangements for a drop to fall periodically from above on to the forehead of a wretched and innocent performer, who was tied by his part to sit in a certain chair and conduct a very serious conversation for many minutes on end.

He was baffling to his friends, and often a problem to himself; he was so easily moved to laughter and to tears, careless one moment and emotional the next, with sudden inexplicable silences and equally sudden indiscretions.

His children were growing up now, and they bewildered him; they were out of his reach in a year, with plans of their own, with friends, with secrets they did not tell. Adolescence was something he had not figured upon; he had not reckoned on that little world of experience that is an imposing barrier between the early and the later 'teens, and the children who had been companions at fourteen were strangers at nineteen.

They seemed old beyond their years, with a queer, half-fledged wisdom picked up from books and odd scraps of gossip; they talked with assurance about things they did not understand; and, instead of laughing at their puppy knowledge and marking time while they should find their feet, he worked himself up into little states of emotion and distress, creating an atmosphere of suspicion and unrest, asking sudden and embarrassing questions, wandering about with books of psychology under his arm, tearing at their privacy, and hurt by their reserve. Like many men, he had a poor memory for his own youth; he could remember only his follies and his indiscretions, which filled him with alarm for fear his children should do the same, and he forgot that their lack of friendliness was a necessary development in character; that they held their tongues even as he had held his tongue before Mummie and Papa.

There is, alas! a world of difference between the girl of eighteen and the man of fifty, especially when they are father and daughter. The one is resentful of the other. The girl mocks at experience and detests the voice of authority; the man yearns for companionship and does not know how to attain it. They stand side by side, with the barrier of years between them, and both are too shy to break it down; both are too diffident, too self-conscious. They chat about superficialities, and avoid each other's eyes, while all the time they are aware that the moments are passing, and the years will not bring them nearer to one another. Gerald was hungry for companionship; he longed for Angela and Daphne to tell him everything, to discuss their friends, to solve their problems, to share their troubles; but the very quality of his emotion made them shy. They could not admit him into their confidence, and they drew back like snails into their respective shells.

It was not only Gerald's tragedy. It is the tragedy of every father and every daughter since the world began. But he took it harder than most. He brooded upon it, and nursed it in his mind. It gave to him a little added bitterness which was peculiar to him and strangely pathetic. But his daughters shut their eyes to it; they pushed it away from their minds; they stood rooted to their generation, and would not admit him to their world. There might have been some hope for him had he allowed himself to become the schoolboy brother that he sometimes tried to be, or even if he had kept firmly to his pedestal as father, a figure of wisdom and respect; but he was so changeful, so inconsequent a man, a judge intolerant and hard one day, and human, all too human, on the morrow. They were never quite sure of him, never certain of his mood, and they walked away from him, leaving him a lonely, rather hesitating figure, to find consolation in his little restaurant lunches, listening to the confidences that might have been theirs.

He was proud of them, too, in a funny, self-conscious way, and if anyone else ventured to criticize his children he was aflame at once, returning thrust for thrust, jealous for their sake, proud for their reputation.

He was tremendously proud when Daphne wrote her first novel, and furious when no salesman could produce it at a bookstall. He was very pleased when Angela played Wendy in *Peter Pan*, and played it exceedingly well, and he demanded the blood of one critic who gave her an indifferent notice. He was excited when Jeanne began to draw in black and white at Papa's old desk, and could prove there was something in heredity. Whatever they said or did not say to him, they were his children, and he loved them better than he loved himself.

And they were not always hard on him; they were not always unkind. Angela took her position as eldest daughter with some sense of responsibility. She sat with him at dinner if Mo was down in London. She put off appointments, dinner engagements, when he was likely to be alone. She played cards with him; she was interested in the theatre; she read plays. Daphne was more elusive; she kept disappearing to Paris and to Cornwall. She was independent. She began to make money on her own, and when she chose to come home from time to time he used to hang about in the hall, shy and pathetically hopeful, wondering whether she would spend the day with him, waiting for her to suggest it on her own accord.

Seeing him more seldom, she learned things about him that she might not have understood had she been continually at home. She was a confidante at times, an ally, a listener to his little moods and tales. He talked about the past and about the present; he confessed his doubts of the future; and once or twice he clung to her like a small boy and whispered his fear of shadows, of darkness, of the grey hours before dawn. He told her about the family; about Papa, about Trixie. He drew a pattern of the old days, the happy, careless days when he was twenty-one, and she laughed with him and at him, and yawned sometimes and did not listen, while the air at Boulestin's grew thick with the smoke of his cigarette and that full, rather meaty smell of after-lunch, and the hands of the clock pointed to half past three. Or his would be a gay mood, a ribald mood, a schoolboy practical-joking mood, and off they would go to a toy-shop to buy a box of tricks; to Fortnum's to buy unnecessary presents; to buy walking-sticks that turned into umbrellas and swords, and which as soon as they were bought became a nuisance to carry, and would be given away. And from the heavy-hearted, discontented man of the morning he developed suddenly, for no reason, as swiftly as a cloud passes away from the face of the sun, into a laughing cavalier ten, twenty years younger than he had been before, walking swiftly, swinging a stick, singing at the top of his voice:

'Why are you so mean to me?'

His practical jokes did not only take place in the theatre. Long and expensive wires containing cryptic messages only understood by himself would be sent with false signatures and from faked post-offices to trembling and bewildered friends. Ingenious and scandalous items of news, presumably genuine press-cuttings but in reality privately printed with immense trouble, arrived in envelopes to cause consternation at the breakfast-table; and there was the famous occasion when he found an old photograph of himself as a child, which he had touched up, renovated, and modernized, attached it to a whining and complaining letter which he wrote himself in a disguised hand, and then sent it through the post to Mo, pretending that it was a photograph of an illegitimate son. As it turned out, this elaborate joke fell flat as a pancake. Mo was not taken in for a moment; she merely said, 'How absurd you are, darling,' and stuck the photograph up on her desk, reminding him that she had seen it amongst Mummie's things from the flat for years.

That he possessed a warped brand of humour cannot be denied, and he was lucky that it never brought him any serious trouble, but when he was not planning these elaborate and somewhat devilish schemes his sense of fun was childish and simple. A conjurer had only to produce a rabbit from a hat for him to clap his hands, open-mouthed like a child at his first party, and a clown who tripped up on a banana peel at the circus sent him into convulsions.

He was such a creature of contradictions, so old in experience, so young in wisdom; a faun one moment and an alderman the next; a child in the morning and a blasphemer at night; a citizen of the Empire with great ideas of justice, a beachcomber with his face in his hands; an unfrocked priest shaking his hand at heaven; a laughing Cockney alone in the wild woods.

There was never a moment, decisive and clear for all time, when you could point a finger and say of his mood, 'There, that is Gerald. That is the man. This is his portrait.' For he would be away, and changed, and lost in the shadows, and the man who stood in his stead had other eyes.

When the last was really seen of *Mrs Cheyney*, and the run, which had lasted for over a year, come to an end,

Gerald decided to stop on at the St James's in association with Gilbert Miller, while Gladys went back to the Playhouse under her own management. Both followed up *Cheyney* with big successes. Gladys, at the Playhouse, presented Somerset Maugham's *The Letter*, which Gerald produced for her, and he, at the St James's, found a winner in *Interference*, a drama by Roland Pertwee and Harold Dearden.

It was in this play that he took the part of John Marlay, a famous specialist, who, suspecting his wife, on damning circumstantial evidence, of having committed a murder, arranges the scene to look like suicide, in a desperate attempt to save her from arrest. Of course, he is suspected himself, and is about to suffer heroically for his wife's sake, when the real culprit – his wife's former husband – turns up and admits his guilt.

It was another very improbable melodrama, but once more it was excellent theatre from beginning to end, intensely exciting, with plenty of action, and Gerald again had proved wise in his judgement.

In the second act, when he was left alone on the stage with a dead body at whose feet lay his wife's handbag, the moment was one which could have been either unconvincing or over-theatrical in the hands of another actor. It may be argued that this was yet one more du Maurier part, and that Gerald was playing himself. Perhaps so. It did not matter. Whether Gerald had entered the skin of John Marlay or Marlay had become Gerald did not affect the issue. The result was the consternation and horror of a man high in public life who is suddenly faced with the appalling evidence that his beloved wife must have committed a murder – justifiable, perhaps, when threatened with blackmail, but murder for all that, for which the penalty is death.

It did not matter whether this man was John Marlay the specialist, fighting for his wife, Faith, or Gerald du

Maurier the actor, trying to save Mo from the stern hand of the law; the audience were given a performance that could not have been surpassed for sincerity, depth, and genuine emotion.

There was something rather terrible in the sight of this man pulling himself together, recovering from the shock, and proceeding with the care and stealth born of desperation to fake the evidence and to cover up his wife's tracks. Softly he moved about the room; silently he replaced an object here, an object there; with his gloves on his hands he wiped the rim of the glass that contained prussic acid, he poured the dregs of the poison into a vase, he placed the empty bottle of poison between the dead blackmailer's fingers. His movements were watched with a fearful interest by every member of the audience, and the passing moments might have furnished an example for the proverbial pin. It was an exquisite piece of silent acting, during which no word was spoken for ten minutes.

To quote Mr Agate,

One might say that Sir Gerald du Maurier's performance gives infinite pleasure. But that would be to speak loosely. His acting last night gave one pleasure of a finite, definite, almost concrete sort. You could pin down, and nail to the counter, each and every one of its many admirable qualities – vigour, ease, precision, attack, balance. He did what only an actor of extreme accomplishment could have done; he remained ten minutes alone on the stage without speaking. There are other rôles besides the philosopher's in which one can be bounded in a nutshell, and count oneself a king of infinite space.

Actually Herbert Marshall as Philip Voze, the murderer, scored the biggest success of the play. There was great personality and much fascination about his ne'er-do-well drunkard, and like Gladys, Nares, Squire, and others, he enjoyed his first real taste of fame under Gerald's management.

Like *Cheyney*, *Interference* also ran for a year, but, alas! it was the final play of Gerald's to do so. It is significant that in the June of '28 the dependable, cautious, and invaluable Tom Vaughan, who had been his business manager since the early Frank Curzon–Wyndham's days, died, having been ill for some little while. Nobody was ever to take his place. Gerald had never been able to cope with money. He knew no more about finance than a child. He was completely lacking in money sense, and he left his business entirely in Vaughan's hands. 'Oh, ring up Tom; he'll settle it,' he would say about any little problem, and the shrewd, practical friend from the Midlands would shoulder responsibilities, large or small. Vaughan knew just exactly how to deal with agents, authors, managers, dissatisfied actors and actresses; he possessed sound judgement, and could guarantee the money-making capabilities of a new and untried play. He had tact, discretion, and a sense of humour. That after his death Gerald chopped and changed theatres, produced a smattering of failures, appeared in plays that with the exception of *Cynara*, never ran longer than a few months, played in films to a poor salary and rotten contract, and never for one moment knew how he stood financially, could not by any manner of means be put down to chance.

He lost in Tom Vaughan a faithful and priceless friend, by whose help he had attained much of his success and most of his financial stability, and, though it was the fault of no one, he was never again to know complete security. It was the death of his business manager that broke down the defences that so carefully guarded him, and made his position vulnerable from all quarters. Meanwhile, two years back, during the run of *Cheyney*, he had met and become friendly with Edgar Wallace, whose crime novels were a household word but who had not then turned his talent to the drama. They met in an odd way. Edgar had written a scathing article in a newspaper condemning a certain school of thought whose members were largely in evidence at that particular time, and Gerald, also a fanatic on the subject, telephoned to congratulate him. They met and became firm friends. Edgar wrote his play, *The Ringer*, based on one of his novels, called *The Gaunt Stranger*, took Wyndham's Theatre, and not only persuaded Gerald to produce the play, but to help in the adaptation. For the latter service he insisted on giving him half of the profits throughout the entire run of the play. His generosity did not end here, and he was lavish with his gifts and his invitations, taking Angela and Daphne off with his own family to holidays in Switzerland, giving parties, presents – keeping open house, as it were, every moment of the day and night.

A novelist himself, no character in fiction clamours more furiously to be put between the pages of a book than the character of Edgar Wallace. His rise to fame, and, it may be said, to power, makes one of the most fiercely interesting studies of human nature that our generation has seen. What a piece of work for a writer with scientific ambitions, to place that mind, that body, and that soul under a microscope; to search deep into the influences that beset him; to trace the why and wherefore of his tremendous energy, his reserve of strength, his sensitive pride, the reasons for his intolerances, his jealousies, his passions, his capacity for love and hatred, work and generosity; to watch the piling fortune that brought to him the things of the world and at the same time destroyed his peace of mind, creating within him doubt, disillusion, and discontent; to discover finally and for ever from what sense of inferiority that seed of sorrow sprang. Edgar's genius lay very near the borderline; he could with truth have pointed to those visionary Napoleons who straddle their little universe of an asylum, and said, 'There, but for the grace of God ...'

His trouble was that he tried to split his great brain as the scientist would split the atom; instead of concentrating his force upon a single purpose, he must scatter his strength in all the fields. He must produce plays, direct films, edit newspapers, own racehorses, plunge into politics, and in wasting his talents thus, he so destroyed himself. He did none of them really well, and this was always jarring on his self-confidence. He could have become a great national figure had he poured all his energy into a definite source, but his ambition prompted him to do otherwise. He became a dabbler at all trades and a master of none, and to hide his fear of failure he built up great walls of defence around himself, shutting out enemies, friends, and his own family; creating a strange atmosphere of strain and unreality that was peculiar to himself, and which one word of courage, one smile of affection and understanding, might, or might not, have broken.

His was a very compelling and somehow tragic personality; but, while his faults pass away with him beyond recall, his generosity and true kindness will never be forgotten, nor will that calm, impassive face, nor the dead-blue eyes, nor the inevitable cigarette-holder and the crumbling ash, and the nervy, ceaseless tap-tapping of his fingers upon the desk before him.

Gerald, who produced *The Ringer* for him, the piece that brought him fame as a dramatist, also produced and acted in the last play he ever wrote, *The Green Pack*, in '32. And, in a lifetime filled with incident from beginning to end, those final six years of Edgar's existence, from the production of the first play to the production of the last, were surely his most significant. Thanks to Edgar's generosity, Gerald did very well financially out of *The Ringer* and handed over the proceeds to Mo, as was his custom. The result was an investment in the form of a house in Cornwall.

Mo was obviously making a last and desperate bid to ensure the annual holidays of happiness. With a natural flair for houses and their renovation, the house on Fowey harbour was bought and played with to her satisfaction. Staircases were built, ceilings were lowered, walls were hacked, floors were dug, bathrooms were introduced, oak was 'pickled', fittings and furniture were added, and when everything was finished, down to the last bulb in the flowerpot, Gerald was bidden for inspection.

Nothing had been forgotten from the launch that rocked at its moorings and was named *Cora Ann*, after *The Ringer* heroine, to the girls in their sea boots and jerseys, and the shrimping-nets poised suitably in the hall (surely a last-minute effort of the resourceful Viola!).

He arrived; he put on the large and disfiguring spectacles that had become his inveterate companions, gazed about him in polite admiration, leaving the usual trail of packages in his wake – field-glasses, cardigans, magazines, bird books, boxes of cigarettes, packs of cards, whisky bottles and two or three changes of hats – and, when the tour of the house was finished, he kissed Mo and said, 'Well, well, how you have coped! It's all very charming, but I should like to get some dynamite and blow up those houses opposite, with the grey roofs. However, what does anything matter as long as the weather's fine and we have cold beef and radishes for dinner?'

At any rate, the place was not condemned; it might, with luck, prove pleasing. Time alone could tell. The first brief holiday was a success. Gerald had not time to be bored, and the family worked at high pressure to provide entertainment. Christmas was also spent at Fowey, with Coley and Geoffrey for companions; and, in spite of the fact that the chimney smoked abominably in the living-room, and the kitchen boiler threatened to crack, Gerald enjoyed himself as much as the others, pulling crackers, wearing paper caps, going for country walks, and playing absurd games in the evening with paper and pencil. It looked as though the holiday problem had been solved at last.

But, alas! the truimph of the family was short-lived. The following summer was a disastrous failure. The weather was bad – it rained as it can rain only in the West Country – the wrong people were invited to stay: little things jarred; fishing and boats began to pall; the atmosphere became sullen with strain and discontent; and everybody, including Gerald, was thankful when the holiday came to an end. That it was immediately followed by two failures at the St James's – one a dreary and rather unattractive play by Arnold Bennett called *The Return Journey*, and the other a pointless Hungarian translation, *The Play's the Thing*, which he produced against his better judgement – did little to brighten the outlook; and, though these happenings of misfortune could not be put down to the enervating Cornish air, one thing after the other had combined to put him against Fowey, and he took no further interest in the place. He would suffer a week or ten days, because his family adored it, but he never really enjoyed it after that first year. Instead, he clung with grim tenacity to his beloved Hampstead, where he had been born and bred and hoped to die. It was a great tragedy, but for that unfortunate summer of '28 he might have grown to love and appreciate the peace and beauty of that healing countryside. The lapping of the water, the crying of the gulls, the distant voices, and the little harbour sounds, might have cast their spell upon him, who in his boyhood had adored his Whitby. He might have sown seed for the future; he might have struck roots in the soil; but he turned his back upon the promised land and returned to the pavements where he held that he belonged. For him there was no place like Hampstead, for all his use of it as a background while he spent his days in London, and no house in the world like

Cannon Hall. He had no wish to travel beyond it, no desire to wander further afield. He found all the country that he wanted in the garden in summer.

Sunday was the great day of the week, when people came up to lunch and tennis, and Gerald was in his element from morning until evening chattering like a magpie as all his sisters had done before him, dressed in white flannels and an old cardigan, changing spectacles about a dozen times a day. With one pair on his forehead and another pair in his hands, and yet another in his pocket, he wandered about the house, before the guests arrived, shouting for Mo, the children, and the parlour-maid to find yet another indispensable pair. 'These aren't the right ones,' he grumbled, and then, while the household searched the building from floor to ceiling, he forgot what he was looking for; and, pottering about the drawing-room, he remembered the gramophone, which he would turn on much too loudly, the strains blaring forth to the next-door houses, and at the same time he would sit himself down at the piano and try to pick out the tune with groping one-handed chords.

By the time that a harassed maid had discovered the missing spectacles in the most obvious place – his desk in the library – he would be turning out the drawers of an enormous cabinet looking for some forgotten drawing of Papa's which he had suddenly decided it was imperative to find, while the gramophone record protested its finish with a jarring needle to his heedless ears.

In the meantime Daphne, who had been ready to go for a walk since half past eleven, shouted up from the hall that it was already twenty past twelve, and did he want to go? Then further minutes would be spent in choosing one of his numerous hats, selecting a stick from his rack of twelve, and deciding whether to wear another cardigan under his coat or go to the other extreme of not wearing a coat at all. These important questions settled, he would make the sudden decision that, instead of walking, they would go to the Zoo, as there was some rare bird he wanted to see; and it was not surprising that, with the change of plans, they would arrive home again at ten past one to find Mo struggling with half a dozen guests and the cocktails unmixed. Lunch would follow in a clamour of conversation, Gerald of course as ringleader, with Angela a good second, Mo, the supreme hostess, with an eye to right and left, while Daphne and Jeanne nudged each other under the table and remained dumb, like critical oysters.

Tennis was the order of the afternoon, and, except for a break for tea and a further influx of guests, continued from three until past seven, with Gerald playing in five sets out of eight. Restrained, but only just in time, from inviting later comers to stop on for supper, he would wave farewell to the last departing taxi from the courtyard at twenty to eight, and then, staggering up to the drawing-room, collapse into the nearest chair in an exhaustion comparable only to the winner of a thirty-mile Marathon.

Instead of going straight to bed, he would revive himself with whiskeys and sodas and become even more talkative at supper, alone with his family, than he had been during the babel at lunch. Sunday supper was the great time for discussions, for revelations, for pronouncements, for sudden questions; and, while Mo twiddled her hair and read a library book, and Jeanne dreamed at the piano, Gerald held forth over his port and cointreau in the dining-room to Angela and Daphne, sprawling on the club fender.

He had a rambling, very individual way of talking, as hard to follow as shorthand, switching from one subject to another without any apparent connexion, and expecting his listeners to supply the missing link.

His imagination was fertile and tortuous; he would

discuss the personalities of the people who had played tennis in the afternoon and make wild suggestions about their private lives.

'Curious creature, x,' he would say. 'I don't trust those eyes, set so close in the head. Brown eyes too. Never trust a brown-eyed man or woman. I should say she's decidedly tricky. Jealous as a tigress. Did you see the way she looked at Y across the table at lunch? I give them a year, no longer. Y is a decent fellow, but don't tell me he was ever in love with her. I should say he's as weak as butter, though. Somebody's only got to come along with a come-hither look in her eyes and he'll be for it. Off the deep end. I thought he rather fell for old z as it was. Now, she's a good sort; can't think why she doesn't marry and have eight sons. She's the marrying sort. Not everyone's money, though, you know – shocking legs, and possibly bad breath; one never knows – but a sterling good sort. Now Q I find very attractive, don't you? No? Funny, I should say she was your type. A lonely mug. Profile off a coin and good eyes, and probably a temper like Hades. I wonder what goes on at the back of her mind? She must join the lunch club. I don't know what you think, but I've come to the conclusion that U is developing into a God-forsaken bore. Pompous too. Talked a lot of un-mitigated rubbish. Frightful old snob. Only bothers about one when one is playing in a success. Wonder if any of 'em would care a damn if one died tomorrow? They're tricky and they're funny when you have the ready money, but try 'em when you're stony broke. Jeanne's a funny child; what does she think about? I wonder if any of you will ever marry? I can't imagine anything more appalling than being a woman. Well, I wish you luck. How frightful if one had had to start all over again, married to somebody else! "Wait till you come to forty year," Papa said. "Now seems it more than ever rich to die, to cease upon the midnight with no pain." It's not much fun when you're fifty. Old Gladys is a funny thing. One can never really get anything out of her. I wonder if she's happy? Who is that fellow you went out with last night, Jill? Are you fond of him? What do you talk about? I don't understand my children. Trixie and Sylvia didn't go out with young men at your age. Are they familiar with you? Ah, well, *ce n'est pas mon affaire.* I found a miniature of Papa this morning. There was no difference between it and you, Daph. Why can't you write me a play instead of scribbling short stories that will never pass the censor? I wish I was your brother instead of your father; we'd have such fun. Did I ever tell you about that time I went to Spain? There's a story for you if you like. Get me another cointreau, one of you. . . .' He rambled on, stray memories trickling from his congested mind – now an adventure, now an indiscretion, now an idea for a play, now the confidence of a friend, now the intricate conversation held over lunch during the past week, now an anecdote of Whitby days. And then suddenly, for no reason, after a great burst of laughter because of a practical joke played on someone at the theatre the night before, which he told with tears running down his cheeks, he would wipe his eyes, sigh despondently, and, with the laughter scarcely controlled, murmur, 'Oh dear, I'm so unhappy.'

The clock struck ten. There would be a thump on the floor above from Mo, and the parlourmaid, who had made several abortive attempts to enter the room to clear away, would rattle the door handle in a suggestive manner.

'We'd better go upstairs,' Gerald would say, finishing his drink; and, his mood changing once more as he wandered into the drawing-room, he would play his favourite tunes on the gramophone and, with energy renewed, give an imitation of Viola dancing at a restaurant, a cushion for his partner, while the manuscript of a play he had promised to read for some unfortunate author lay crumpled on the floor under a panting Pekinese.

The next morning he would complain of being so tired and stiff that he was unable to move, and he would fall in with Mo's suggestion that the following week-end should be spent quietly, reading and resting in the hammock in the garden; but by Wednesday or Thursday he had forgotten all his resolutions, and, while Sybil thumbed the telephone directory in a feverish search for addresses, he wandered about in pyjamas, half shaved and very vague, finally calling from the bathroom, 'Let's have the So-and-So's up next Sunday, and try old Stick-in-the-Mud and his girl for a fourth, and then perhaps one other man . . .'

And so it continued, week after week, the little ritual of his Sundays, and, like all children with new toys and all women with new dresses, he would take sudden fancies and sudden dislikes. The same face would appear for three or four weeks in succession – would be seen, to put it bluntly, just twice too often; while another, inoffensive to all intents and purposes, would be dropped for at least six months and not resurrected until a dearth of players brought the name before his notice again for further trial.

But, whoever came, whether failures or successes, bores or comics, old or new faces, he would enjoy his day. From the first peal of the front door bell to the last hoot of the departing taxi he flung himself with abandon into his own special relaxation; laughing, talking, arguing, playing, he fulfilled that instinct which was strongest in him, which endeared him to his friends, and to which, after all, he had devoted a not inglorious lifetime – the art of entertaining.

CHAPTER TWELVE

THE long run of *Interference* was followed by a mild
success which, if it did not draw all London, at least kept
the theatre open for a few months, chiefly because one
of the leading ladies was Gracie Fields.

This importation was another of Gerald's 'stunts', but
the fact of the matter was that it did not quite come off.
Poor Gracie Fields, it was not fair to take her out of her
element and expect her to act everyone off the stage, but
she had humour enough and common sense enough to
carry on during the run, and her generosity and high
spirits made her the most popular member of the company.

Gerald, of course, adored having her in the theatre.
He took her out to lunch and gave her presents, as he
did to all the women who acted with him, and at first
she could not make him out at all. She was not at all sure
that she approved of him, which was a great source of
gratification to the sadistic Gerald. He started off by
playing one of his practical jokes, and, buying a fake
diamond ring for ten and sixpence, he wrapped it up in
a box from Cartier's and threw it on to Gracie Field's
lap in his careless off-hand manner.

'Wear it for me,' he said; 'it only cost seven hundred
pounds.'

The poor girl blushed with anger and outraged pride
and handed it back.

'How dare you give me that?' she said. Gerald, in an
ecstasy of secret delight, warmed to his part, and could
scarcely restrain himself from twirling an imaginary
moustache like the villains of melodrama.

'Come on,' he said roughly, 'don't be a silly little fool.'

Furious at his insulting manner and his dark insinuations, Gracie Fields walked up to him and gave him a ringing slap on the face. Gerald burst into a shout of laughter, and explained to the bewildered Gracie that he was only trying out one of his peculiar forms of humour, that the ring cost ten and sixpence, that hers was the easiest leg to pull of any woman he had ever met, and when was she coming up to Cannon Hall to meet the family?

Gracie gave one ringing mill-hand laugh, relapsed into broad Rochdale tongue, and they were life-long friends from that moment.

Gerald certainly squeezed every ounce of satisfaction out of his practical jokes, but not every woman would have forgiven him for this one as freely as Gracie did; and with certain 'victims' it might have proved disastrous. One or two women would find a ten-and-sixpenny ring the reverse of a compliment!

Gerald was getting fed up with the St James's Theatre, and Tommy Vaughan was dead, and it looked as though he were in for a run of bad luck. Then Audry Carten, the girl who had made such a big success in *The Dancers*, and with it had taken such a dislike to the stage that she left it, wrote, with her sister, a play called *Fame*, and gave it to Gerald to read.

He thought a great deal of it, and decided to produce it. It was an unequal play, at times very good and at times very bad, and showed too obviously that two people had worked in collaboration. It did not hang together. It was as though one sister had said, 'Let's do a play about the hunting crowd,' and the other replied, 'No, let's do a dreary play about Pegwell Bay in the rain,' and they both said, 'Well, anyway, let's do a play for Gerald and see what happens.' The result was a mixture of farce and tragedy, exaggeration and realism, none of it properly knit together but possessing at any rate excellent dialogue, a capacity to hold the audience, and giving Gerald a longer and more interesting part than he had acted for years.

For the first two acts he had nothing to do except to look like a musician who can think of nothing but his violin and be abnormally sensitive at the same time. But in Act 3, at the seaside lodging-house, when paralysis has robbed him of his fame and turned him into an irritable, miserable, and appallingly selfish invalid, with nothing left but an artistic temperament at its worst, he gave what was certainly one of the best performances of his career. It was an unattractive part, and could never be a popular success, therefore he received little credit for it. There was none of the charm in Paolo Gheradi that there had been in Harry Dearth; he was bitter all through, and clamoured to be disliked, and the Carten sisters had remained sincere in their determination that public taste should not be pandered to by permitting him one glimmer of light, one suggestion of softness. Artistically they were right, but from the point of view of the box-office they had made a mistake. The public could say what they liked about 'du Maurier always being the same'; they would not allow him to be anything else. That wretched invalid in the third act of *Fame* was a piece of acting that was memorable and beyond praise, but the audience did not appreciate it. Perhaps they might have forgiven him had he lit a cigarette and kissed his wife, followed by a slap on the face in true du Maurier style, as the curtain fell; but he did none of these things, and the play ran for only a few months. It served at any rate as a gesture of farewell to the St James's Theatre. The year was 1929, and the position was critical. Gerald had no theatre and no play, and at fifty-six he was thoroughly weary of his profession.

In the old pre-war days an actor-manager of his standing and his years would have retired in peace and contentment to a property in the country, with a bank balance large enough to keep him in comfort to the end of his days. Gerald could never afford to do so. He had made no attempt to save money, and the small fortunes of *Bulldog, The Dancers,* and other big successes had been scattered on the holidays abroad, on cars, on keeping up two houses, on giving presents, on entertaining, and on charity.

He lived extravagantly. He had no idea of economizing, and, like everyone else who lives over and above his income, he suddenly discovered that he owed vast arrears to that hungry consumer of capital, the Inland Revenue.

This menace became the darkest cloud on his horizon; it was like a beast from the jungle, a sort of Kong that must be fed at intervals to be kept at bay. It looked as though Gerald must continue to act, not to keep house and home together, but to satisfy those gaping jaws that waited, ready to snap. The theatre, too, was passing through a lean period, and the talkies were in the first flush of success. Cinema houses like the Empire, the Plaza, and the Tivoli were packed every hour of the day, while the theatres were half empty. A play that would have had a fair chance of success a few years back failed now to draw at all, and screen stars from Hollywood bathed in the glamour that had once invested English actors and actresses. The new talkies had seized the public fancy, developing into as great a craze, and with the same popular appeal, as the dancing boom of the immediate post-war years.

It was *démodé* to go to the theatre and it was fashionable to wander into the Empire or the Plaza between dinner and supper and listen to American wise-cracks, leaving two or three hours later with a theme-song on the lips and a variety of expressions of the 'And how!' and

'Sez you!' brand. That three and sixpence bought a comfortable chair, the right to smoke, and a programme packed with incident, weighed heavily in the balance with the twelve-and-sixpenny stall, the boiled shirt, and the long intervals that awaited the audience in the legitimate theatre.

The screen could show both Africa and the North Pole within the space of a few minutes, whereas the theatre could only offer false walls and a painted backcloth. The screen could skip generations and continents without losing conviction, which the stage, for all its revolving platforms and tricks of lighting, never quite succeeded in doing.

This sudden overwhelming invasion of the talkies found the London theatre unprepared, and Gerald, like everyone else, was unable to cope with the situation. Like others of his calling, he might have gone off to Hollywood and started life all over again, with a villa in Beverly Hills and a swelling bank balance, but he had long ago taken one of his famous oaths about America, and not even the shrillest demands from the Inland Revenue would have persuaded him to cross the ocean. Besides, he was tired; his energy and his restlessness were beginning to foresake him at last; the monotony of making up his face and saying the same line night after night began to strike him as another form of hell. He had said all he wanted to say, done all he wanted to do. Acting any sort of part, whether good or bad, was a thankless task and a weary grind. Even producing had lost all interest for him. Gladys, the courageous, who had married again and was going to have a baby, came to the rescue with the offer of the Playhouse Theatre, and Gerald took it over in September as a stop-gap and presented a half-hearted revival of *Dear Brutus*. It was a poor affair compared with the original play of twelve years before; everyone was miscast, and Gerald seemed to make no effort with the production. The magic had gone; the enchanted wood was nothing but a group of painted trees; the characters drifted on and off the stage as though it was an easy though rather boring way of passing the regulation two and a half hours, and Gerald himself was a lost and rather puzzled Harry Dearth who looked as though he might turn to the audience any moment and say, 'It's no good. I don't feel it any more. I've forgotten what it was all about. Harry Dearth isn't here; he disappeared for ever in the real wood in 1917. Go back to Wyndham's in the middle of the night, when the watchman's dozing in his chair and the boards are creaking; you'll find Dearth there with little Lob and the rest. . . . But he's not here.'

What remained of *Dear Brutus* was given a decent burial after a hundred and eight performances, which was just about a hundred too many for an admirer of Barrie. At Christmas, Gerald took a really big jump into the past and appeared in his original parts of Mr Darling and Captain Hook in *Peter Pan*. It was meant to be great fun, and it was fun up to a point, but you can't really enjoy leaping about the stage with a toy sword and a wig when you are fifty-six as you did when you were thirty; you can give almost as good and as spontaneous a performance, but it plays the devil with your back, your voice, and your temper the next morning. Secretly, too, you had an uneasy feeling that it was all rather undignified, like impromptu charades after three glasses of port, and that to appreciate *Peter Pan* you should have left something of your mind for ever in the nursery. There are two schools of thought about Peter – the school who rock in silent ecstasy throughout the nine long scenes, and the school who consider it the most unmitigated rot that pen ever put to paper. If Gerald did not venture to either extreme, at least he had outgrown his early enthusiasm. He found shouting his lungs out to excitable schoolchildren neither very restful nor particularly amusing The scenery was shoddy, the props were ready to fall to pieces, the clothes were threadbare with age, and, while the whole play clamoured to be pulled together and produced properly all over again, acted by children with a boy playing Peter, it was not his business to suggest it, and anyway he had not the energy. Fifteen years ago perhaps; ten years; six years ... but not now. It was all too late, all too tiring, and, if you came to think of it, not worth while. To what end, anyway? Why cope? Why struggle? No, with a voice hoarse from shouting, with a back that ached, with the pain that he called 'Mummie's pain' worrying his inside, with the income tax knocking at the door, with no play in prospect, it was not much fun being fifty-six.

And yet he continued day after day, because, after all, it was expected of him, and there was a certain duty to be performed to his profession and his self-respect. But often he could not help wondering what it was all about. Success is not always joyous; popularity palls and becomes a test of endurance; responsibilities accumulate; professional ties are binding and develop into duties, and friends can be too clinging. Even with a home one adores and a wife one worships, sometimes there is a loneliness in the blood: a need for that first happiness and quiet content, a desire to hear Trixie shake with laughter and talk twenty to the dozen, to watch Sylvia's profile and her smile, to argue furiously with May, to kiss Mummie and amuse Papa, and above all to look up and see brother Guy come into the room with a twinkle in his eye – 'Well, young 'un, what is it?'

But they were all gone and had left him alone. And, although he believed neither in God nor in man, he did his best for their sake, because of Papa, because of Guy; helping poor mugs down on their luck, and working for his profession; keeping certain standards and certain ideals as a tribute to them, so that in some odd way he should not have lived entirely in vain. And, lighting a cigarette, he would shout for Buckley, his dresser, to fetch him his coat and his hat, and to pour him out a last whiskey and soda, thinking, as he swallowed it down, that to pull a poor mouth about life was the one unforgivable crime, and that at all costs a sense of humour must be preserved, and so out of the dressing-room and along the passage, swinging his stick and humming a song, feeling in his pocket for the usual half-crown to give the fellow who loitered with such expectancy outside the public-house at the corner.

'Home, Allen,' he would say to the waiting chauffeur, and would climb into the car, waving his hand to the small group of fans who had collected in self-conscious excitement to watch his departure.

He wondered how much he had changed in mind and body since those old days at the Garrick and the Haymarket, when, dashing into his clothes after the performance, he had gone round to the Green Room and played cards until three or four in the morning. It seemed an almighty long time ago. What an idle, excitable young fool he had been, completely lacking in every sort of sense. A proper waster if it had not been for Guy, and an unscrupulous blackguard if it had not been for Mo. What would he have been like if he had never married? He supposed he would have drunk himself to death long ago. Or committed suicide. Or been in jail. Funny that the girls did not marry. He did not understand them. They were growing up like strangers. Perhaps it was inevitable. Generations were always poles apart. Probably Papa and Mummie had felt the same about him. He wished he could see into their minds. He wished the children would come up to him and say, 'Look here, such-and-such a thing has happened. What am I going to do about it?' But they never did. They led their own lives. Where did Angela go when she went out in the evenings? Why was Daphne always going to stay in Paris? Whom did Jeanne have interminable conversations with on the telephone? They were not the companions they might have been. Perhaps it was his fault; perhaps it was theirs. It was all very disappointing. He wished they were children again, playing cricket on the lawn. What were they doing now, this minute? He had a furious desire to know. Supposing they were like himself at the same age? It was unthinkable. Thank God he had not got a son. Mo sometimes said, after an argument with Angela and anxiety about Daphne, who had not come home until three in the morning, that perhaps boys would have been easier. He did not know. He washed his hands of them. All he knew was that his sisters had not stayed out to all hours of the night. How happy were they in their lives, though? How little one knew about one's family. How little one knew about anyone. How little, deep down, one really knew about oneself. He wished he knew more about birds. He wished he knew what went on at the back of a bird's mind. Did they only think of food and sleep, or did they get fond of each other? Of course, that was the only thing that mattered really. The whole meaning of life boiled down to one thing: affection; being fond of one another. Men and women. Not necessarily being physical, but being companions, swinging hands, yawning in company, eating side by side, saying, as one picked one's teeth or scratched one's head, 'A funny thing happened this morning driving the car'; little intimacies, little conversations, humming a tune; not talking; eating cold beef and cos lettuce.

If one could do that in life one had not done so badly. If one could do that, living was worth while.

The car swung into the courtyard and drew up before the fountain. Home.

In the June of 1930, Gladys and Gerald, remembering the enormous success of their last venture, *Cheyney*, joined forces once more and acted together at the Playhouse. The play was *Cynara*, by H. C. Harwood and Gore Browne, and with the competition of the talkies on every hand the authors had borrowed something of the cinema's technique. The play was chopped up into several scenes for variety, one or two of which, if amusing, were superfluous, and it was obvious that the play had been adapted from a novel. It was a good story of the type that is known as 'strong', and, once really under way, moved swiftly to a crisis which was both tense and surprising. Gerald's part provoked discussion. He was a barrister who allows himself to be led into an affair with a shop-girl while his wife is away on holiday, and, tiring of it, is threatened with notoriety when the girl commits suicide. The character was held to be unsympathetic. It was a difficult and not very satisfactory part, and there was something rather unconvincing about a man like Jim Warlock's being led astray from a wife like Gladys, whose part was an entirely sympathetic if rather secondary one, for all the gentle and timorous appeal of the shop-girl, beautifully played by Celia Johnson. However, Gerald did as much with Jim Warlock as it was humanly possible for him to do, and, banishing the lethargy that had overtaken him with *Dear Brutus*, he took infinite pains with the cast and the production. He was careful to give the best of himself and to do nothing second-rate when Gladys was about. In spite of what the critics call a mixed reception, the play was a success – not the glorious riot that *The Last of Mrs Cheyney* had been, but a good honest seven months' sitter. It was the combination of Gladys and Gerald that drew the audiences, with the added interest of Celia Johnson as another example of Gerald's flair for young talent.

Before the production of *Cynara*, Gerald had been busy

making his first talkie. According to a newspaper correspondent, Galsworthy's *Escape* was to 'represent the biggest effort yet made to establish British prestige at home and abroad.' With Basil Dean as director, and Gerald, Edna Best, Madeleine Carroll, Lewis Casson, and others in the cast, and the whole of Dartmoor as a background, it certainly sounded a great undertaking on paper. Everybody was very enthusiastic, and there was much talk of 'beating the Yanks at their own game'. But making films is a heart-breaking business even in the most up-to-date studio, worked with every conceivable gadget; and when a scene, consisting of two lines and a movement to a door, has been played for the fortieth time, and is still not right, and it's hours over time and you've a headache like a load of bricks and an empty stomach, there was nothing, according to Gerald, which bore a greater similarity to unadulterated hell.

The actual shots on Dartmoor were not so bad; if the day was fine, Gerald sat about on boulders and squinted at birds through field-glasses while Dean shouted himself hoarse at cameramen, and Mo, who had come down to keep Gerald company, brought her knitting and a book and a stick in case of snakes.

Then, after hours of waiting for a cloud to pass, a scene would be 'shot'. And Gerald, as the wretched fugitive from prison, had to scramble about ditches and climb over walls, panting for breath and feeling almost as exhausted as if he were a genuine convict, only to discover, when he had played his scene, that it would have to be taken all over again. He had thought that playing the same part for eight performances a week in the theatre was tiring and monotonous enough, but it was a paradise of ease compared to this.

It didn't help matters either to be reminded that every penny he was going to make personally would have to be paid over to the Inland Revenue. However, with a tankard of beer in his hand, cracking jokes with the cameramen in the pub at Tavistock, no one would have thought him other than the most carefree and light-hearted of men, enjoying every moment of his excursion into the new talkie world.

Escape turned out to be a moderate success, with Gerald giving a convincing and moving performance as Galsworthy's hero, but it did not take the film world by storm any more than did other English pictures of the same vintage. Gerald himself did not know what to make of the whole business. He knew that the industry was still in its infancy, in England at any rate, and he suspected that nobody in the country had really the faintest idea how to handle it. It was easy to talk, so easy to walk on to a set and shout through a megaphone. But it was not so easy to get everyone working in harmony, and deliver a picture that was both technically and artistically perfect, and, what was more important still, a success from the point of view of the box-office.

Had he been ten years younger he might have done something about it. He might have brought all his talents to bear upon this new branch of entertainment, and, with his producing experience tucked away at the back of his mind, have allowed himself to forget all that was immaterial to the production of pictures and settle down to learn this new job from the beginning. The stories were there; the opportunities were there; the American and German experts were there, if you cared to pay for them; the actors and actresses were there; the whole English countryside and the whole of English literature were there to pick and choose from. It only required someone with courage, imagination, and sufficient driving-force and the machine would be set in motion, the adventure of a lifetime would begin. If it had been 1920 instead of 1930!

And yet – and yet – perhaps even then it would have

been too late; perhaps even then the clamour and confusion, the vulgarity and greed, the grasping mercenary outlook, the double-faced backhanded methods that made the film industry nothing more nor less than the lowest form of gamble, would have proved too strong for the determined and the brave.

When you are approaching sixty, unless you have led the life of an ascetic, or possess a tremendous faith in yourself and your achievements, you have neither the force nor the inclination to set out on a crusade. The days of battling are over, and you want to sit back and have things made easy for you. Younger people must carry banners and storm cities.

Gerald felt this way about the film racket. He had served his profession for over thirty-five years to the best of his ability, and it seemed to him that he could do no more. He did not want to conquer this new world. It was up to somebody else. Besides, he had lost his old initiative and had not much belief in himself. His day was over. People flattered him or lied when they said he had only to go out to Hollywood to create the sensation of a lifetime. He knew better. He had done all that he would ever do. He had played his little part. He had had his say. There was nothing more degrading than the popular favourite who clings to his pedestal, and with anxious eyes watches the faces of his friends. Thank God he had the sense to know when his time had come. A few more years, and then oblivion. But in the meantime he had to live. Even the delectable cold beef and radishes had to come from somewhere, and Cannon Hall wasn't a two-roomed flat. One must pay for one's comforts. One must swallow one's pride and stand about all day with yellow make-up on one's face, playing small parts that didn't matter; being knocked into by electricians and carpenters, while raucous-voiced fellows in shirt-sleeves wiped their mouths on the backs of their hands, and, amidst a babel of sound where every language and every accent but English was spoken, lifted up their voices and yelled, 'Qui-et there, please. Are you ready? Start yer motors.'

The constant glare of yellow lights, the whine of machinery, the arid, lifeless atmosphere, the attentions of the 'make-up' man with his perpetual powder-puff and clothes-brush, the microscopic, impersonal stare of the continuity writer, the good-humoured – though, after a time, a little wearisome – familiarity of the cameramen, the laboured and somewhat insincere politeness of the foreign director who was never really very sure of one's name and murmured something about Sir George or Sir de Mure, the interminable hanging about, standing, sitting, hanging about ... it all combined to fray Gerald's nerves.

On the set at nine, ready with make-up, and then not wanted until half past three. One shot, perhaps a failure, and then sent home again, and a whole day wasted. Or twenty and thirty re-takes of a slow walk across the room, until from very weariness one prayed that one might die. And smiling all the time, saying, 'Yes, of course it doesn't matter at all; I'm in no hurry,' because long ago one had taken an oath never under any circumstances, on any stage, to lose one's temper, and what held for the theatre held for the films. It was perhaps, after all, a form of retribution for one's selfishness, one's cruelty, one's little careless sins. It was the cadet corps at Bushey in a new guise, but without the jovial *camaraderie*, and the feeling that one was doing something for one's country, that had made even the grimmest day at Bushey worth the while. It was a lesson to what shreds of self-conceit one might possess, and a profound and steady hammering to one's pride.

The first experience of *Escape* was like a picnic compared to the later films, where there was not the fresh air of Dartmoor to relieve one temporarily from the atmosphere of chaos and monotony which was calculated to drive even the most patient of men to a state bordering upon insanity.

In 1931, however, Gerald had only done the Galsworthy picture, in which he played the leading part. He had not entered the final phase when, with a shrug of the shoulder and a philosophical whistle, he allowed himself to become the bearded doctor in *I Was a Spy* and the obsequious valet in *Catherine the Great*.

To return to the theatre: *Cynara* gave way in February to a revival of *The Pelican*, a play by Harwood which had been a great success at the Ambassadors six years before. Its short run now was another proof that revivals seldom pay. Gerald stood in the background and played a very small part.

Gladys then went off on a holiday and left Gerald to produce a play on his own, *The Church Mouse*, which also turned out to be a disappointment.

The summer and autumn loomed ahead, and the outlook was not a particularly cheerful one. Gerald could not afford to be idle, but he had no play in mind. Something had got to be done. The old successful days at Wyndham's seemed very long ago, with Tom Vaughan sitting in a corner of the dressing-room sipping his whiskey and soda, and announcing in his solid, confident voice that there wasn't a seat bookable in the house for six months, and that the new play was in for a year's run. It was no use sighing and regretting the days that had gone for ever; the present clamoured for security, and the future was a menace. Advice, of course, was cheap. Go to America. Go to New York. Go to Australia and South Africa. There was heaps of money to be made. You only had to get on the boat. It was so easy to talk, so easy to conjure up ideas of the income tax paid off at last, of a bank balance that could be looked at without shuddering, of a triumphant return to England with pockets full of banknotes and hysterical press-cuttings.

But, when he really got down to it, the picture was not quite so brilliant. Like all the big undertakings in life, it required confidence and energy, and he wasn't sure if he had either any more. The very thought of setting out on a long journey, from which one might not return for two years; of travelling, of continually meeting new people, of being entertained by governors and viceroys, of staying in hotels, railway carriages, ships ... no, he was too old, too tired; he simply could not cope. England one might manage; after all, one had toured the provinces with Tree and Forbes-Robertson so often in the past, they would be familiar ground. So there was an idea. And Gladys had done it a few years ago and made a packet of money. It was true that Gladys had a courage and a determination that was hard to equal and impossible to defeat, whereas he was never certain, never sure; but, even so, he might get away with it with a slice of luck.

If only Frank Curzon had been behind him, and Tommy Vaughan at his side! The trouble was to find a play, and a new one, to give the provincial audiences. Films had rather spoilt the market, for one thing; there were big cinemas in every town, and almost every old play had been adapted and turned into a film story which was old history by now. There were no new plays – nothing, at least, that was worth producing, and certainly nothing that was worth risking for the first time. It looked as though he would have to take an old play that was a proved success. *Bulldog* had been done to death in the provinces; besides, it had been made into a film. *Dear Brutus* – no, not again so soon; and anyway it was not suitable. *Diplomacy* might suit, and he owned the rights, but apparently a tour of it had been done not long ago. Wherever he looked it seemed as though the plays had been done before. What about *The Ware Case*? It was a rattling good play, had not dated, and would always bear revival. Nor had it been on tour – or, at least, not for many years. The more he thought about it the more he liked the idea of *The Ware Case*, and finally it was decided upon.

A four-months tour of the provinces was arranged, the cast was engaged, and, in August, Gerald, accompanied by Mo, drove off to Southsea to appear before a provincial audience for the first time for thirty years.

There was something rather strange about arriving in his own car and staying at the best hotel, with reporters waiting for him at the theatre door and his name in huge letters above the entrance, when once he had herded with six or seven others in a third-class carriage, and shared dingy lodgings in a back-street, had bacon and eggs for supper and sung 'Frosty Weather' amid shrieks of delight. It had been very pleasant living without responsibilities. Whether this tour was a success or not, at least he had made up his mind to one thing, and that was that he would make some money for charity. Besides being President of the Actors' Orphanage and of Denville Hall, a home for aged actors and actresses, he had this year been elected President of the Actors' Benevolent Fund, and he was determined to work hard for it in his first year. Shy and diffident about his own financial affairs, and utterly incapable of striking a bargain for himself, Gerald would go to any lengths to raise money for his charities, and during the tour of *The Ware Case* he set himself the huge task of raising a thousand pounds for the Actors' Benevolent Fund. Originally starting as a bet, and by saying half jokingly, 'I know it can be done,' this task developed into the most serious and vital object of the tour, and the success of *The Ware Case* became a minor affair. It was characteristic of his whole life that the tour, as a tour, was not the brilliant triumph that everybody but Gerald himself had anticipated. The play had dated slightly, and it had been seen before; and the box-office returns were disappointing even if the reception was enthusiastic. But the Actors' Benevolent Fund over-topped its thousand pounds by a large margin.

Gerald deliberately made his task more difficult, and more exciting, by wagering that he would raise over a hundred pounds in each individual town, and he did not fail. It spoke well for the generous sporting spirit of the provincial audiences, whom he took into his confidence, that they never let him down; and it became a matter of honour for Nottingham to beat Birmingham, and Leicester to beat Leeds. After the curtain had fallen on each performance, Gerald would come in front and make a personal appeal, which would be received with good-natured cheers and promises to respond. He asked those who had not, until the last act, discovered the murderer in *The Ware Case*, to put a sum of money in the box towards his thousand pounds, or, better still, to send him a cheque. Although tired after playing the exhausting part of Hubert Ware all the evening, he gave his audience another little performance on his own, and made up as Henry Irving, the founder of the Actors' Benevolent Fund, speaking to them with his voice and his mannerisms as he remembered them over forty years ago. As a guest to various Rotary Club luncheons he made speeches on behalf of his charity, and, mixing up his appeal very cleverly with some reminiscences and anecdotes, he would relieve the members of their pocket-money in the space of a few minutes.

Nobody escaped from his eagle eye, from the Mayor of the city to the smallest schoolboy in the pit on matinée days, and in all the fourteen weeks of the tour he met with no refusal from any member of the community.

It was a triumph for the Actors' Benevolent Fund and a really wonderful piece of work by its President. Gerald felt that for the first time for years he had accomplished something that was worth while, something which more than made up for the little disappointments and depressions of middle age.

After all, it showed a small mind and an ungrateful memory to grumble. He had enjoyed over thirty years in the profession which had brought him so much success and happiness, and the least he could do was to make some small gesture in return. What did it matter if *The Ware Case* had not turned out to be a big financial proposition? At least the company had enjoyed themselves, they had all had plenty to laugh about, there had been many excellent opportunities for practical joking, and Mo had looked after him in her own inimitable way.

They returned to London in time for Christmas, and celebrated, as usual, with holly and mistletoe, turkey and plum pudding, crackers and a conjurer. And Gerald, with a paper cap on his head and a whistle in his hand, talked at the top of his voice, hid half-sovereigns in his neighbours' mince pies, and looked as though he had never heard the word depression.

Edgar Wallace was writing a play for him. It was to be produced at Wyndham's. He was entering upon his sixtieth year, and damnation to all who stood in his way, and particularly the Inland Revenue!

The responsibility of *The Green Pack* lay upon his shoulders entirely, as Edgar was out in Hollywood, and the only means of communication was by cables or by long-distance telephone calls at a prohibitive cost.

Scenes had to be altered, and characters changed, and a new ending to the play worked out. Edgar had written it in his usual tearing hurry – twenty-four hours or something phenomenal – and, though it looked good on paper, it did not look quite so good at rehearsal. The play could not be produced as it stood; that was obvious. It would have to be turned upside down and pulled about like a jig-saw puzzle, which, with Edgar's cabled permission, Gerald proceeded to do. Actually it came to every member of the company walking about with pencils and pieces of paper, lips moving silently, foreheads creased in a frown, and every now and then one of them breaking into a cry: 'Look, what about this for an idea?' It was not the way the greatest plays of all time have been written, but, then, nobody was suggesting for a moment that *The Green Pack* was a great play. It was doubtful if it was even a moderately good play. The only thing Gerald and the company hoped to do was to make it into a good enough play to warrant full houses at Wyndham's Theatre for three or four months.

'Do what you like with the play,' Edgar had wired from Hollywood, 'and God love you, Gerald.' The message of faith and affection made Gerald more determined than ever to produce a success and to be able to repay Edgar for his trust and generosity. By a tremendous effort the play was pulled into shape and presented to the public on the 9th of February, but it was overshadowed on the opening night with the grave news that the author was dangerously ill in Hollywood with a sudden attack of double pneumonia. The following day the message came that Edgar Wallace was dead.

It was a terrible blow to all his friends and the world in general. It seemed unbelievable that the flame of his personality should be quenched at last, his great, generous heart be stilled, and his dynamic force and brilliant brain be silenced for evermore. That Edgar should die – Edgar, with his superhuman energy, his strength, his grip upon life; Edgar, who, sinister and serene, with his Napoleonic head, should have straddled the world when the rest of us lay dead. It was a shock to faith and an attack upon courage. It was one more argument in favour of futility. Not until Time had brought a light of reason and understanding to bear upon it did the mind accept with thankfulness that Providence or God Almighty had chosen both wisely and well. It is known now that Edgar would have been an invalid had he lived longer, without hope of recovery, and probably in pain. With the supreme good fortune that had favoured his meteoric path through life, he went out of his little world at the right moment, with a smile on his lips and without a gesture of farewell.

With heavy hearts and saddened spirits the company at Wyndham's continued the performance of *The Green Pack*. But with Edgar dead, it was a joyless undertaking, almost in the nature of a requiem, and neither actors nor audience could forget the tragedy of the author and lose themselves whole-heartedly in the story of the play. It did not possess the excitement of *The Ringer*, nor the grim realism of *On The Spot*, nor, yet again, the quick pace and vivid story that made *The Calendar* memorable. It was, and always had been, an indifferent play that all the artifices of production could not turn into a winner. It ran for nearly five months, however, which was not so poor in these days of short runs, and Gerald considered that, taking into account the tragic circumstances that had overshadowed it from the beginning, the play had done very well. It was like old times, too, being back at Wyndham's, with the original staff and his original dressing-room. It only needed Tommy Vaughan to wander in with his inevitable handshake and his genial, 'Well, Gerald, old man', to bring back the old days of ease, and enthusiasm, and security.

With the final night of *The Green Pack* it was a plunge once more into the unknown, a last farewell to Wyndham's, and another lone and weary search for the right play to produce at the right time.

For the first time, Gerald began to look a little older, a little weary, a little worn. He complained of not sleeping, of feeling eternally tired, of having 'Mummie's pain' under his heart. He was always going into chemists' shops and buying quack medicines with mysterious names. He wandered about with great medical volumes under his arm, profusely illustrated, which told him in a wealth of detail all the diseases from A to z. He was losing his eagerness, his curiosity about people and their ways of living; it was an effort to think clearly about things, to give an opinion, to make plans.

He spent much of his time pottering in the drawing-room and looking through old letters of Guy's, old sketches of Papa's. It was as though he wanted to soak himself in the past and shut away the present and the future.

Fewer people came to the Sunday lunches. He began to appreciate quiet days, sitting about, playing bridge with Angela and Jeanne. Daphne suddenly wrote from Fowey and said she was going to be married, and Gerald burst into tears, just as Kicky had done over Trixie, and said, 'It isn't fair,' like a little boy. At any rate, the fellow was a soldier, and Guy had been a soldier, so perhaps it was all for the best, he sighed, and she would settle down like the du Maurier girls in pictures that Papa had drawn – like Trixie, and Sylvia, and May; but oh! damn and blast! Why did one's daughters fall in love?

Getting married, bearing children, growing old ... things happened so swiftly in life, and the moments passed. He pondered on the why and wherefore of little things, and he never came to a definite understanding. He never learnt wisdom finally and for ever.

And here he was, the head of his profession, nearly sixty, and sick to death of acting; frittering away the days in doing nothing, in lunching with a pal, in having a yarn, in hanging about; wondering at the back of his mind why he was alive at all, and if there was any riddle to the universe after the long day was over. And, in spite of everything, he had to go on acting, because he could not afford to retire.

'Which do you prefer, Sir Gerald?' asked an anxious and hopeful reporter, his stub of pencil in his hand. 'Acting for the films or acting on the stage?' 'I prefer strolling down the street,' said Gerald, smothering a yawn. It was a typical reply, and must have astonished the young journalist, used to interviewing actors and actresses who declaimed about their Work with a capital letter. 'And your plans for the future?' continued the newspaper man in some trepidation, while Gerald solemnly wound up a clockwork animal and placed him on the floor. 'I'm going to read the most amazing play in the world which has not yet been written, by a man I don't know, and who doesn't exist,' Gerald answered. 'And,' he went on, 'if I accept it, I shall produce it in a theatre which has not yet been built.' The reporter thanked him for his information and went away wondering why Sir Gerald had ever been knighted – which sentiment serves as a reminder of one of Mo's classic remarks. When asked by one of the children suddenly out of the blue, 'Mummy, why was Daddy knighted?' she looked up from her knitting, pushed back her spectacles, thought solemnly for a few minutes, and then replied, 'I don't think we've ever quite known.'

Gerald was certainly not a satisfactory person to interview from a journalistic point of view. He never answered questions in the right way, and always wandered from the point; and, as he had never in his whole life 'truckled to the Press', as he called it, newspaper proprietors could hardly be blamed for disliking him. One or two unfortunate experiences had led Gerald into declaring a vendetta against the Press in general, and he was often deliberately rude. This was not a helpful factor in his public life, and he was obliged, especially in the last years, to fight a lone battle, without allies, against Time and depression in the theatre, a battle which a little tact and good will on either side might have made entirely unnecessary.

They thought Gerald snobbish and conceited when he was merely bored or not particularly interested, and he thought them rude and offensive when they were merely earning their daily bread. They could not believe that his dislike of publicity was genuine and not a pose, and he could not believe that their general attitude was critically honest and not deliberately malicious. Circumstances had combined to make the Press unpopular with Gerald and Gerald equally unpopular with the Press, and so the vendetta continued to the end. Meanwhile, in '32, Gerald was still looking for a play. Recent evidence had shown him that the public no longer came to see a play for the sake of one big name alone; they liked a combination and a variety of talent. *Cynara* had been a success because both he and Gladys had played in it together. Therefore as well as a play he must find a leading lady whom stalls and gallery and pit would pay to see. His choice fell upon a play by John van Druten called *Behold, We Live,* and he presented it in August at the St James's, with Gertrude Lawrence playing the part of the woman. It was a gloomy story, surely written under the stress of some emotion, and did not have much popular appeal, but it managed to survive through the autumn. At the same time Gerald and Gertrude Lawrence took part in a film, *Lord Camber's Ladies,* that was being directed at Elstree. His dislike of film-acting increased tenfold during this period, though no one would have believed it to look at him, with his pockets full of tricks and practical jokes that he let fly amongst the feet of cameramen, electricians, and directors in a sort of desperate effort to relieve the tedium. Practical joking during these months developed to a pitch of positive frenzy, until both theatre and studio resembled another Bedlam. The nervy, highly strung Gertie was a boon companion in mischief, and the round-faced Hitchcock a surprising ally down at Elstree. It was a wonder that the picture was ever completed at all, for hardly a moment would pass without some faked telegram arriving, some bogus message being delivered, some supposed telephone bell ringing, until the practical jokers were haggard and worn with their tremendous efforts, and had lived so long in an atmosphere of pretence that they had forgotten what it was like to be natural.

It was a game that could be carried too far, and, settling as it did into a daily routine, ceased before long to be genuinely amusing, and almost developed into a vice. It served, however, as a form of safety-valve, and prevented Gerald from dwelling too deeply on his future, which to his discerning eye appeared to be forbidding. Half-heartedly he would read plays, none of which seemed to him worth while producing, and he would turn them down with a shrug of his shoulder and 'I don't know; perhaps I've lost my sense of judgement, but it seems unholy muck to me.' And then, a few weeks later, he would hear that the play he had refused had been read and accepted by someone else; and it would be produced, and become a moderate or even a definite success.

This would not annoy him in the least. He would not grudge the success that might have been his. Instead, he would shrug his shoulders again and say, 'All right; I suppose I was wrong. Thank God I'm not acting in it all the same.'

In the spring he revived that hardy veteran, *Diplomacy*, and produced it at the Prince's Theatre. The public had not seen it since '24, when Gladys gave it ten months' run at the Adelphi, and now Gerald took some little trouble with the wording of the play itself, substituting certain modern expressions for some of the decidedly Victorian phrases. It was always an actor-proof play, and could be relied upon, like a dependable car, to run smoothly, despite its age, and tide over a difficult period. Gerald played his original part of Henry Beauclere, which had always suited him admirably, and made no great demand upon his strength or his powers of concentration, especially now that he had brought this particular type of acting to perfection; and, with his years of experience behind him, he could not fail to give an accomplished, polished, absolutely first-class performance.

It survived through the early summer, and, in August, Gerald and Mo went off to Wales for a holiday, finishing up at Fowey in September.

For the first time for many years Gerald appeared to enjoy his holiday, both at Port Merion and in Cornwall. He did not complain of boredom, he was not restless, and he did not hanker after London. He seemed happy pottering about, and reading, and laughing at everything and everybody; the weather was generally fine and he had none of his fits of depression. It seemed premature to talk, but was it possible that he was going to enjoy resting at last, and would be content to pass quiet holidays, lying about, playing bridge with the girls, sleeping in the sun? There had been a great agitation earlier in the summer to sell the house at Fowey and thereby cut down one of the expenses. Gerald's dislike of the place had been the chief argument in favour of the plan. And then, with the motion practically carried through and the paper signed, Gerald made one of his sudden decisions. 'Don't do it,' he said. 'I can't explain why, but I feel it would be a terrible mistake. It's a thing that might be regretted for a lifetime. Never do anything like that in a hurry.' And so the house was not sold, and in that month of September at any rate Gerald appeared to be content. Films claimed him once again in the autumn, much as he detested them, and the weary grind of early rising and being ready made up at the studio at an impossible hour in the morning, only to find he was not wanted for some hours, became once more the order of the day.

By this time he was resigned, more or less, to the confusion and the delay that is apparently a necessary feature to the making of pictures. He did not expect anything else. It was all part of the show. Even if he loathed every poisonous moment, it was something that had to be endured; it was not his concern; he was only a unit out of a thousand other units; he was not even playing a leading part. He did it because he could not at the moment bring himself to consider any other means of making money; it was one stop-gap after another, one more straw floating on the surface of the water.

He persisted in being vague about his plans. When urged to consider the future, he began to talk about birds, or a new trick from Hamley's, or somebody he had been lunching with the day before. 'I can't be bothered with the income tax, Billy dear,' he said when a distraught Sybil presented him with buff-coloured forms; 'they're probably quite decent fellows. Write and tell them I haven't any money. Look, there's a starling outside my window, behaving in the most curious way.' And he would put on one of his enormous pairs of glasses and lean out of his window to make an inspection.

At one moment there would be suggestions of a big tour in the Dominions; at another, tentative plans would be discussed as to the production of a new film, engagements in London, engagements in South Africa, contracts to appear in a stated number of pictures; but none of these ideas came to maturity.

Gerald would not make up his mind, he would not come to an agreement; it was as though something whispered in his heart and behind his brain that these things were to no purpose. He was like one who, glancing at his watch and smoking a last cigarette, stands on the brink of an adventure, marking time ...

CHAPTER THIRTEEN

GERALD leant out of his bedroom window and looked out across the garden. It was hushed and still, and no distant hum of traffic broke in upon the silence as a reminder that the city lay below; only the warm glow of a million lights was reflected in the sky from the great heart of London that glittered like a jewel. It was a view of which he had never tired, which had stirred him in his happy moments and been a comfort to him in the lonely hours. It was here he had taken his oaths, sworn vengeance and forgiveness, come to his decisions; here that he dared projects, meditated upon friendship, laid bare his heart, entered into communion with the dead.

It was his meeting-ground, his place of refuge, his confessional. Here his little superstitions held their tryst; here he would stand at midnight with Mo at his side, listening to the last moments of the Old Year, waiting for the first chimes of Christ Church bells to ring in the New. Peace could be found here, high above the city, far from the petty turmoil of the day. There was no need to pretend, no necessity to play a part; he could be honest with himself and speak the truth.

This was much the same view that, over sixty years ago, Papa and Mummie had looked down upon from their window in Church Row; but their eyes had not seen as far, their range was limited, and the lights were not so bright nor yet so many. They had been contented with obscurity; they had not ventured far, and had dreamed dreams amongst the firelight and the shadows.

Guy had seen this view as a boy; with his chin cupped

in his hands he looked beyond the lights, beyond the murky chimney-pots and roofs, to the unseen spaces and the distant hills. Trixie and Sylvia, as little girls in striped petticoats, pressed their noses against the window-pane and made problematical guesses about the future, Trixie with a gay infectious laugh and an imperious toss of her head, Sylvia more solemn, more uncertain, her arms already cradling a doll. May would have been too young to join in their play; and had she been old enough she might have found the lights of London not altogether to her liking, too suggestive of people and of parties; and, with a child's quick powers of fantasy, have turned them into the lights of a frigate, with herself as midshipman left in sole command. Only Gerald, who had not been born, was to watch those lights with longing and frustration, with satisfaction and content, with a strange intermingling of many emotions because they would represent for him his earth, his little world, his kingdom.

He stood at the window now and looked down upon them, remembering the many times that they had beckoned to him and he had followed, called to him and he had not gone. They stood for success and for disillusion, for pleasure and for pain, for a life that had been uneven in promise, rich in experience, courageous sometimes and cowardly too; lights which for all the shadows and the dark moments shone with a little glamour of its own. The bitterness and the depression had been birds of passage, frail and temporary things, and now they hid their faces as though they were ashamed, and gave way to memories that would endure for ever, moments of beauty, of friendliness, of fun.

These would remain when the others had departed; they would be the last colours he would nail to his mast as a triumphant signal that he had not been defeated. They would blow in the air like tattered and rather gallant banners, to fortify his family and his friends, to whom, in his secretly shy and inarticulate way, he could leave no other message.

He wished he had been less difficult this last year, had shown greater forbearance, and possessed more patience, had been kinder to people. The spoken word and the lost opportunity – those were two of the things that Barrie said never came again in a lifetime. *Dear Brutus* and the second chance. Had he his life over again, would he have chosen differently, done other things, walked stranger paths, loved different people, sung other songs?

He did not believe so. In the clearness of his mind and in the truth of his heart he knew that he would live as he had lived before. He was thankful for his blessings, for his good fortune, for the laughter and the tears. It had been an adventure, and he regretted nothing. It was over now, and he was tired, immeasurably tired. People were kind, but they did not understand. And he could not explain. Sometimes words were hard to put together especially these words, and he was afraid to wound. He had tried to tell Mo the other day, and she had looked at him with frightened eyes and he had not continued. He had always been curious about death and, now that he believed it near, it was astonishing how calm he felt, how indifferent, how lacking in interest. He had so passionately minded the deaths of other people, and now he was unmoved at the prospect of his own. Whatever people might believe, he was not deceived, not for a moment. One did not often have a major operation at sixty-one and get away with it. Not in his family. He knew the du Mauriers too well. He did not mind for himself, but it meant that Mo would be unhappy, and it was a thought on which he did not care to dwell. The girls would be all right; they were young, and they had their own lives, their friends, their interests; perhaps Angela and Jeanne would one day marry as Daphne had done, have babies, make discoveries, wander in fresh fields. They would be all right; they were not like puppies any more; they had attained a certain understanding. The aftermath of death was trying, though, a nuisance, a bore to people. He wished he could spare them that. Funerals were a menace; they should be stopped by law. He smiled as he remembered his own zeal at burials. The old undertaker, the children had called him, the ghoul, always first to don a black tie and to view the corpse. It must have been a bourgeois strain in his nature, a sort of hark-back to his French ancestry. And he remembered how even at the most solemn moments a ribald thought would cross his mind and he would see the funny side. His life had been full of moments like that, now he came to think of it. Laughing when he should have been serious, and solemn when he should have smiled. What a tremendous amount of acting one had done off the stage! More than most of his friends had ever realized. More than he had perhaps realized himself at the time. And yet so often there had been a demon at the back of his mind, whispering in satisfaction, 'That was a remarkably good performance, Gerald.' Never on the stage, funnily enough. Then one was merely straightforward, like a plumber, doing one's job, earning one's daily bread. He would have liked to have been more useful in life. He wished that he had not been quite so inefficient with his hands; had known how to mend fuses, wind engines, understand the insides of cars; had not been so infernally helpless. He felt he should have read more about birds; spoken several languages; lived with costers in the slums; met Mussolini. There were several things, after all, that he had never done. Much about men and women he knew he had never learnt. There were many problems still unsolved. Where from? Where to? Why? For what reason? Those were secrets that had never been told. They held a certain interest for him; he could not entirely forget them. Perhaps that was why he had been inattentive lately, had pottered about in an absent-minded way, whistled a half-tune, worn a puzzled frown. It was as though he wanted to ask a question and did not know whom to ask. Sometimes he felt like a child stumbling in the dark. It was a funny sort of business.

The lights of London were very bright tonight; they would make a lovely background to a play. He had always meant to put this view on a stage, but the right play had never appeared. First nights had been fun in the old days. The only time he had ever enjoyed acting. He was not nervous then. How the public had shouted their heads off at Wyndham's when the last curtain fell! And the party round at the back afterwards, with Mo as hostess, and a buffet from Gunter's, and all one's friends. Tommy Vaughan whispering in his ear that the libraries had done a deal. Driving back in the car and talking it all over. We must tighten up the second act, cut that scene that dragged, tell old Stick-in-the-Mud to speak up. Of course, it had been a lot of fun.

Croxley days, the birds singing, and Mo wandering about gardening, the children in sun-bonnets. Himself in an old tweed hat with a spy-glass in his hand looking for birds. Friends and laughter, and the early tours with Tree. Playing poker till three or four in the morning; sneaking back to New Grove House; with his shoes in his hands, creeping past Mummie's door. Mummie, bless her, nodding her head and twiddling her hair, rubbing his chest with camphorated oil when he had a cold in the head. Papa blinking behind his glasses, singing a song in French, going off for his favourite walk on the Heath with Chang. Guy, his companionship, his great fidelity. 'What's wrong, G?' – sauntering into the room, his head on one side. Funny how he felt that Guy had never deserted him, had always, in some inexplicable way, been close to him.

A little prayer, a little message invoking help, and all was well. Bless his old heart! There was Christ Church striking the hour; he must stop dreaming and go to bed. Mo still had her light on, through the open door. She was lying in bed, twiddling her hair as Mummie had done, while she read, and her lips moved as she read the words to herself. He had always teased her about this. Strange to think they had been married thirty years, had their silver wedding a few years back. It seemed incredible. It was last week. It was yesterday. It was not all that long time ago that they had been young together. He had begun to lose count; the years had rolled away from him tonight as though they had never been. Perhaps he had looked too long upon the lights of London and they had blinded him a little to reality. He must sleep tonight, because in the morning doctors had to be faced, and decisions taken, and wearisome formalities gone through. A bore, but never mind. He went through his little routine of kissing the family photographs.

He stood by the window and took a deep breath of air.

'Now then, Guy, for the last time perhaps, a little help, please ...'

Far below him the lights of London flickered and danced, flooding the sky with brilliance, bright and undiminished, like symbols of eternity.

MORE ABOUT PENGUINS
AND PELICANS

Penguinews, which appears every month, contains details of all the new books issued by Penguins as they are published. From time to time it is supplemented by *Penguins in Print*, which is our complete list of almost 5,000 titles.

A specimen copy of *Penguinews* will be sent to you free on request. Please write to Dept EP, Penguin Books Ltd, Harmondsworth, Middlesex, for your copy.

In the U.S.A.: For a complete list of books available from Penguins in the United States write to Dept CS, Penguin Books, 625 Madison Avenue, New York, New York 10022.

In Canada: For a complete list of books available from Penguins in Canada write to Penguin Books Canada Ltd, 41 Steelcase Road West, Markham, Ontario.

Also by Daphne du Maurier

THE BLUE LENSES AND OTHER STORIES

Eight stories by the well-loved authoress of *Rebecca* which enlarge our understanding of human nature while exploring the half-forgotten world of childhood fantasies and the subtle dreams which condition all our actions:

The Blue Lenses is the terrifying post-operative nightmare of a woman who 'sees' anew . . .

Ganymede is a cameo of an ageing homosexual's experiences with a young boy and his predatory relatives.

In *The Alibi* a would-be murderer-turned-artist is hoist with his own petard.

The Pool delicately evokes the fantasy world of a young girl on the brink of puberty.

The Lordly Ones is a simple poignant tale of a deaf child.

The Archduchess is an ironical fable about revolution and change in the perfect mini-duchy.

The Menace and *The Chamois* each throw a different light on aspects of modern sexuality.

Also by Daphne du Maurier

THE BIRDS

AND OTHER STORIES

Daphne du Maurier has a rare gift for dragging up those irrational fears that lurk behind the smooth plaster of existence. In *The Birds* she somehow lends probability to an impossibility which is nearly too fearful to imagine. United by mad hatred, the birds – the gulls, finches, crows and tits – have combined to wipe out humanity. This strange, haunting fantasy was chosen by Alfred Hitchcock for the making of a horror film.

There is also a supernatural element in 'The Apple Tree', but 'The Little Photographer' and 'Kiss Me Again, Stranger' reach their macabre climaxes by way of a natural and even humorous realism. In addition to the long mystery story, 'Monte Verità', which recalls the mood of her great novel, *Rebecca*, this volume also contains a surprise in 'The Old Man'.

'Anyone starting this book under the impression that he may sleepily relax is in for a shock . . . Continually provokes both pity and terror' – *Observer*

Also published
THE FLIGHT OF THE FALCON
THE GLASS-BLOWERS
HUNGRY HILL
THE PARASITES
THE INFERNAL WORLD OF BRANWELL BRONTË
VANISHING CORNWALL